Paul, Politics, and New Creation

Paul, Politics, and New Creation

Reconsidering Paul and Empire

Najeeb T. Haddad

LEXINGTON BOOKS/FORTRESS ACADEMIC
Lanham • Boulder • New York • London

Published by Lexington Books/Fortress Academic
Lexington Books is an imprint of The Rowman & Littlefield Publishing Group, Inc.
4501 Forbes Boulevard, Suite 200, Lanham, Maryland 20706
www.rowman.com

6 Tinworth Street, London SE11 5AL, United Kingdom

British Library Cataloguing in Publication Information Available

Library of Congress Cataloging-in-Publication Data

Library of Congress Control Number: 2020946487
ISBN 978-1-9787-0894-5 (cloth)
ISBN 978-1-9787-0895-2 (electronic)

For my mother.
In memory of my brother, father, and uncle.
ἵνα πᾶς ὁ πιστεύων εἰς αὐτὸν μὴ ἀπόληται ἀλλ᾽ ἔχῃ ζωὴν αἰώνιον.

Contents

Preface and Acknowledgments

This study is a revised and edited form of my doctoral dissertation completed at Loyola University Chicago in the spring of 2018 under the direction of Thomas H. Tobin, SJ. I owe special thanks to him not only for his mentorship but also for his friendship. Tom and I share a similar history, primarily because we were both raised in Chicago's Southside. Though he is a fan of the Chicago White Sox, I never held it against him. This project was also informed by my readers Edmondo F. Lupieri and Christopher W. Skinner. Their criticisms and responses helped make my work and experience at Loyola Chicago a golden time in my life. I also thank Chris for our continued collegial relationship. I would be remiss if I did not acknowledge Wendy Cotter CSJ and Robert Di Vito who have positively influenced my studies while at Loyola Chicago. An especial word of thanks to my undergraduate mentor, now colleague and friend Troy W. Martin. He helped cultivate my love for biblical scholarship and continues to read my work and counsel me in more ways than one. Troy is very dear to my heart.

I completed the revisions to this monograph as assistant professor of religious studies at Notre Dame of Maryland University. My colleagues in the Department of Religious Studies as well as the university have welcomed me with open arms, making my transition to NDMU and Baltimore Maryland a joyful experience.

During dissertation writing and defense, my family experienced great grief. My brother Walid tragically lost his life in a motor vehicle accident in April 2015, and my father Turki-Munier fell asleep in the Lord after a long battle with cancer in January of 2016. My beloved uncle Raymond, a second father to me, reposed in February 2018. Their memory is my continued inspiration. My mother is one of the strongest women I know, and her love and dedication to her family are evident to all who know her. She is a model of intelligence and integrity. This monograph is dedicated to her and to the memory of my loved ones.

List of Abbreviations

SBL abbreviations apply throughout, supplemented by the IATG³. The following abbreviations are also used in this study.

Epigraphical, Numismatic, and Papyrological Abbreviations

AGWR   Ascough, Richard S., Philip A. Harland, and John
        S. Kloppenborg, *Associations in the Greco-Roman*
        World: A Sourcebook. Berlin/Waco: de Gruyter/Baylor
        University Press, 2012.

AAM   Herbert Musurillo ed., *The Acts of the Pagan Martyrs*:
        Acta Alexandrinorum. New York: Arno Press, 1979.

CIL   *Corpus inscriptionum latinarum*, Consilio et Auctoritate
        Academiae Litterarum Regiae Borussicae editum.
        Berlin: Georg Reimer, 1863–1974.

CPJ   *Corpus Papyrorum Judaicarum. Edited by Victor A.*
        Tcherikover and Alexander Fuks. 3 vols. Cambridge:
        Harvard University Press, 1957–64.

GRA   Kloppenborg, John S., Philip Harland, and Richard
        Ascough. *Greco-Roman Associations Texts,*
        Translations, and Commentary. BZNW 181. Berlin:
        Walter de Gruyter, 2011–. Vol.1. Attica, Central Greece,
        Macedona, Thrace (2011).

IBosp   Struve, V. V., ed. *Corpus inscriptionum Regni Bosporani*
        (CIRB): Korpus bosporskikh nadpisei. Moskva and
        Leningrad: Nauka, 1965.

Ieph   Engelmann, H., H. Wankel, and R.
                  Merkelbach. *Die Inschriften von Ephesos.* IGSK
                  11-17. Bonn: Rudolf Habelt, 1979–84.
IG II²   Kirchner, Johannes, ed. *Inscriptiones Atticae*
                  Euclidis anno anteriores. 4 vols. Berlin: Walter de
                  Gruyter, 1913–40.
IG V/1   Kolbe, W., ed. *Inscriptiones Laconiae et*
                  Messeniae, part 1. Berlin: Georg Reimer, 1913.
IG V/2   Von Gaertringen, F. Hiller. *Inscriptiones*
                  Graecae V. Inscriptiones Laconiae, Messeniae,
                  Arcadiae, fasc. 2. Berlin: Inscriptiones Arcadiae, 1913.
IGLAM   Le Bas, Philippe, and William Henry
                  Waddington. *Voyage archéologique en Grèce et*
                  en Asie Mineure, Tome III: Inscriptions grecques
                  et latines recueillies en Asie Mineure. Paris: Chez
                  Firmin Didot Frères, 1870.
IGLSkythia II   Pippidi, D.M. *Inscriptiones Scythiae Minoris*
                  graecae et latinae: Volumen primum. Inscriptiones
                  Histriae et Viciniae. Inscriptiones Daciae et
                  Scythiae Minoris Antiquae. Bucharest: Academiei
                  Scientiarum Socialum et Politicarum Dacoromana, 1983.
IGRR   Cagnat, R.L., J.F. Toutain, V. Henry, and G.L.
                  Lafaye, eds. *Inscriptiones graecae ad res romanas*
                  pertinentes. 4 vols. Paris: E. Leroux, 1911–27. Vol
                  1: (nos. 1–1518) ed. R.L. Cagnat, J.F. Toutain, and
                  P. Jouguet (1911); Vol 2: never published; Vol 3:
                  R. Cagnat and G. Lafaye (1906); Vol. 4: Asia (nos.
                  1–1764) ed. G. L. Lafaye (1927).
IGUR   Moretti, L. *Inscriptiones graecae urbis romae.*
                  4 vols. Studi Pubblicati dall'Istituto Italiano per
                  la Storia Antica 17, 22, 28, 47. Rome: Istututo
                  Italiano per la Storia Antica, 1968.
IKosPH   Hicks, E. L., and W. R. Paton. *The Inscriptions of*
                  Cos. Oxford: Clarendon Press, 1891.
ILS   Dessau, Hermann. *Inscriptiones latinae selectae.* 3
                  vols. Berlin: Weidmann, 1892–1916. Repr. Dublin:
                  Weidmann, 1974; repr. Chicago: Ares, 1979.
ISardBR   Buckler, W.H. and D.M. Robinson, eds. *Sardis.*
                  VII, 1: *Greek and Latin Inscriptions.* Leiden: E.J.
                  Brill, 1932.

Ismyrna	Petzl, Georg, ed. *Die Inschriften von Smyrna.* IGSK 23-24/1-2. Bonn: Rudolf Habelt, 1982–90. Vol. 1 (1982); Vol. 2.1 (1987); Vol 2.2 (1990).
NewDocs V1-5	Horsley, G. H. R. *New Documents Illustrating Early Christianity.* North Ryde, Australia: Ancient History Documentary Research Centre, Macquarie University, 1981–89.
PH	Paton, W.R. and E.L. Hicks. *The Inscriptions of Cos.* Oxford: Clarendon Press, 1891.
PMich	Boak, A.E.R. *Papyri from Tebtunis* (Michigan Papyri II and V), 2 vols. Ann Arbor: University of Michigan Press, 1933–44.
RPC I	A. Burnett, M. Amandry, P. P. Ripollès, *Roman Provincial Coinage I. From the death of Caesar to the death of Vitellius (44 BC–AD 69)* (London and Paris, 1992); reprinted 1998, 2006.
Res gest. divi Aug.	*Res Gestae Divi Augusti.* Translated by P.A. Brunt and J. M. Moore. Oxford: Oxford University Press, 1967.
SEG	*Supplementum epigraphicum graecum.* Leiden: Brill, 1923–Present.
Syll³	Dittenberger, Wilhelm, Hiller von Gaertringen. *Sylloge inscriptionum graecarum.* Leipzig: apud S. Hirzelium, 1915–24.
TAM	Österreichische Akademie der Wissenschaften. *Tituli Asiae Minoris.* Wien: Hoelder, Pichler, Tempsky, 1901–. I: Ernst Kalinka, *Tituli Lyciae lingua Lycia conscripti* (1901); II/1–3: Ernst Kalinka, *Tituli Lyciae linguis Graeca et Latina conscripti.* 1 vols in 3 (1920–44); III: Rudolf Heberdey, ed. *Tituli Pisidiae linguis Graeca et Latina conscripti* (1941); IV: Friedrich Karl Dörner, and Maria-Barbara von Stritzky, eds. *Tituli Bithyniae linguis Graeca et Latina conscripti* (1978); V/1–2: Peter Herrmann, *Tituli Lydiae linguis graeca et latina conscripti* (1981, 1989).
TM	Trismegistos numbers for papyri. These numbers can be used at http://www.papyri.info /# or http://www.trismegistos.org.

Chapter 1

A Counter-Imperial Paul?

The State of the Question

There has been a recent surge of interest in Paul's relationship to the Roman Empire. In more recent history, recalling the work of Dieter Georgi, it has been suggested that Paul's preaching in Rome and in the eastern provinces critiques the Roman government.[1] Georgi's seminal study has led to several significant publications on this very subject, including three volumes of essays edited by Richard Horsley.[2] Taking a cue from Georgi, the essays in these edited volumes discuss political, sociohistorical, and postcolonial readings of the letters of Paul. There is also discussion within a number of these essays of Paul's counter-imperial, and even subversive, agenda. Sometimes, they argue, these attitudes are manifested in plain sight and at other times, one must search for the *hidden* meaning within the text.

This chapter seeks to investigate the state of the question regarding the counter-imperial agenda in Paul. It will evaluate representative authors who hold the position that the letters of Paul contain a counter-imperial rhetoric. However, I will argue that many of these scholars, though they make many worthwhile arguments, often argue from inadequate evidence regarding Paul's subversive agenda. Their evidence relies on a series of arguments that seem to build on unfounded notions in the Pauline letters. I will attempt to make the case that there is little positive evidence to support their counter-imperial claims.

This chapter will be divided into two sections. The first section will critically analyze arguments made for a counter-imperial agenda within Paul's undisputed letters.[3] Some political interpreters of Paul often locate direct challenges to Rome in Paul's letters. These challenges are characterized as Paul against the imperial cult, namely, against the cultic worship and/or veneration of the Roman imperial family. The Roman imperial cult never claimed a revealed or transcendently valid doctrine, but many scholars point to it as a monolithic

1

phenomenon across the empire. Critically analyzing these counter-imperial arguments within the context of Paul's letters will show that a counter-imperial Pauline agenda is difficult to reconcile with what is found in his letters.

The second section will analyze two larger issues which appear in discussions of a counter-imperial agenda in Paul, namely, parallelism of terms and the notion of "hidden transcripts." Some political interpreters of Paul will locate terms found in the letters which mirror terms used by the Roman imperial authority in their descriptions of the emperor and empire. They argue that Paul intentionally used parallel terms in order to draw a distinction between Christ, the true "Lord," and Caesar, the imposter "Lord." Though parallel language may aid in our study of Paul, the argument that Paul incorporated parallel terminology to subvert Rome must be reevaluated.

"Hidden transcript" or "coded speech" is another argument some interpreters appeal to make counter-imperial arguments. They suggest that Paul, for the fear that Roman government may intercept his letters, described his counter-imperial agenda in coded language (e.g., 1 Thess 2:13–16, Phil 3, and Rom 13:1–7). In this way, his readers will know his true intention, leaving those outside the Pauline community oblivious to Paul's agenda. As it will be shown, however, the notion that Paul appealed to some kind of "coded speech" in his letters demands both historical and rhetorical evidence, which some political interpreters are hard-pressed to find.

SCOPE

Recent critiques of Paul and empire have led to a convoluted understanding of the terms "postcolonial" and "anti-imperial." Though postcolonial scholars can critique any empire as a "colonizer," and are described as "anti-imperial," not every New Testament anti-imperial interpretation can be described as postcolonial. Postcolonial studies include a critique of both imperialism and colonialism. Edward Said defines imperialism as "the practice, the theory, and the attitudes of a dominating metropolitan center ruling a distant territory." He defines colonialism as "the implanting of settlements" on that distant territory.[4] If scholars suggest that Paul was critical of the Roman Empire and their analysis critiques contemporary notions of colonization, then this assessment is described as *postcolonial*.[5] These scholars attempt to map out Paul's thought, being attentive to his political imagery, and attempt to draw out historical parallels. Paul can become either an agent for change, becoming a contemporary anti-imperial hero, or a colonized colonizer by shifting the tyrannical Roman hierarchical structures into the church.[6]

This study, however, is not a postcolonial reading of Paul.[7] It is a critique of counter-imperial interpretations of Paul. It will argue that Paul's relationship to the civic authority is much more nuanced than previously suggested, without labels akin to "anti" or "pro" *imperial*. Though some may draw parallels to postcolonial interpretations, that is not the intention of this work. To suggest Paul is counter-imperial is to say he was writing against the authority, order, and power structures of the Roman Empire. These scholars, discussed in some detail below, as noted by Daniel Oudshoorn, "are attempting to restore Paul not only to his *ethnic* Judean and *cultural* Greco-Roman contexts but also to his rootedness within the *political and economic* empire that existed under the Julio-Claudian dynasty."[8] I will consider these counter-imperial arguments and map out ways Paul understood the relationship between his communities and the civic authority.

LETTERS OF PAUL

1 Thessalonians

An account of Paul in Thessalonica is recounted in Acts 17:1–9. The author of Acts offers a strong impetus for an anti-imperial reading of 1 Thessalonians because of the Jewish response to Paul. Acts 17 recalls Paul's missionary journey to Thessalonica, where he preached the crucified and risen Christ to those in attendance. The author of Acts says that some of the Jews, as well as others in attendance, became believers. But "other Jews" became angry by Paul's successful mission, and they made accusations against Paul and his community. When they could not find Paul, they brought a believer of Christ, Jason, before the authority. The accusations made against Jason before the politarchs (πολιτάρχας), on account of Paul's preaching, are "because these that disturbed the world are also here . . . they are all defying the decrees of Caesar, saying that there is another king, Jesus" (Acts 17:6b, 7b).[9]

Edwin A. Judge argues that the claim made against Jason before the politarchs, namely, "defying the decrees of Caesar," probably refers to personal loyalty oaths made to the Caesarian house.[10] The loyalty oaths were administered by the provincial authorities, like the oath of loyalty from Paphos to Cyprus sworn to Tiberius on his assumption to power.[11] This oath included a pledge to serve, revere, and obey the emperor. Another oath in particular, which Judge gives special importance to, is the oath that the Paphlagonians swore to the emperor Augustus, which included a pledge to report and attack anyone who disregarded that oath (*IGR* III, 137).[12] This leads Judge to conclude that the Thessalonians could have treated the oaths as a "decree" of Caesar. Because Acts 17:8 says the accusations made against Jason incited the anger of the Thessalonian authority, Judge argues their anger is a result of their having sworn a loyalty oath to the emperor ("the decrees of Caesar").

The theory behind his interpretation of Acts 17 is to connect it to certain verses in 1 Thessalonians, linking the accusations made against Jason to Paul's preaching. Paul, he argues, "covertly" calls for a change of ruler (e.g., 1 Thess 2:3, 4, 5, 8; 4:16; 5:2–3). To call for a change of ruler is to ultimately inquire into predictions about the Caesar's death, which was "prohibited by Caesarian edict." Hence, for Judge, Paul is defying the decrees of Caesar in 1 Thessalonians.

Mikael Tellbe supports Judge's conclusion by arguing that the Thessalonians had a deep commitment to the imperial cult.[13] He finds that the accusations made against "the believers" in Acts 17:6–7 work in two fundamental ways that, he argues, will help our reading of 1 Thessalonians. First, Paul's urging of the Thessalonians to live peacefully (1 Thess 4:11–12) is a response to the accusation that the believers have disturbed the world (Acts 17:6). Second, the charge of proclaiming another king (Acts 17:7) is affirmed through Paul's distinct use of the title "Lord" (κύριος) coupled with a unique eschatology.[14] Tellbe does not conclude that Paul was a revolutionary but does suggest Paul required political quietism in the face of such adversity (cf. 1 Thess 4:11–12; 5:15).[15]

Karl P. Donfried, as well as others, argues that Paul proclaimed the gospel in Thessalonica in direct opposition to the "imperial gospel."[16] They point to the prevalence of the imperial cult in Thessalonica as support for their argument. Part of their argument rests on the use of imperial terms which they identify in 1 Thessalonians such as "presence" (παρουσία), "meeting" (ἀπάντησις), "peace and security" (εἰρήνη καὶ ἀσφάλεια), "savior" (σωτήρ), and "hope" (ἐλπίς). Donfried builds upon Judge's hypothesis that the followers of Christ in Thessalonica were persecuted because of their refusal to take oaths of loyalty to the emperor. Paul attacked the "peace and security" (εἰρήνη καὶ ἀσφάλεια) of the empire (1 Thess 5:3).[17] When Paul speaks of Satan hindering his visit to Thessalonica (1 Thess 2:18. cf., 1 Thess 3:5), it is possibly an indication of a strong political opposition which made a visit to the city extremely difficult.[18] Donfried takes his counter-imperial reading even further when he suggests the Thessalonian believers suffer martyrdom (2:14) on account of their refusal to take oaths of loyalty, making reference to the Paphlagonian oath of loyalty.[19] Therefore, they suffer persecution and, in some cases, death.

The apocalyptic language of 1 Thess 4:13–18 serves to support Donfried's conclusions. He says, "Paul attempts to assure the community that those who have died will not be forgotten and that those who are alive at the parousia will not have precedence."[20] For Donfried, Christian martyrdom is at the heart of the issue in Paul's letter to the Thessalonians. He argues that oaths of loyalty, those which included rules for infractions of such oaths, were administered by the politarchs of Thessalonica (cf. Acts 17:1–9). Because

Paul's preaching could have been perceived as politically inflammatory, his Thessalonian community was not only being persecuted but "occasionally" its members were being killed.[21] Donfried suggests that Paul is arguing that those believers who are martyred do not have precedence at the parousia over those believers who are still alive.[22]

A concern for martyrdom in 1 Thessalonians likely rises from reading Acts 17:1–9 as the immediate background for the letter. In his book *Christ and Caesar*, Seyoon Kim gives a more tempered interpretation of Paul's relationship to empire as presented in Acts.[23] Though some have read Paul's preaching to be a challenge to empire, and though this is the claim made against him in Acts, Acts does not interpret Paul in such a manner. Kim observes,

> Luke makes clear that the political interpretation of Paul's gospel was mistaken and the Roman procurators Felix and Festus actually knew that it had not anti-Roman or treasonous characteristic (Acts 24:22–27; 25:18, 25; 26:30–32). Just as in his first volume Luke shows that Pilate nevertheless yielded to the pressure of the Jewish leaders and wrongly condemned Jesus to crucifixion, so in his second volume he shows that Felix and Festus yielded likewise to the pressure of Jewish leaders and failed to administer justice in their trials of Paul.[24]

Indeed, most of the unrest against Paul in Acts was instigated by Jewish opposition (cf. Acts 9:23–25; 13:12; 13:50; 14:5; 14:19; 16:22–23; 17:10; 17:14; 18:12–17; 21:28). The author of Acts does not want to present Paul as a political revolutionary, which his opponents make against him. Rather, Paul's gospel is not recognized as treasonous by the civil authority. Even though charges are brought against Jason in Acts 17:7, the magistrates only request money from Jason disregarding the severity of the allegations brought against him and Paul.

The matter is the fate of believers who have died before the parousia, not martyrdom. As Kim observes, if Paul was addressing Christian martyrdom "he did a poor job with his argument that those martyrs would not suffer disadvantage over against the surviving believers at the *parousia* of the Lord Jesus."[25] Paul does not make clear that the martyrs would be rewarded at the eschaton by Christ, the true "Lord" (κύριος) and the true "savior" (σωτήρ), at which time Christ will return to lay waste to the Caesar, who is the false "Lord" (κύριος) and the false "savior" (σωτήρ).[26]

According to James R. Harrison, Paul's use of imperial terminology in 1 Thessalonians is set up directly in opposition to Augustus's *imperial gospel*.[27] Paul warned believers in no uncertain terms of the idolatry of the imperial cult (e.g., Rom 1:23; 1 Cor 8:5–6) and he established Jesus's superiority over the "apotheosized Augustus" (1 Thess 4:13–5:10).[28] Harrison also argues that the imperial terms Paul employs in his epistle were terms that were also employed in Jewish apocalyptic texts.[29] He suggests that Paul is using Jewish apocalyptic imagery intentionally to critique the "imperial eschatology and Augustan apotheosis traditions."[30] Harrison concludes that "the apostle was summoning his Gentile converts back to the Jewish roots of their faith which had found its eschatological fulfillment in the house of David and not in the house of the Caesars."[31] I agree with Kim that Harrison has a "strange view."[32] He observes that 1 Thessalonians does not mention anything explicit about the Jewish roots of the Christian faith, let alone an eschatological fulfillment of a Davidic prophecy.[33]

In response to Kim, Harrison argues that Kim overlooks 1 Thess 1:10, "his son from heaven" (τὸν υἱὸν αὐτοῦ ἐκ τῶν οὐρανῶν), which he regards as a messianic reference to Jesus.[34] But in other Pauline passages a reference to God's son emphasizes the close relationship between God and Christ, namely, that Christ is the agent for bringing about eschatological salvation (cf., 1 Cor 15:24–28; Gal 2:20; 4:4–8; Rom 5:8–11; 8:3, 32).[35] Similarly, in 1 Thess 1:9–10 Paul is not concerned with Davidic messianic references to Christ. Rather, he is concerned with the eschatological implications associated with belief in Christ. Christ is God's son from heaven who will rescue the Thessalonian believers, since they turned away from their "idols" (εἰδώλον) (1 Thess 1:9b; cf., 1 Thess 4:13–5:11).[36] Indeed, there is neither explicit mention of the Jewish roots of the Thessalonian community nor any notion of Davidic prophecy. The only time Paul mentions the Jews is in his condemnation of them for having "killed both the Lord Jesus and the prophets," and because of their hostility toward the church (1 Thess 2:14–16). But his mention of the Jews was not in relation to the Davidic household. Rather Paul made a comparison to them being persecuted by their own kinsmen just like their "persecuted" (ἐκδιωξάντων) counterpart in the Judean church.[37] Harrison makes a presumption with little evidence to support his conclusion.

Like Donfried, Harrison argues that the eschatological language found in 1 Thess 4:13–5:11 is set up in opposition to imperial authority. Paul, he says, is critiquing the imperial propaganda of his day.[38] There is only one *epiphany* and one *parousia* for which the believers are waiting. It is not that of the emperor but that of Christ.[39] Using imperial terms, Paul makes apparent that Christ, not the emperor, is the true *Lord* and *Savior*. Like Donfried, however, Harrison's reading of 1 Thessalonians is also problematic because Paul is arguing about the fate of dead believers. He is also arguing that believers should not be anxious about the day of the Lord. Paul says, "For if we believe that Jesus died and rose, even so God will bring them with him those who have fallen asleep through Jesus" (1 Thess 4:14). He goes on to say how the Lord will return to usher in the eschaton; with Christ's return he will bring about the resurrection of the dead and "take up" (ἁρπαγησόμεθα) into the clouds all the believers who are still living (1 Thess 4:16–17). A larger point of the passage in 1 Thess 4:13–18 is that the living should not grieve for their dead, because both the dead believers and the living believers will meet the Lord at the *parousia*. The dead are not at a disadvantage; all believers will meet the Lord when he returns.[40] It is difficult to conjecture that this passage is arguing against a Caesarian imperial eschatology. Paul does not mention Caesar or the imperial authority at all. As I will argue, one of the major reasons for assuming a counter-imperial rhetoric in 1 Thessalonians is because of the so-called "prominence" of the imperial cult in Thessalonica.

Those who argue for a counter-imperial agenda in 1 Thessalonians often begin their discussions by observing that the imperial cult flourished in Thessalonica. Many appeal to the unpublished ThD dissertation of Holland Lee Hendrix, *Thessalonicans Honor Romans*.[41] They conclude that because of the prominence of the imperial cult in Thessalonica, Paul's use of specific terms, which are also used in the imperial cult, stands in direct opposition to the imperial cult.[42] However, on the one hand, Hendrix does show that there was an imperial cult in Thessalonica but on the other hand, he also makes it clear that because of scant evidence, it is important to ascertain how and to what extent the imperial cult functioned in Thessalonica.[43]

Harrison points to numismatic evidence to suggest the pervasiveness of imperial cult in Thessalonica. By appealing to this evidence, he suggests that the emperor Augustus's exercise of power was perceived there as "Zeus-like."[44] After the ascendancy of Octavian, Thessalonica manufactured a series of coins to honor Octavian. RPC I 5421 shows on one side the laureate head of Julius Caesar with the legend ΘΕΟΣ. On the reverse side, it was the bare head of Octavian with the legend ΣΕΒΑΣΤΟΥ. Alternatively, RPC I 1555 shows on one side Julius Caesar identified as ΘΕΟΣ, but on the reverse Augustus with the imprint ΘΕΣΣΑΛΟΝΙΚΕΩΝ. Even though the title "son of god" (θεοῦ υἱός) does not appear on the side with Octavian on any of these coin varieties, the juxtaposition of the Divine Julius with his adopted son may reflect the Thessalonian awareness of the emperor's divine status. This may indicate that the Thessalonians recognized the divine status of Octavian as the "son of a god" (*divi filius*). But there is an implicit relationship between the authority of Greek communities to mint coins with Roman ruler's images, and the Romans whose authority the coins declare the communities respect. This is not to declare religious dedication, but to recognize the benefaction of the emperor.[45]

With respect to the imperial cult, one must recognize that the imperial cult was not a sort of unified doctrine across the Roman Empire. In fact, the cult in the east was a voluntary matter, "absorbed within preexisting structures."[46] What does it mean when we claim that an imperial cult existed in Thessalonica? One cannot assume that "imperial cult" is comparable to, for example, the cult of Zeus. Hendrix suggests, from extant archaeological evidence, that there are neither altars for Julius nor Augustus in Thessalonica, or any evidence of honors beyond that which appear on coinage and in the games.[47] At the temples of the emperors at Gytheum and at Ephesus, sacrifices were not offered to the emperor but were made on their behalf for the continuance of their rule. If the temples at Thessalonica were not used for worship or sacrifice, what was their function? Hendrix suggests

> It was constructed *not* to honor Julius, but Augustus. In effect, the temple was an honorific monument. Reverence for the divine Julius and sensitivity to the importance of Octavian attached to his relation to the deified forbear suggested perhaps the specific form of the monument at Thessalonica and in other Greek cities, but the act itself was essentially that of a civic honorific. As such, it was an extension of Thessalonica's earlier policies of monumental recognition for distinguished Romans whose benefactions were important for the city.[48]

Though there was a priest associated with the temple of Caesar in Thessalonica, the responsibilities of the priest seem to be of an honorific quality.[49] At the heart of the matter was the forging of a link, through the priest, to imperial benefaction. Hendrix concludes that the religious categories of divine royalty which were associated with the emperors were articulated in the context of the city's honorific traditions. They were also articulated "according to a hierarchy of benefaction extending from the gods to the emperors and Roman patrons to the citizens of Thessalonica."[50]

During the Ptolemaic period, inscriptions highlight that sacrifices were made to a god on behalf of (ὑπέρ) the ruler or the ruling family.[51] During the Hellenistic period, sacrifices were more often made on behalf of the king to the god. Though in some instances we have sacrifices made to the ruler, they were made *to* him in thanksgiving for some kind of temporal benefit "he had bestowed on a city or institution, [yet] it is still clear [from the inscriptions] that they were essentially honorific."[52] These divine honors given to a ruler, which was a conventional way of showing the proper gratitude to those who made some kind of grand contribution to a particular people, was carried over into the Roman period.[53]

With regard to the Roman emperor, it appears that no one would say prayers or offer sacrifices to the living emperor in the hope of some kind of supernatural blessing.[54] It must be noted, however, that there is some ambiguity in a number of inscriptions where the relationship between the emperor and a god are blurred.[55] Nonetheless, inscriptions with vows show that a vow is paid to a god while the dedication is to the emperor.[56] In a number of inscriptions (e.g., CIL 13, 4624 = ILS 3453; CIL 3, 5935), the god to whom the vow is paid is mentioned explicitly and the name of the emperor is associated in the dedication. In other words, the emperors are not treated as gods who, for example, answer prayers.[57] There is no unequivocal documentation of an ex-voto offering made to the living emperor.[58] Ex-voto offerings were "made in recognition of supposed deliverance in some invisible manner from sickness or other peril. This we do not find directed to rulers dead or living."[59] The lack of ex-voto offerings shows that the common people did not regard the ruler as a god akin to the Olympian pantheon.[60] Rulers were not thought of as having supernatural powers and the lack of ex-voto offerings should not be surprising. This is not to deny that homage was paid to the emperor, but rather a distinction should be made regarding how the emperor was *worshipped* and how, for example, Zeus was worshipped. Duncan Fishwick concluded from his examinations of ancient inscriptions that the living emperor was not seen as a personal god of saving or healing to whom a community would turn in times of crisis.[61] An emperor could be associated with a god if an emperor performed some kind of magnificent deed (e.g., some type of benefaction or conquering of a land), or was perceived to be endowed with great beauty or strength reminiscent of a god.[62] Even after the emperors' death, however, their divinity was never at the level of the Olympian gods.[63]

Many of the arguments for a Pauline counter-imperial rhetoric in 1 Thessalonians are based on half-true information. Indeed, the imperial cult was present in Thessalonica but that did not entail understanding the living emperor in terms of a personal god or even as a personal *savior*.[64] Neither sacrifices nor ex-voto offerings were made to the living emperor. As Nock, Fishwick, and Hendrix observe sacrifices and ex-voto offerings were made to the gods on behalf of the emperor. The *divine* emperor was more of an honorific title and the lack of any ex-voto offerings and of prayer inscriptions to living emperors shows that the people understood the *divinity* of the emperor as honorific. This is not to deny that the political realm lacked a spiritual dimension. I am not seeking to distinguish a political reality from a spiritual one, which would be unheard of in the ancient world.[65] I do want to emphasize, though, that the cult of the emperor was a recognized organization of benefaction.

The argument being made by Tellbe, Donfried, and Harrison, considering this evidence, would suggest that Paul is applying these parallel terms to Jesus in an honorific sense. For example, if Jesus is *divi filius* like Augustus, then this defeats the purpose of Paul's Christology. Augustus is *divi filius* because of Julius's divinity. For Paul, Christ is the Son of God not because of mere relationship. Christ is the God-Man who saved humanity from sin and death (e.g., Phil 2:5–11; Rom 8:1–4, 31–34). One can conclude that in Paul's letters, Jesus's divinity is beyond any honorific term(s). Regarding the emperor, extant evidence shows Greco-Romans understood to some degree that the divine honors given to the emperor were just that, namely, divine honors. At the outset of this evidence, it does not seem that Paul was in direct competition with the imperial cult. Paul, however, recognized both imperial authorities and ecclesial authorities as servants and ministers of God (e.g., 1 Cor 3:5; Rom 13:1–7; 15:16). Furthermore, Christ becomes a personal savior, unparalleled in the imperial cult, and he will bring those who have fallen asleep into eternal life (1 Thess 4:14). I have attempted to show that Paul is not intentionally making any sort of comparison to the Roman emperor. To suggest that he does so by appealing to the imperial cult does not agree with the existing evidence. Therefore, to make appeal to the imperial cult, to support a counter-imperial reading of 1 Thessalonians calls for a critical reevaluation.

1 Corinthians

Some political interpreters of Paul find a counter-imperial agenda most clearly in 1 Corinthians 2:6–8 and 15:24–28. These passages concern the eschaton, when the "rulers of this age" will pass away, and when "every rule and authority and power" will ultimately be destroyed. Richard Horsley understands these two passages as speaking directly against the Roman imperial powers.[66] Horsley understands the crucifixion and resurrection of Christ as the pivotal moment when all history was transformed. In apocalyptic terms and perspective, the Christ-event has brought humanity to the imminent judgment and the "appointed time of fulfillment" drawing ever closer.[67] In other words, Horsley sees Paul's political agenda as quite apparent. One should "immediately notice" how politically Paul understands the events of "this age" and how the Christ-event inaugurates the new age.[68] For Horsley, Paul is attempting to build up his Corinthian community to stand "over against the dominant society."[69] Paul is using a deliberative rhetoric in 1 Corinthians to persuade his community to stand in solidarity against the larger society; against the imperial society, which he suggests is "the present evil age" (Gal 1:4), "the present form of this world [that is] passing away" (1 Cor 7:31).[70]

Horsley suggests that Paul is arguing for his community to be fully independent and autonomous from the Roman powers. He gathers that Paul's prohibition of eating foods sacrificed to idols (εἰδωλοθύτων) acts as a means of the Corinthians' political-religious solidarity against the dominant Roman society.[71] He suggests that those who share in the food sacrificed to idols shared that food also with demons (1 Cor 10:14–22). These are the Greco-Roman social bonds of sharing and for the Corinthians to withdraw from such social dimensions, Horsley suggests, means to withdraw from the dominant imperial society.[72] Paul is insisting that the Corinthian believers are now an exclusive alternative community to the dominant society.

He further illustrates this point by arguing that Paul, in refusing economic support from the Corinthians (1 Cor 9), is directly assaulting the Greco-Roman patronage system.[73] The Corinthians who were "examining" Paul *"must have"* had the patronage system in mind.[74] Rather, Paul embodied the biblical visions of support which regarded God as a divine estate owner and himself as the steward. Horsley says, "Such imagery fits with similar controlling metaphors, such as God as a monarch, Christ as the alternative emperor, and himself as the Lord's 'servant' or 'slave.'"[75] But what Horsley says about God reflects the incorporation of a similar patronage system. Did Paul criticize one patronage system in exchange for another? Horsley seems to be undermining his own argument.

Horsley's argument on idol worship and its relationship to the patronage system is very difficult to argue for because of the lack of any explicit reference to the imperial powers which he claims are apparent in 1 Cor 8–10. What seems to be at the heart of 1 Cor 8–10 is Paul's admonition to the believers in Corinth to live considering their new calling in Christ and not to be conformed to their former pagan ways of living. The false worship of the Corinthians is in the notion of false worship as improper practice and association (κοινωνία).[76] False worship for Paul is anything that directs a believer's devotion away from Christ. In essence, Paul is not concerned with the activity of the pagan political authorities but how idolatry is a danger to those within the community.[77]

It is also not clear how Horsley derives an argument against the patronage system in 1 Cor 9.[78] It is more likely that 1 Cor 9 serves as further development of Paul's argument in 1 Cor 8, namely, that the strong should consider more than themselves in the overall concern for the community and for Christ. Trent Rogers observes the argument in 1 Cor 9, writing, "The contrast is between Paul and the Strong, and can be summarized: for the sake of others, Paul does not exercise legitimate apostolic rights, and how much more then should the Strong be willing to sacrifice their pseudo-right."[79] An "economic" argument is not apparent. Rather, as Rogers observes, the argument is for the strong to exercise their Christian rights (ἐξουσία) out of love (ἀγάπη), to not harm another believer's conscience (συνείδησις).[80]

Neil Elliott also argues the case for a counter-imperial reading of 1 Corinthians.[81] Elliott regards the crucifixion of Christ as "one of the most unequivocally political events recorded in the New Testament."[82] Elliott therefore understands the political turmoil around Christ's crucifixion as underscoring Paul's counter-imperial agenda in 1 Corinthians. The cross of Christ becomes that which has brought forth "the dissolution of the Roman order," and the Christ-event must be understood as central to the counter-imperial rhetoric found throughout the letters of Paul, most especially in 1 Corinthians.[83]

Like Horsley, Elliott highlights the apocalyptic terminology suggesting that the Christian is no longer obligated to that which is of the world because it is ultimately passing away (1 Cor 7:31). Rather they are to obey God.[84] Elliott concludes,

> Paul has not obscured the nature of the cross as historical and political oppression; rather he has focused it through the lens of Jewish apocalypticism. Only a gentile church unaccustomed to that perspective, and more familiar with the sacrificial logic of the blood cults, could have transformed Paul's message into a cult of atonement in Christ's blood (the letter to the Hebrews) and a charter of Israel's disfranchisement (the *Letter of Barnabas*). Paul's own letters show that he recognized these tendencies within the gentile church of his own day, and opposed them.[85]

It is difficult, however, to reconcile Elliott's conclusion with much of what is found in Paul's letters. Though this age is passing away, there is still value in this age which Paul expresses in cosmic terms rather than political.[86] For Paul it is Christ's crucifixion and resurrection that have reshaped the world as he knew it (e.g., Rom 6:1–7; Gal 6:13–15). The emphasis seems to be that all things of this world, including the political realm, will fade away (1 Cor 7:31) and all that will remain is the new creation in Christ (2 Cor 5:17). Furthermore, to emphasize a political meaning to the cross of Christ, by noticing only the instances of possible political meaning, as in 1 Cor 2:6–8 or 1 Cor 15:24, is to bypass the numerous references made to Christ's atoning death in the Pauline corpus (e.g., Rom 3:21–26; 4:24–25; 5:5–11; 8:3–4, 32; 14:15; 1 Cor 5:7–8; 6:20; 7:23; 8:11; 11:23–25; Gal 1:3–4; 2:19–20; 1 Thess 5:9–10).

To regard the Roman Empire as the only reality or manifestation of evil in Paul's letters, does not serve his Christological agenda. That the Roman Empire is at center stage is never made apparent by Paul. As we shall see, Paul's more fundamental foci are the cosmic enemies of humanity, which for him are sin and death (e.g., Rom 3:9–20, 22b–23; 5:12–14, 21; 6:9–23; 7:4–13, 22–8:2; 8:2–17; 1 Cor 15:21–26, 54–56; Gal 2:16, 3:10–12, 21–22).[87]

Philippians

There are three passages in Philippians that are suggested to be key indications of Paul's counter-imperial agenda: Philippians 1:27; 2:5–11; 3:20–21. In Phil 1:27, Paul calls the Philippians to "live a life of citizenship" (πολιτεύε σθε). The translation of this imperative has long puzzled scholars, since this is the only place outside of Acts 23:1 where the term appears.[88] Nonetheless, the term carries the connotation that one participates dutifully in civic life being mindful of one's civic duties.[89] In his commentary on Philippians, Markus Bockmuehl suggests that Paul's use of πολιτεύεσθε acts in direct opposition to Rome and the emperor. Bockmuehl says, "Paul interposes a counter-citizenship whose capital and seat of power are not earthly but heavenly, whose guarantor is not Nero but Christ."[90] Bockmuehl understands Philippi to be under the direct patronage of "Lord Caesar" but Paul's community is first and foremost a colony of "Christ the Lord."[91]

Bockmuehl understands The *Kenotic Hymn* of Phil 2:5–11 as a counter-imperial passage suggesting that this hymn is parodying encomia bestowed on the emperor. This hymn, he argues, highlights Christ as *Lord* over and against the claims of the imperial cult. Furthermore, he understands this passage, at the very least the expression that "Jesus Christ is Lord," as standing in direct opposition to Caesar. One cannot proclaim "Christ is Lord," and agree at the same time that "Caesar is Lord." "A Christian," says Bockmuehl, "is forbidden to render to other powers, or to require from them, the allegiance that belongs to Christ alone."[92]

Similarly, Gordon Fee recognizes this passage as placing "Christ in bold contrast to 'Lord Nero.'"[93] Fee link's Paul's opposition to the emperor with the prominence of the imperial cult, which he says plays a significant role in Philippi.[94] Peter Oakes, however, disagrees with Fee's suggestion and instead argues that Christians were a marginalized community in Philippi.[95] First, Oakes suggests that the imperial cult is not a concern in this letter. The Kenotic Hymn is emphasizing an ascendancy to imperial authority rather than an apotheosis. Furthermore, he observes, "His [Christ's] enthronement prepares for his saving return in 3:20–21, which is like the action of a ruling emperor rather than a dead one who has been divinized."[96] Second, Oakes explains that the emperor is at the center of Greco-Roman society. But because of a marginalization of Christians at Philippi, pointing to Paul's imprisonment as evidence, Paul moves Christ to the center of authority, effectively replacing the emperor (2:6–11). Upon hearing that "Christ is Lord" the Philippian community would have recognized that Paul was replacing the emperor with Christ; that Christ's power has eclipsed the power of the emperor.[97] Insofar as a rhetoric of political subversion is concerned, Oakes rejects such a notion suggesting that Paul is not concerned with overthrowing Rome. Instead, Paul focuses on the plight of the marginalized Christians.[98]

N.T. Wright, who was Peter Oakes's dissertation director, employs Oakes's thesis to support his conclusion of a counter-imperial rhetoric in Philippians.[99] Wright makes a distinction between the salvation offered by the emperor and the salvation offered by Christ. In Phil 2:12, Paul says, "Therefore, my beloved, just as you have always believed, not only in my presence only but now much more in my absence, continue to work out your salvation with fear and trembling." Wright says that Paul knows that the Philippians live in

a world where there is "salvation" offered. The salvation of the emperor can
be achieved only if one lives by the rules of the empire and submits "to its
lord."[100] Wright says, "[Paul] is urging them to recognize that, as they have
a different lord, so they have a very different salvation, and they must, with
fear and trembling, work out in practice what it means to live by this salvation rather than the one their culture is forcing upon them."[101] In other words,
Wright sees a dueling ideology; a salvation offered by the empire over against
a salvation offered by Christ. The salvation offered by Rome is temporal. He
explains that if there was a crisis in the city, the emperor would leave Rome
to rescue and liberate his people, "transforming their situation from danger to
safety."[102] But what Christ offers is eternal, a future-saving activity. This is
something the emperor cannot offer. Paul's message is set up directly against
this temporal "imperial eschatology."[103] The Philippian community, as the
faithful, will therefore choose the eternal salvation offered to them by Christ.
Wright agrees with Oakes insofar as there is no counter-imperial rhetoric in
Phil 2. But with respect to what he calls a "clear challenge to imperial ideology and eschatology" in Phil 3:20–21, the letter must be seen in terms of a
challenge to the empire.[104]

The major evidence of a counter-imperial reading of Philippians appears to
be in Phil 3:20. Paul says, "For our citizenship (πολίτευμα) exists in heaven,
from which we eagerly await a savior (σωτῆρα), the Lord Jesus Christ." With
regard to the term πολίτευμα, Wright argues that this is a coded message for
those who are both Roman citizens and believers in Christ to give up their status and privilege as Romans.[105] Using the Kenotic Hymn as a springboard for
his hypothesis, he says that the critique of the Jews in Phil 3:2–11 should not
be understood as a warning against Judaism but as a coded warning against
the Caesar-cult. Wright says,

> [Paul's] concern is to warn them against the Caesar-cult and the entire panoply
> of pagan empire. But his method of warning them, and of encouraging them to
> take a stand for the counter empire of Jesus, is given for the most part in code.
> He tells them his own story, the story of how he had abandoned his status and
> privileges in order to find the true status and privilege of one in Christ, and he
> encourages them to imitate him.[106]

The central argument is Paul's call to the Philippians to be imitators of him.
Paul had pride in his Judaism and it is this similar pride which the Philippians
may have in their Roman status which could hinder them from understanding
the gospel of Jesus Christ.[107] Their true πολίτευμα is in heaven, in the hereaf-
ter, and therefore must take seriously their new status as followers of Christ.

Another key term in Phil 3:20–21 is "savior" (σωτήρ).[108] Wright suggests
that this term is the same term which is used to describe the Caesar. To
describe Christ as "savior" is to suggest that Christ is the true emperor of

the true empire. The gospel reveals that true citizenship is associated with Christ. Their only rescue from their struggles is the one true Lord and savior.[109] Others who also argue for a counter-imperial rhetoric in Paul often appeal to similar language to emphasize that Paul indirectly challenges the imperial cult.[110]

The counter-imperial readings of Philippians, however, have difficulties. The first is the overall dependence on what is termed *emperor worship*. As noted earlier, to suggest that there was "emperor worship" seems to say something to the reader, namely, that worship could be interpreted as offerings and sacrifices to the living emperor as to an Olympian god. This, however, is not the case. Benefaction in the imperial cult is how a city would honor the living emperor. As Lynn Cohick shows, references to "emperor worship" seem to overlook this idea of honoring, even so far as to ignore other dimensions of honoring in the imperial cult. The imperial cult not only included the emperor but also included members of his family, as evidenced by Livia's deification declared by Claudius (cf., Suetonius, *Divus Claudius*, 11; Dio Cassius, *Roman History*, 60.5.2; Seneca, *Apolocyntosis*, 9).[111] If Livia, the wife of Augustus, was honored in Philippi, that suggests that Paul could not be setting up a contrast between Caesar and Jesus since the imperial cult was more than just the emperor.[112]

With respect to the letter to the Philippians, to argue for a counter-imperial rhetoric based solely on a notion of hidden transcripts in Phil 3 stands in contrast to the letter as a whole. Paul, in the very beginning of the letter, proclaims that he is defending and proclaiming the gospel in his imprisonment (1:7). Furthermore, Paul is emboldened by his situation and does not encourage the Philippians to be quiet or act in secret. Rather, Paul's imprisonment served to advance the gospel among the "whole praetorian guard" and now those other followers of Jesus are likewise emboldened "to speak the word [of God] fearlessly" (1:13–14). Paul's agenda is the preaching of the gospel, and he is not hesitant to proclaim it. To suggest that Paul employs a hidden transcript is to contradict Paul's open stance as a preacher of the gospel, especially in this letter.

Paul's association of "citizenship" with "heaven" in Phil 3:20 evokes a heavenly focus, not a temporal one. Andrew Lincoln observes that Paul uses "heaven" to talk about a realized eschatology. He says heaven is the space where "the benefits of salvation awaited at the end are already present . . . the place where Christ rules as Lord from God's right hand."[113] As Dorothea H. Bertschmann rightly observes, this heavenly focus keeps with the theme of the letter.[114] She says,

> Looking forward to this ultimate horizon [the day of Christ (cf. Phil 1:6, 11; 2:16)] the believers are also looking upward, where Christ has already realized what will ultimately be true for all. This Christ-reality is the defining vantage

point for the present. All moments of outward looking (like resisting heresies, standing firm in the face of opposition), and inward looking (living harmoniously and lovingly) are under the pull of this "upward call." ([Phil] 3:14)[115]

Bertschmann further notes that the church in Philippi is not the heavenly *politeuma*, "but that it *has* a heavenly *politeuma*."[116] There is not a call for loyalty over another entity. "There are not two commonwealths or governments contrasted but two foci: one that ponders earthly things and one that looks to the heavenly government."[117]

Considering this point, I would agree with commentators who suggest that Paul's use of πολιτεύεσθε in Phil 1:27 also evokes a sense of commitment to the local community of believers. Paul is calling his community to live in a distinct manner in which commitment to their community, by means of the gospel, comes first. Bockmuehl, despite his counter-imperial reading, shows that this verb in LXX texts and other Hellenistic Jewish texts connotes "a Jewish way of life."[118] In the examples referred to by Bockmuehl the verb connotes, "a deliberate, publicly visible, and (at least in a broad sense) *politically relevant* act which in the context is distinguished from alternative lifestyles that might have been chosen instead."[119] To reiterate, Paul is calling the Philippians to commit first to their community and the gospel. From the very outset of this letter, Paul informs the community that his major concern is to advance the gospel of Jesus Christ.

ROMANS

Neil Elliott is one of the more rigorous advocates for a political reading of the Letter to the Romans.[120] Elliot argues that the Letter to the Romans is "Paul's attempt to counteract the effects of imperial ideology within the Roman congregations."[121] He understands the Jews of Rome to be in a precarious situation following the expulsions under Tiberius (19 CE) and again under Claudius (49 CE). For this reason, Paul writes in a counter-imperial manner due to the anti-Jewish sentiments among the Roman intelligentsia which had seeped into the Christian congregations.[122] He argues that the gentile members of the early Christian communities adopted the ideological perspectives of the empire, understanding the Jewish Christians to be *weak* (Rom 14:1–2; 15:1); they are powerful while, somehow, the Jewish followers of Christ are "weak." Those gentile believers have even begun to confuse their status as being "in Christ" with a status that "imperial ideology promised them as participants in the civilization of wealth."[123] Romans is a "defiant indictment of the rampant injustice and impiety of the Roman 'golden age.'"[124] Paul is therefore concerned with counteracting the imperial ideologies which existed in the community. Paul writes for the sake of creating a new community, focused around "a more authentically Judean scriptural perspective."[125] This new community will ultimately challenge the ritual and ceremony of the empire through civility and solidarity.[126]

Like Elliott, N.T. Wright argues for a counter-imperial agenda in Romans. Wright locates an *inclusio* in Paul's letter to the Romans. It begins in Rom 1:3–4 and ends at Rom 15:12.[127] Wright finds in Rom 1:3–4 Paul's Christological affirmation that Christ is not only the Jewish Messiah but fulfills messianic prophecies of being the one true king of the world.[128] The phrase "Son of God" has overtones of Davidic messiahship and Wright sees Paul asserting that the resurrection of Jesus installed Jesus as the Messiah of Israel; this is Christ's *euangelion*.[129] Paul concludes the main body of his letter in Roman 15:12 with a quote from Isaiah 11:12, which refers to one from the "root of Jessie" who will rise to rule all the nations. The *inclusio* emphasizes Jesus's Davidic Messiahship in a very traditional sense of an earthly rule over all the kingdoms of the world in peace. The letter should therefore be read in this regard, over and against the Caesar.

Because of this *inclusio* Wright understands the terms of κύριος and δικαιοσύνη not only regarding their Jewish (LXX) usage but also as a "pagan challenge" against the Roman imperial authority. Paul referring to Christ as κύριος was a direct challenge to the lordship of Caesar. Because Caesar demanded worship (sacrifices) as well as "secular" obedience, he became the "supreme divinity" in the Greco-Roman world. Not only was Caesar seen as divine, argues Wright, but as servant of the state he provided justice and peace "to the whole world." He was therefore declared "Lord and trusted Savior." This was the world in which Paul declared Jesus, "the Jewish Messiah," to be "Savior and Lord."[130]

Wright makes a similar argument for God's δικαιοσύνη in Romans. In Rom 1:16–17 Paul declares that the gospel reveals the righteousness of God (δικαιοσύνη θεοῦ). Wright understands δικαιοσύνη, like the term κύριος, in terms of Roman imperial ideology of justice as well as in the Jewish sense of covenant promises. He writes, "Paul was coming to Rome with the gospel message of Jesus the Jewish Messiah, the Lord of the world, claiming through this message God's justice was unveiled once and for all."[131] The gospel stood in direct opposition to the Roman imperial authority. Wright goes on to say, "Paul's declaration that the gospel of King Jesus reveals God's *dikaiosynē* must also be read as a deliberate laying down of a challenge to the imperial pretension. If justice is wanted, it will be found not in the *euaggelion* that announces Caesar as Lord but in the *euaggelion* of Jesus."[132] Ultimately, Wright sees the letter to the Romans as a direct challenge to the Roman

Empire. Paul sets up this letter in such a way that he is emphasizing that Jesus is the true Lord and that Caesar is not. Nevertheless, I will argue that there is no apparent indication that Paul is laying down such a claim in Romans.

There are, however, significant problems with the positions of both Wright and Elliott. The *inclusio* Wright finds in Romans is at odds with Paul in Romans 13:1–7. Wright argues that the letter is written in direct opposition to the Roman imperial authority but Romans 13:1–7 affirms that Paul does not see any reason for resisting the authority of Rome. Even though he proclaims Jesus to be the risen Lord (Rom 1:4) and a messianic king (Rom 15:12), Paul calls on the followers of Christ to respect and honor the authority (Rom 13:7). Though distinct, Rom 13:1–7 exhibits parallels to what is found elsewhere in the letter, namely, the theme of conduct toward outsiders (Rom 12:17–18), especially to be at peace with "all humanity" (πάντων ἀνθρώπων).[133] With regard to Wright's *inclusio*, Paul is not speaking of the Messiah's political reign but instead presents the Messiahship of Jesus in terms of eschatological acts of redemption procured for humanity through Christ's death and resurrection (Rom 3:24–26; 4:25; 5:6–11; 8:3–4, 32; 14:15).[134] Paul does not understand Jesus's Messiahship in a traditional Jewish sense of a political reign over the nations. Rather, Paul understands Jesus's Messiahship in a transformed sense of a "reign of redemption from the powers of sin and death," that can be seen across his letters (e.g., Rom 3:9–20, 22b–23; 5:12–14, 21; 6:9–23; 7:4–13, 22–8:2; 8:2–17; 1 Cor 15:21–26, 54–56; Gal 2:16, 3:10–12, 21–22).[135]

In Wright's understanding of Paul's use of κύριος and δικαιοσύνη, namely, that Paul uses these terms in direct opposition to the empire, are less than convincing. Seyoon Kim suggests,

> Why, then, being concerned to present God's righteousness in Christ as a challenge to the Roman imperial propaganda, Paul says nothing about the fake "justice" of the Roman Empire or the parody character of the imperial *euangelion*, but concentrates his whole argument only on the sinfulness of all human beings (Gentiles and Jews) and their inability to achieve "justification" by the works of the law.[136]

Paul writes to the followers of Christ in Rome to address certain misgivings about him and his gospel.[137] What seems to be at the heart of Romans is concern whether or not the observance of the Law of Moses justifies one before God. Furthermore, many commentators agree that the purposes for Paul's writing the letter are varied but a great majority do not reckon a political, subversive, intention as one of them.[138]

In similar fashion, Elliott's argument of the letter being a "defiant indictment of the rampant injustice and impiety of the Roman 'golden age'" does not reflect the viewpoint we find in Romans. In each stage of his letter, Paul is dealing with issues which do not correlate to an attack on the Roman imperial authority. I agree with Thomas H. Tobin, who observes four major stages in Paul's overall argument in the letter (Rom 1:18–3:20; 3:21–4:25; 5:1–7:25; 8:1–11:36).[139] The arguments take shape in three stages: (1) an appeal to commonalities between him and the Roman followers of Christ; (2) Paul then develops the beliefs to support a central aspect of his gospel; (3) he shows how the controversial aspects of his gospel should be understood as acceptable and should not give way to certain misgivings about him or his gospel. Where Rome's imperial authority figures into these arguments is not apparent. If the proposition of Paul's letter is that the gospel reveals the righteousness of God for all who believe, Jew and Greek (Rom 1:16–17), an overtly political reading of Romans becomes difficult to ascertain.

ARGUMENTS FROM SILENCE

Parallelism

Investigation in modern scholarship on the politics of Paul often begins with reference to the work of Adolf Deissmann who, in 1927, suggested that there is a "polemical parallelism" between the language of the cult of the ruler (Rome's emperor) and the cult of Christ. Deissmann argues that when the first followers of Jesus Christ began their missionary journey across the Greco-Roman world, they began using terms for Christ which were normally associated with the divine. Some words which Deissmann highlights as "polemical parallelism" are "god" (θεός), "lord" (κύριος), "king" (βασιλεύς), and "savior" (σωτήρ).[140] Deissmann acknowledges, however, that Christian terms were derived "from the treasury of the Septuagint and the Gospels and happen to coincide with solemn concepts of the imperial cult which sound the same or similar."[141] He continues and writes, "I am sure that in certain cases a polemical intention against the cult of the emperor cannot be proved; but mere chance coincidences might later awaken a powerful sense of contrast in the mind of the people."[142] Deissmann, therefore, showed considerable restraint in his discussions on parallel language.

Samuel Sandmel, in his 1961 presidential addresses to the Society of Biblical Literature, warned against "parallelomania."[143] Sandmel defined *parallelomania* as the "extravagance among scholars which first overdoes the supposed similarity in passages and then proceeds to describe source and derivation as if implying literary connection flowing in an inevitable or predetermined direction."[144] Sandmel is not denying the existence of parallels and their possible usefulness in interpreting a text; he is rather warning against exact parallels which can be devoid of meaning.[145] An example of "exact parallels" can be found in the work of Adolf Deissmann, but he calls it "independent parallelism."[146] Independent parallelism (or "exact parallels") is when one finds a term or a phrase in a New Testament text which parallels a source from the greater Greco-Roman world. Deissmann uses the example of Paul's expression in 1 Cor 10:21, "the table of the Lord" with the analogous Egyptian expression, "the table of the Lord Serapis." As Deissmann explains, with regard to table-fellowship, Paul's expression was most probably influenced by Septuagint parallels (e.g., Mal 1:7. 12; Ezek 39:20; 44:16) than by anything to do with "the table of the Lord Serapis."[147] Nevertheless, Sandmel wants to emphasize context. For example, in what context is Paul using the term κύριος when referring to Jesus? With regard to Paul, Sandmel says that our knowledge of parallels may assist us in our understanding of Paul, "but if we make him mean only what the parallels mean, we are using the parallels in a way that can lead us to misunderstand Paul."[148]

Recalling Sandmel's presidential address to the SBL, N. T. Wright notes, correctly in my opinion, that some contributors to the edited volume by Richard Horsley have not abandoned the misleading method of *parallelomania*.[149] They understand the relationship between Rome and Paul as polemical and point to the common language which is used both by Paul and by Roman imperial propaganda. Yet how far removed is Wright himself from this phenomenon of *parallelomania* in some of his own interpretations of Paul? Wright finds numerous "echoes" of Roman imperial ideology in the terms Paul employs in his letters.[150] As previously noted, Wright understands the terms κύριος and δικαιοσύνη, especially in Romans, to stand in direct opposition to the Roman imperial authority.[151] Likewise in the letter to the Philippians, Wright understands the terms πολίτευμα and σωτήρ as standing against not only the citizenship which Rome offered but also against the "salvation" which was offered by the emperor.[152] These parallels, partly, lead Wright to conclude that Paul has deeply counter-imperial and subversive attitudes toward the Roman Empire.[153]

In his study on 1 and 2 Thessalonians, James R. Harrison contends that Paul's use of particular terminology in 1 Thessalonians is contrary to Augustus's imperial *gospel*.[154] Harrison locates in 1 and 2 Thess the terms "presence" (παρουσία), "appearance" (ἐπιφάνεια) "meeting" (ἀπάντησις), "peace and security" (εἰρήνη καὶ ἀσφάλεια), "savior" (σωτηρ), and "hope" (ἐλπίς), suggesting that these essential terms, which are used in imperial propaganda, are Paul's attempt to critique the empire intentionally. These terms appear in contexts dealing specifically with the emperor, for example, the "παρουσία of the god Hadrian in Greece."[155] Paul, therefore, may be using the term in the context of Christ's παρουσία at the eschaton (1 Thess 4:15–16), that points to the "glory and pomp accompanying the advent of the heavenly *Imperator*."[156] Similar arguments are made for the other terms mentioned and Harrison concludes that there is "little doubt" that in 1 Thessalonians Paul is critiquing the imperial propaganda and, subsequently, imperial rule.[157]

A discussion on parallelism can also be found in the work of Joseph D. Fantin. In his work *The Lord of the Entire World*, Fantin seeks to reconstruct the historical context of Paul in order to see if there were conflicting views on worship in the titles used for Jesus and the emperor (e.g., κύριος and κύριος Ἰσοῦς). "The goal of this study," says Fantin, "is to determine whether or not it is probably that Paul intended a polemic against the living Caesar in some of his uses of κύριος for Jesus."[158] Unlike the other counter-imperial scholars already mentioned, Fantin argues that Paul was not primarily counter-imperial but Paul's declaring the Jesus is Lord is highly suggestive that Jesus's lordship is both superior to and supplants all other earthly rulers. Unlike James Dunn who sees the lordship of Christ and the lordship of Caesar on two different plains, not necessarily contradicting each other, Fantin argues only Christ or Caesar can be the *supreme Lord*.[159]

John M. G. Barclay suggests that the relationship between Pauline terms and those terms found in imperial propaganda are not as exact as others claim. Namely, the antithetical constructs that they locate in Paul's letter.[160] The major question for Barclay is whether the overlap of vocabulary implies a negative relationship between Paul and Rome. He observes that the use of common language, political or religious, does not necessarily imply a hostile relationship between two or more entities who use the same words.

Barclay shows how Paul can speak of ecclesial leaders as both διάκονοι and λειτουργοί of God (1 Cor 3:5; Rom 15:16), as well as the political authorities as διάκονοι and λειτουργοί θεοῦ (Rom 13:4,6).[161] Neither claim challenges the other, nor does it suggest that if Paul is a διάκονος θεοῦ, that "Caesar is not."[162] With regard to the term κύριος Barclay says,

> In relation to Christological titles, precisely this sort of antithesis is present in 1 Cor 8:4–6: whatever beings other people may honour as "Lords" and "Gods," "for us there is one κύριος and one θεός" (1 Cor 8:6). Given this evidence it is no surprise that Paul does not refer to political authorities as κύριοι. But we know of his sensitivity regarding this title only because he explicitly marks this antithesis. This is not the case with regard to some other terms (διάκονος), and we cannot assume it to be the case elsewhere. Everything depends on precise analysis of the linguistic and rhetorical contexts in which such terms are used.[163]

Barclay makes a crucial observation about parallel terminology. What is the precise meaning of the term with respect to its linguistic and rhetorical contexts? As he demonstrated with the term κύριος, if we merely think of Paul using the term to critique and undermine the Caesar then we lose focus of how Paul really understands the term κύριος, as well as how he understands the soteriological-eschatological function of Christ. For Paul, the main influence on his thought being the LXX, κύριος, as well as θεός, is a title only reserved for the God of Israel. Paul may not understand the emperor as κύριος or θεός on account of his Judaism, but he can understand him as διάκονος. What should guide our reading of Paul is foremost Paul's Jewishness; he believed that Jesus was the unique Son of God, and his understanding of both Jesus's Messiahship and his gospel has precedence in the Jewish scriptures.[164] But to assume Paul writes against Rome merely on the basis of common language is to lose focus on what Paul wants to convey and the Jewish context in which he is doing it.

Christopher Bryan makes similar observations with regard to the traps of *parallelomania*.[165] Bryan observes that Paul did not live in seclusion as he wrote his letters but wrote in the midst of a society which was heavily influenced by notions of the sacred. Bryan says, "They all had to use *some* vocabulary and concepts to speak of the things that they held sacred, and if they were to communicate at all, they all had to draw on more or less the same vocabulary and concepts as everyone else. Hence, there were bound to be parallels between them."[166]

Like Barclay, Bryan is arguing that one must be aware of linguistic and rhetorical contexts. Bryan convincingly argues to this point with regard to the phrase "Son of God." He says,

> Romans spoke of living emperors as "son of god," "lord," and "savior." Paul and other Christians did the same for Jesus. Does it follow . . . that for Christians "to proclaim Jesus as Son of God was deliberately denying Caesar his highest title, and that to announce Jesus as Lord and Savior was calculated treason"? No, it does not. Certainly Christians were using some of the same words about Jesus as pagans used about Caesar, but they were hardly using them in the same context, or meaning anything like the same thing by them.[167]

Bryan then goes on to show the difference between Octavius's title as "son of god" and Jesus's title as "Son of God." When Octavius was called *divi filius* it was because he was the son of the divinized Julius, a title which demonstrated great honor and prestige that the Greco-Roman world had for both Julius and Octavius.[168] But Paul, a Jew, believed Jesus to be "Son of God" because "he believed him to have been 'sent' in the fullness of time by the one God of Israel."[169] Paul understands Christ's sonship as deriving from Jewish traditions. How could Paul be countering Caesar when he speaks of Christ as "the Son of God, who loved me and gave himself up for me" (Gal 2:20) or that "God has sent the Spirit of his son in our hearts crying, 'Abba Father'"

(Gal 4:6). Bryan says, "to suggest that at such moments as these Paul was concerned with denying something to Caesar is surely a spectacular example of placing the cart before the horse."[170]

Seyoon Kim also shows how *parallelomania* can lead to two further weaknesses in counter-imperial methodologies; deductions from assumptions and proof texting.[171] He argues that some political interpreters of Paul form a deductive argument starting from various assumptions: (1) the imperial cult was pervasive through all social and religious aspects in the Eastern Empire where Caesar was worshipped as lord and savior of the world. Therefore, worship of Christ as Lord and Savior was necessarily subversive toward the imperial cult.[172] (2) Paul, "an heir to Jewish apocalypticism," thought in terms of two ages, one passing (1 Cor 2:6) and the other, the new age personified by the King of God and the Lord Jesus Christ.[173] (3) Because Jesus died by means of crucifixion ultimately administered by the Roman authority, his gospel, namely, the gospel of the crucified and resurrected Messiah—the Lord and the Savior of the world—already had an inherently counter-imperial character.[174] (4) Paul's use of the term ἐκκλησία already carried with it connotations of Greco-Roman civic assemblies. By using the term to designate his communities, Paul is attempting to set up an alternate community which stands against the Roman imperial system.[175] (5) The patronage system of benefaction was an integral part to the Roman imperial system. Paul's refusal to accept the patronage of the Corinthian community shows Paul's rejection of the imperial patronage system.[176] (6) Paul was often under investigation for his counter-imperial preaching and was also imprisoned on account of this appealing as witnessed in Acts 17:1–9.[177] If one takes these assumptions as fact, one could easily deduce from them that Paul's preaching included a counter-imperial, and even subversive, rhetoric.

Having made these assumptions, some political interpreters of Paul then look for terms in Paul's letters which parallel terms found in imperial propaganda (e.g., "Lord," "citizen," "savior," "gospel," "righteousness," "faith," "peace," "liberty," "hope"). They then connect these terms with those assumptions, "so that the terms take on counter-imperial meanings, regardless of the contexts in which they appear. Then they read the counter-imperial meanings out of the whole passage, regardless of the chief concerns and intentions of the passage itself."[178] As Kim notes, these interpreters are imposing counter-imperial meanings on these terms. The passages where these terms appear are then read as subversive. At times, these passages are then used to extrapolate the meaning of one passage to another, so that they may claim that Paul preached in a deliberate counter-imperial manner.[179] Because they read the assumptions as true they impose their assumptions on the parallel terms, thus fashioning a counter-imperial rhetoric in Paul.

Nevertheless, I have attempted to show how parallel language does not necessarily imply a particular meaning. In this context, parallel language does not suggest a Pauline counter-imperial agenda. Parallel language can, possibly, help inform a specific situation, but one cannot come to conclusions without understanding linguistic and rhetorical contexts of the Pauline texts themselves. Those political interpreters of Paul who suggest that this parallel terminology *clearly* demonstrates Paul's counter-imperial agenda are basing their conclusions on several assumptions. They then impose political meaning not only on Paul's use of the term but also to the larger passage and even to Paul's letter as a whole. However, an explicit counter-imperial interpretation of Paul using parallel language has its complications. Since it is problematic to elicit a counter-imperial rhetoric by appealing to parallel language in Paul, some political interpreters of Paul will often appeal to what has been called "hidden transcript" or "coded speech." We now turn to the argument for Pauline "hidden transcripts."

Hidden Transcripts and Recognizing Their Presence

It is argued that Paul could not openly declare a counter-imperial sentiment for fear of political repercussions. Therefore, Paul had to write in 'hidden transcripts.'[180] One of the earlier, if not earliest, mentions of a Pauline hidden transcript was Adolf Deissmann. Deissmann suggested that when Paul confesses Jesus Christ to be "the Lord," it acted as a "silent protest against other 'lords,' and against 'the lord'" who was Caesar.[181] Deissmann, on the basis of parallels, thought Paul made silent protests against Rome and Caesar. But he also showed restraint and does not press the issue any further.

The argument for Paul's use of hidden transcripts is often drawn from E.R. Goodenough's discussion of Philo's *De Somniis 2*.[182] *De Somniis 1–2* are part of a group of Philo's writings which are called the *Allegorical Commentaries*. These treatises were written for a group of people with extensive biblical and philosophical insight.[183] Drawing from the passage in *Somn.*, 2.81–92, Goodenough argues that Jews would have seen in this passage the Romans who Philo calls "beasts and asps."[184]

Throughout the work, Philo compared the harsh rulers to savage and deadly animals (ἀγριώτεροι καὶ ἐπιβουλότεροι) but, at the same time, explicitly calls his readers to honor the rulers. Goodenough draws from *Somn.* 2.91–92, which he suggests has a double meaning:

And what? Are not we also, whenever we may be spending our time in the market-place, accustomed, on the one hand, to be astounded by the rulers and also, on the other hand, to make way for the pack-animals? But [we make way for these] because of different, and not the same, purposes; for, on the one hand, to those rulers out of honor and, on the other hand, the pack-animals on account of fear lest we are injured from them. And when occasion allows it, it is good to destroy by subjugation the violence of enemies; and to be safe, lest it is not permitted, be silent; but if we desire to find that same benefit from them, it is more appropriate to propitiate them. (Philo, *Somn.* 2.91–92, my translation)[185]

Goodenough calls attention to Philo's sarcasm in this passage by comparing the rulers to the pack-animals in the marketplace. It was a reality that Jews in Alexandria lived with in the first century CE. On the one hand, both the ruler and the pack-animals are revered, but, on the other hand, that reverence is due to different reasons. Like the pack-animals, the rulers could crush those who came in their way. If Philo's intentions in his writing were ever raised by the Romans, he could easily deflect any criticism by insisting that he was speaking in general and not toward the elite ruling class. But Goodenough highlights *Somn.* 2.91–92 saying, "And the Jews would also have understood by the last sentence that if Philo had been able to destroy the Roman power he would gladly have done so. The propitiating attitude he was advising was the only one a sensible Jew . . . could take under the existing circumstances."[186] Goodenough does not depend on parallel language to make his argument, that is, parallel language found between Philo and Alexandrian imperial propaganda. He argues, however, from Philo's use of rhetoric.[187] Whether or not a hidden transcript can be located in Philo is not our concern, however, Goodenough's methodology is relevant for this study.[188]

Specifically, Goodenough's work is often appealed to when a discussion about Pauline hidden transcripts arises.[189] For instance, Neil Elliott, in his discussion on Pauline rhetoric, suggests that the "hidden transcripts" found in Philo's *Somn.* 2.81–92, present to us how Jewish intelligentsia reacted under Roman colonial pressures.[190] Elliott argues that Goodenough's work demonstrates that one should not expect to find in Paul or any of his Hellenistic Jewish contemporaries an "unequivocal 'pro-Roman' or 'anti-Roman' posture," but should look for the "traces of [Paul's] response to the pressures of Romanization."[191]

Elliott, as well as others, argues that Paul wrote in "hidden transcripts" or in "coded speech," lest the documents were intercepted by the authority who would in turn persecute Paul and his communities.[192] Part of their argument for bolstering the proposition that Paul writes in hidden transcripts rests on the work of sociologist James C. Scott.[193] In his analysis of public transcripts, Scott argues that the public discourse of subordinate groups, which takes place in the presence of the dominant group, will often contain a hidden message which only the subordinate groups understand. In other words, the subordinate group presents a hidden message which goes undetected by the dominant group. Scott calls this type of subordinate discourse "offstage" and coins the term "hidden transcript." It is "offstage" because even though a discourse may be public, the hidden transcript takes place "offstage," undetected by the dominant group.[194] Hidden transcripts take place "offstage" and consists of "speeches, gestures, and practices that confirm, contradict, or inflect what appears in public transcript."[195] Scott identities examples of "hidden transcript" in codes, gossip, ritual, songs, or euphemisms which take place on the public stage but can be interpreted differently by different groups of people.[196] These types of discourse which take place in the public eye are not the "hidden transcript" itself, but they contain trace elements of a larger polemic against those in power.

John Barclay warns against those who appeal to Scott's work for their arguments for a Pauline counter-imperial agenda.[197] Scott's work rests on forms of public discourse and public documents. Paul's letters are not public documents; they are not addressed to nonbelievers and Paul does not anticipate his letters will be intercepted by the Roman authority. Paul's letters are private documents written to a small group(s) of believers across the empire. Barclay comments, "There is every reason to think that we have here, in pure form, a Christian 'hidden transcript'—that is, what they said among themselves 'offstage' in freedom and without fear."[198] Rather than finding some kind of coded dialogue, we find the full expression of what Paul believes since this document is what Scott would consider "offstage." Barclay suggests that the letters are offstage because it takes place in private, not on the public stage. Paul, then, speaks openly and in undisguised language. So, if these are Paul's undisguised words, then one does not find openly subversive or counter-imperial language. Paul does not make any direct comment against Rome's "gospel" or the Roman Empire. In other words, Scott's analysis actually "argues directly *against* those who would regard Paul's letters as a coded discourse which masks what he or other early Christians really thought."[199]

Christoph Heilig, however, makes two critical remarks against Barclay's analysis of James C. Scotts's work. First, Barclay underestimates how the small size of Christ follower groups could still attract the gaze of the civil authority. For outsiders, the Christ followers may have resembled Roman *collegia*. They did not meet monthly like other associations but gathered weekly, which could possibly raise suspicions against them. Second, and I think most important, is that Paul's letters are not wholly private documents since they are read aloud in the community where outsiders are said to be present (cf. 1 Cor 14:23). As Heilig notes, Paul would have had to consider the possibility that his correspondence could be heard or intercepted by others who were not the intended recipients. He had to consider the possibility of his letters being heard by outsiders and could be affected "by public scrutiny and the rules of public discourse."[200] Therefore, for Heilig, it is not a matter of "if" the Roman Empire occupied Paul's thought but how much of it occupied Paul's mind. Although Heilig does not state whether aspects of Paul's letters are counter-imperial, he does help nuance why Paul may have not felt the need to be explicitly counter-imperial.[201]

And yet, Paul was a Jew and those of the Jewish faith openly and at length criticized Rome and its emperor. Why would Paul hide his belief that the emperor was neither God nor the Son of God? Among other examples, Philo speaks at length against the Roman authority in his *Legatio ad Gaium* (e.g., *Legat.* 357) and his *In Flaccum*. Likewise, Josephus in his *Contra Apionem* criticizes the imperial cult saying:

> our legislator—not as if he were prophesying that Roman authority should not be honored but because he disdained a means that is useful neither to God nor to human beings, and because an inanimate object is proved to be inferior to every animate creature, and much more to God—forbade the making of statues. He did not prohibit that good men be paid homage with other honors, secondary to God: with such expressions of respect we give glory to the emperors and to the Roman people. (Josephus, *C. Ap.* 2.75–76 [Barclay])[202]

Though he cautiously criticizes the imperial cult, he nonetheless still criticizes Rome. Both Josephus and Philo can write in their documents, which are generally understood to be public and were sometimes even presented to emperors, that they were genuinely dissatisfied and openly critical of some aspects of the Roman Empire and its practices.

Likewise, among the Alexandrian Greeks, there was open criticism of the Roman emperors for their apparent favor toward Alexandrian Jews.[203] The *Acts of the Alexandrian Martyrs* (*AAM*), the stories of Alexandrian Greek heroes who die at the hands of the emperors, are semi-literary documents based in some way on historical documents.[204] These heroes died because they sought to defend the rights of Alexandrian Greeks before the Caesars. In essence, the *AAM* were written primarily to ridicule the emperor.[205] One of the more outlandish criticisms of the emperor Commodus (180–192 CE) can be found in the *Acta Appiani* (P.Yale.1536; P.Oxy.33). Appian, an Alexandrian gymnasiarch, is condemned to death (extant evidence is not clear as to why he is condemned). The text says that as he was being led away to suffer the death penalty, he was again called back to the chambers of the emperor. When Appian again appears before the emperor he says,

> Who is it this time that called me back a second time as I was about to greet Death again and those who died before . . .? Was it the Senate or you, the leader of gangsters (ὁ λῄσταρχος)?[206]

Appian was again led to his death, in part, on account of his name-calling the emperor "the leader of gangsters" (ὁ λῄσταρχος). Though this collection of papyri dates from the late second and early third centuries CE, they represent an outcry against the emperor whom Alexandrian Greeks were quite displeased with for some time. If Tcherikover and Fuks are correct about the private nature of these documents, their distaste for the emperor is quite apparent in these "private transcripts."

What these documents, as well as the texts from Philo and Josephus, represent is that a public outcry or subtle denunciation of the emperor or imperial institutions is by no means done in secret. Considering Paul found it necessary to deride or even to try to subvert Rome's government in code lacks plausibility. If Paul spoke in code, then he broke the code when he openly admitted that some in the household of Caesar accepted the gospel (Phil 4:22)! Therefore, arguments for a Pauline "hidden transcript" seems to fall by the wayside.

While studies have argued for and against the Pauline "hidden transcript" none of those studies have adequately read Paul's documents regarding ancient rhetorical devices. The notion that Paul has incorporated "coded speech" or "hidden transcripts" into his writings is related to the larger topic of "figured speech" in ancient texts. Figured speech is a rhetorical device that ancient authors or orators incorporated into their texts to signal a coded or hidden message. To suggest that Paul used hidden transcripts is to argue that he incorporated figured speech into his letters. In the following chapter, I will attempt to show that Paul does not incorporate any of the rhetorical devices associated with figured speech in those passages commonly identified as *hidden* critiques of the empire.

CONCLUSION

This review highlights several significant points for the investigation of Paul and the political. First, it has been argued that the imperial cult did not play such a significant role in the daily lives of ancient Greco-Romans. Indeed, as some counter-imperial interpreters of Paul note, the imperial cult was quite widespread in the first century CE. However, extant archaeological evidence shows that the emperors were never on a par with the Olympian gods. Furthermore, even though temples were constructed in honor of the living emperor, epigraphic evidence has shown that sacrifices were rarely offered to the living emperor. Rather, victims were offered on the emperor's behalf to a god, for his continued reign.

Second, it has been suggested that a Pauline counter-imperial agenda rests on Paul's use of specific parallel terminology, found in Roman imperial propaganda, that Paul incorporates to undermine the religiopolitical authority. Some political interpreters of Paul argue that because Paul writes against Rome he declares Jesus Christ to be the true "Lord," the true "Savior," and the true "Son of God" despite what the imperial cult claims about the Caesar. However, one must account for Paul's Hellenistic Jewish background. Paul preached Christ whom he understood to be the fulfillment of the Jewish scriptures (Rom 10:4). He used and understood the terms he incorporated into his letter primarily in the context of the LXX. Moreover, if Paul preached in a Greco-Roman society it should come as no surprise that certain terms used in Greco-Roman society to describe the sacred were also employed by Paul.

The final point is the argument for the presence of hidden transcripts in Paul's letters. Some interpreters have suggested that Paul could not openly declare the gospel for fear of persecution and, therefore, in particular passages wrote in hidden transcripts to avoid detection by the imperial authority. Yet, as I have argued, a hidden transcript in those passages does not seem fit the bill. Because Paul's letters were private documents, namely, letters written to believers about the gospel of Jesus Christ, then it would not be necessary to incorporate figured speech into his writings. As previously mentioned, if Paul spoke in code then he broke the code when he openly admitted that some in the household of Caesar accepted the gospel (Phil 4:22).

This study considers Paul within his sociohistorical context, and how this context falls into place with his theology. It will nuance our understanding of Paul's relationship with the civic authority. This study, therefore, will proceed in the following manner: chapter 2 will investigate the rhetorical device known as figured speech. I will attempt to show that Paul does not incorporate any of the rhetorical devices associated with figured speech into specific passages to subvert Roman power.

Then, moving away from a rhetorical-critical examination of the letters, chapter 3 will seek to place Paul within the larger context of the Eastern Roman Empire. Examining the history of the late Republic and early Principate will help explicate Rome's relationship with foreign cults. In particular, the cults of Bacchus, Isis, and Yahweh will be used as examples to help determine Rome's possible relationship with Paul's communities of Christ followers.

Chapter 4 will seek to understand how Paul understood his communities and their function amid the Roman Empire. This chapter will attempt to show how Paul's "churches" functioned similarly to Greco-Roman ancient associations, and the significance of how his "churches" may have differed from ancient association. One of the more important differences is how Christians were to practice their faith. In this regard, the Christian groups were exclusive in a way that others were not. In order to be included you must be "baptized into Christ." Once baptized, the Christian is to practice and live out their faith. It is a call to "live by the Spirit" (e.g., Gal 5:16–25). The Christian associations seems to be calling for a type of "resocialization" within the wider Greco-Roman world. They required that their members' primary allegiance be to the community, while maintaining a proper relationship with the larger world. We will ask the question of what it means for these Christ followers to be "re-socialized" in the context of their social environment.

Having put aside an overtly political interpretation, chapter 5 will attempt to understand Paul's eschatological and soteriological understanding of the world in terms of cosmology and anthropology. As we shall see, Paul's language of "world" (κόσμος) and "creation" (κτίσις) impinges upon Paul's relationship with the Roman Empire. Paul's statement embraces both a new anthropology and a new cosmology that are intrinsically linked to the Christ-event. The Christ-event is central to this concept of "newness" and Paul says that he can only boast "in the cross of our Lord" (Gal 6:14). The cross is what leads to this "new creation" (Gal 6:15). Paul's enemies are also not of this world. In Rom 8, which takes up the framework found in 1 Cor 15, Paul preaches deliverance or vindication not over human enemies but over the cosmic forces of death and decay (cf., Rom 8–11). Paul was not primarily concerned with the Roman Empire. In fact, the Roman Empire seems to play little explicit role in Paul's letters. Paul is more concerned with his eschatological soteriology; the gospel of Jesus Christ and how it has reshaped the world. I will ultimately contend that Paul is counter-imperial, insofar as Rome plays no significant role in Paul's eschatological soteriology. By disregarding a place for the empire in his theology, Paul has made a most subversive that he could have made.

NOTES

1. Dieter Georgi, *Theocracy in Paul's Praxis and Theology* (Minneapolis: Fortress, 1991). See also, Dieter Georgi, "Who is the True Prophet," *HTR* 79 (1986): 100–126.

2. Richard Horsley, ed., *Paul and Empire: Religion and Power in the Roman Imperial Society* (Harrisburg: Trinity Press International, 1997); Richard Horsley, ed., *Paul and Politics: Ekklesia, Israel, Imperium, Interpretations: Essays in Honor of Krister Stendahl* (Harrisburg: Trinity Press International, 2000); Richard Horsley, ed., *Paul and the Roman Imperial Order* (Harrisburg: Trinity Press International, 2004).

3. This section will be subdivided into arguments made for each of Paul's letters that have been directly evidenced toward an anti-imperial reading. The ordering of the subdivisions is in chronological order of Paul's writing. It should go without saying that the chronological order of Paul's letters is disputed. But I shall follow the consensus dating that places 1 Thessalonians as Paul's earliest letter and the letter to the Romans as the last one. It should be noted that the ordering has no significance to this chapter but is only used for the sake of organization. For a discussion of Pauline

chronology and authorship of the New Testament letters, see Stanley E. Porter, *The Apostle Paul: His Life, Thought, and Letters* (Grand Rapids: Eerdmans, 2016).

4. Edward W. Said, *Culture and Imperialism* (New York: Vintage Books, 1993), 9.

5. See Andrew C. Hebert, "God and Caesar: Examining the Differences between Counter-Imperial and Post-Colonial Hermeneutics," *CTR* 11 (2014): 91–100.

6. For a postcolonial critique of Paul, as one who embraces an imperialistic/colonial ideology, see Joseph A. Marchal, "Imperial Intersections and Initial Inquiries: Toward a Feminist, Postcolonial Analysis of Philippians," in *The Colonized Apostle: Paul Through Postcolonial Eyes*, ed. Christopher D. Stanly (Minneapolis; Fortress Press, 2011), 146–160; Joseph A. Marchal, *The Politics of Heaven: Women, Gender and Empire in the Study of Paul* (Minneapolis; Fortress, 2008).

7. For some Pauline postcolonial studies see Davina C. Lopez, *Apostle to the Conquered: Reimagining Paul's Mission* (Minneapolis: Fortress Press, 2008); Harry O. Maier, *Picturing Paul in Empire: Imperial Image, Text and Persuasion in Colossians, Ephesians and the Pastoral Epistles* (London: Bloomsbury, 2013).

8. Daniel Oudshoorn, *Pauline Politics: An Examination of Various Perspectives*, vol. 1 of *Paul and the Uprising of the Dead* (Eugene: Cascade Books, 2020), 58.

9. All translations of the New Testament are mine, unless otherwise noted. The Greek text of the New Testament is from Nestle–Aland, *Novum Testametum Graece*, 28th edition.

10. Edwin A. Judge, "The Decrees of Caesar at Thessalonica," *RTR* 1 (1971): 1–7.

11. T. B. Mitford, "A Cypriot Oath of Allegiance to Tiberius," *JRS* 1 (1930): 75–79.

12. Judge, "The Decrees of Caesar," 5–6.

13. Mikael Tellbe, *Paul between Synagogue and State: Christians, Jews, and Civic Authorities in 1 Thessalonians, Romans, and Philippians*, ConBNT 34 (Stockholm: Almqvist & Wiksell International, 2001), 118–123.

14. Ibid., 126–130.

15. The issue of "parallelism" will be addressed later within this chapter.

16. Karl P. Donfried, "The Imperial Cults of Thessalonica and Political Conflict in 1 Thessalonians," in *Paul and Empire: Religion and Power in the Roman Imperial Society*, ed. Richard A. Horsley (Harrisburg: Trinity Press International, 1997), 215–223. Also Helmut Koester, "Imperial Ideology and Paul's Eschatology in 1 Thessalonians," in *Paul and Empire: Religion and Power in the Roman Imperial Society*, ed. Richard A. Horsley (Harrisburg: Trinity Press International, 1997), 158–166; James R. Harrison, *Paul and the Imperial Authorities at Thessalonica and Rome: A Study in the Conflict of Ideology*, WUNT 273 (Tübingen: Mohr Siebeck, 2011); Craig Steven de Vos, *Church and Community Conflicts: The Relationships of the Thessalonian, Corinthian, and Philippian Churches with Their Wider Civic Communities*, SBLDS 168 (Atlanta: Scholars Press, 1999).

17. Donfried, "The Imperial Cults," 217. In an important study on the phrase "peace and security" Joel R. White demonstrates that the phrase "peace and security" was not a common Roman imperial slogan when Paul was writing 1 Thessalonians. Though "peace" does evoke Roman sensibilities of the Pax Romana, "security"

is more of a Hellenistic aspect with regard to the *polis* than to Roman imperial propaganda. Analyzing eighteen pieces of evidence that have commonly been used by counter-imperial scholarship, White concludes that the phrase "peace and security" does not appear as Roman imperial propaganda prior to Paul's writing of 1 Thessalonians. In the one instance it appears in Velleius Paterculus's *Historia Romana* 2.98.2 (ca. 30 CE), it does not have a slogan like quality to it, nor is he alluding that it does. Ultimately, White says, those who use evidence in support of this phrase as an imperial slogan have not shown "sufficient sensitivity to the diachronic aspects of their analysis." See Joel R. White, "'Peace and Security' (1 Thessalonians 5.3): Is It Really a Roman Slogan?" *NTS* 59 (2013): 382–395, esp. 393. Also, see his study on the tradition-historical provenance of the use of Paul's phrase in 1 Thess 5:3; Joel R. White, "'Peace' and 'Security' (1 Thess 5.3): Roman Ideology and Greek Aspiration," *NTS* 60 (2014): 499–510.

18. Donfried, "The Imperial Cults," 219–220.

19. Ibid., 222.

20. Ibid., 223.

21. Ibid., 216, 222.

22. Ibid., 223.

23. Seyoon Kim, *Christ and Caesar: The Gospel and the Roman Empire in the Writings of Paul and Luke* (Grand Rapids: William B. Eerdmans Publishing Company, 2008).

24. Kim, *Christ and Caesar*, 76.

25. Ibid., 8.

26. Ibid.

27. Harrison, *Paul and the Imperial Authorities*, 47–62, 88–95.

28. Ibid., 95.

29. Ibid., 51–56.

30. Ibid., 86–90; esp. 89.

31. Ibid., 69.

32. Kim, *Christ and Caesar*, 8.

33. Ibid.

34. Harrison does respond to Kim saying, "Kim has disagreed with my proposal, saying that Paul does not mention the house of David in 1 Thessalonians, preferring instead to emphasize the wrath of God coming upon the Jews (1 Thess 2:14–16). In each case, Kim's exegesis is somewhat selective. Inexplicably, Kim overlooks Paul's messianic reference to Jesus as the 'Son' from heaven (1 Thess 1:10: τὸν υἱὸν αὐτοῦ ἐκ τῶν οὐρανῶν)." See Harrison, *Paul and the Imperial Authorities*, 69 n. 90.

35. Charles A. Wanamaker, *The Epistles to the Thessalonians: A Commentary on the Greek Text*, NIGTC (Grand Rapids: William B. Eerdmans Publishing Company, 1990), 86.

36. Ibid. See also M. Eugene Boring, *I & II Thessalonians: A Commentary* (Louisville: Westminster John Knox Press, 2015), 68–69.

37. Cf., Wanamaker, *The Epistles to the Thessalonians*, 114–116.

38. Harrison, *Paul and the Imperial Authorities*, 62–63.

39. Ibid., 59.

40. Earl J. Richard, *First and Second Thessalonians*, SP 13, ed. Daniel J. Harrington (Collegeville: The Liturgical Press, 1995), 232.

41. Holland Lee Hendrix, *Thessalonicans Honor Romans* (ThD diss., Harvard University, 1984).

42. E.g., Tellbe, *Paul between Synagogue and State*, 82–85; Neil Elliott, "Paul and the Politics of Empire," in *Paul and Politics: Ekklesia, Israel, Imperium, Interpretations: Essays in Honor of Krister Stendahl*, ed. Richard A. Horsley (Harrisburg: Trinity Press International, 2000), 17–39, p. 24; Donfried, "The Imperial Cults," *Paul and Empire: Religion and Power in the Roman Imperial Society*, ed. Richard A. Horsley (Harrisburg: Trinity Press International, 1997), 217; Harrison, *Paul and the Imperial Authorities*, 55–56.

43. Hendrix, *Thessalonicans Honor Romans*, 286.

44. Harrison, *Paul and the Imperial Authorities*, 56.

45. Though numismatic evidence is helpful in New Testament studies, limited engagement with extant evidence can skew our claims. In his helpful study on systematically studying coinage, examining Corinthian numismatic evidence, Bradley J. Bitner ["Coinage and Colonial Identity: Corinthian Numismatics and the Corinthian Correspondence," in *The First Urban Churches*, ed. James R. Harrison and L.L. Welborn, vol. 1 (Atlanta: SBL Press, 2015), 151–188, esp. 154.] says, "the types and legends of the Corinthian coinage were chosen by the colonial elite . . . depending on the denomination it was handled primarily by people of certain socio-economic levels. . . . If New Testament scholars insist on regarding coins as 'numismatic windows,' we should at least acknowledge they are *ancient* windows indeed, and will almost always provide us with a refracted and restricted view of our objects of inquiry." Cf. Richard Oster, "Numismatic Windows into the Social World of Early Christianity: A Methodological Inquiry," *JBL* 101 (1982): 195–223. For a general introduction to coin-evidence, see William E. Metcalf, ed., *The Oxford Handbook of Greek and Roman Coinage* (Oxford: Oxford University Press, 2012).

46. Mary Beard, John North, and Simon Price, *Religions of Rome: A History*, 2 vols. (Cambridge: Cambridge University Press, 1998), 1:349.

47. Hendrix, *Thessalonicans Honor Romans*, 296.

48. Ibid., 298–299.

49. See the unique case of a Thracian client-ruler, Caesar Julius Rhoimetalces, who was both priest and *agonothete* of the Imperator at Thessalonica.

50. Hendrix, *Thessalonicans Honor Romans*, 318. Also, Beard, North, and Price, *Religions of Rome*, 1:358–359.

51. Peter M. Fraser, *Ptolemaic Alexandria*, 3 vols. (Oxford: Clarendon Press, 1972), 1:190, 226.

52. Duncan Fishwick, *The Imperial Cult in the Latin West: Studies in the Ruler Cult of the Western Provinces of the Roman Empire*, 3 vols. (Leiden: Brill, 1987), 1:37.

53. Ibid., 46.

54. Arthur Darby Nock, "Deification and Julian," in *Arthur Darby Nock: Essays on Religion and the Ancient World*, ed. Zeph Stewart, 2 vols. (New York: Oxford University Press, 1986), 2:833–846. This is true insofar as it regards sources

contemporaneous with living emperors. Later sources, however, do attribute miracles to the apotheosized emperors. This is likely due to the growing popularity of the Jesus miracle tradition. See Wendy Cotter, ed., *Miracles in Greco-Roman Antiquity: A Sourcebook for the Study of New Testament Miracle Stories* (New York: Routledge, 1999).

55. S. R. F. Price, *Rituals and Powers: The Roman Imperial Cult in Asia Minor* (Cambridge: Cambridge University Press, 1986), 215.

56. Duncan Fishwick, "Votive Offerings to the Emperor?" *ZPE* 80 (1990): 121–130.

57. Fishwick, "Votive Offerings," 126–127.

58. No ex-voto offerings were made to Augustus, or any other living emperor. Regarding the new honors given in response to Augustus's divinity, there was a senatorial decree that a libation be poured to his Genius at every banquet, both public and private. This coincides with Roman tradition of sacrifices to the Genius. The proper offering was not a sacrificial victim but flowers, incense, or unmixed wine. See Lily Ross Taylor, *The Divinity of the Roman Emperor* (Middletown: American Philological Association, 1931), 150–153.

59. A.D. Nock, "Religious Developments from the Close of the Republic to the Death of Nero," in *Cambridge Ancient History*, ed. S.A. Cook, F. E Adcock, and M.P. Charlesworth, 14 vols. (Cambridge: Cambridge University Press, 1934), 10:465–522, esp. 481. See also in Fishwick, *The Imperial Cult in the Latin West*, 1:43

60. Fishwick, *The Imperial Cult in the Latin West*, 1:43.

61. Fishwick, "Votive Offerings," 130.

62. Fishwick, *The Imperial Cult in the Latin West*, 1:41.

63. Fishwick, "Votive Offerings," 130.

64. A number of inscriptions ascribe the term σωτήρ to Augustus. See Taylor, *The Divinity of the Roman Emperor*, 270–271, 272, 275. The terms σῴζω and σωτηρία have several meanings in the Hellenistic world. The action of "saving" or "being saved" could be used in a number of situations, for example, when gods or men rescue others by force from danger. It can also have the connotation of being protected from danger or being cured from diseases. Also, being a *savior* does not suggest a superiority over the one who is being saved. In regard to the imperial cult Werner Foerster [Werner Foerster, "σῴζω, σωτηρία, κτλ," *TDNT* 7:965–1024. Esp. 1010–1011] says, "When a kind of golden age seemed to come under and with Augustus, there was still no established link with σωτήρ. . . . There is a whole set of examples to show that σωτήρ was not reserved exclusively for the emperor (e.g., Augustus) and that it did not necessarily imply the divinity of its bearer or the concept of a world ruler . . . it may be noted that the emperor is very seldom called σωτήρ or *conservator* or *salvator*. In emperor worship, then, σωτήρ is a form of the Greek σωτήρ extended by the range of Roman rule."

65. Beard, North, and Price, *Religions of Rome*, 1:359.

66. Richard A. Horsley, "1 Corinthians: A Case Study of Paul's Assembly as an Alternative Society," in *Paul and Empire: Religion and Power in the Roman Imperial Society*, ed. Richard A. Horsley (Harrisburg: Trinity Press International, 1997), 242–252; Richard A. Horsley, "Rhetoric and Empire—And 1 Corinthians," in *Paul*

and Politics: Ekklesia, Israel, Imperium, Interpretations: Essays in Honor of Krister Stendahl, ed. Richard A. Horsley (Harrisburg: Trinity Press International, 2000), 72–102. See also Richard A. Horsley, *1 Corinthians*, ANTC (Nashville: Abingdon Press, 1998).

67. Horsley, "1 Corinthians: A Case Study," 243.

68. Ibid., 243–244.

69. Ibid., 251.

70. Ibid., 251–252.

71. Ibid., 247–249.

72. Ibid., 248.

73. Ibid., 250.

74. Ibid. Emphasis mine.

75. Ibid.

76. Trent A. Rogers, *God and the Idols: Representations of God in 1 Corinthians 8–10*, WUNT 2/427 (Tübingen: Mohr Siebeck, 2016), 321.

77. Ibid., 321–322.

78. Many debates deal with the place of 1 Cor 9 in the schema of Paul's argument in 1 Cor 8–10. For a concise summary of the positions on 1 Cor 9, see Alex T. Cheung, *Idol Food in Corinth: Jewish Background and Pauline Legacy*, JSNT 176 (Sheffield: Sheffield Academic Press, 1999), 137–143.

79. Rogers, *Gods and Idols*, 259.

80. Ibid., 259. For a fuller treatment of the argument, see pp. 231–257.

81. Neil Elliott, "The Anti-Imperial Message of the Cross," in *Paul and Empire: Religion and Power in the Roman Imperial Society*, ed. Richard A. Horsley (Harrisburg: Trinity Press International, 1997), 167–183.

82. Ibid., 167.

83. Ibid., 181.

84. Ibid., 182.

85. Ibid., 183.

86. It may be anachronistic cynicism to consider Paul's apocalyptic thought as particularly counter-imperial. In the ancient Mediterranean world, many regarded Rome's success in expansion as divine blessing. Likewise, in the Greek east, there is a large amount of evidence that shows a general appreciation of Rome's political and economic stability due to the larger civic authority. See Clifford Ando, *Imperial Ideology and Provincial Loyalty in the Roman Empire* (Berkeley: University of California Press, 2000), 49–69.

87. See a similar conclusion reached by Kim, *Christ and Caesar*, 23.

88. Lynn H. Cohick, "Philippians and Empire: Paul's Engagement with Imperialism and the Imperial Cult," in *Jesus Is Lord, Caesar Is Not: Evaluating Empire in New Testament Studies*, ed. Scot McKnight and J. B. Modica (Downers Grove: InterVarsity Press, 2013), 166–182, esp. 171.

89. Ibid., 171.

90. Markus Bockmuehl, *The Epistle to the Philippians*, BNTC (Peabody: Hendrickson, 1998), 98.

91. Ibid.

92. Ibid., 147.

93. Gordon D. Fee, *Paul's Letter to the Philippians*, NICNT (Grand Rapids: Eerdmans, 1995), 197.

94. Ibid., 197.

95. Peter Oakes, "Re–Mapping the Universe: Paul and the Emperor in 1 Thessalonians and Philippians," *JSNT* 21 (2005): 301–322. See 320.

96. Ibid., 319.

97. Peter Oakes, *Philippians: From People to Letter* (Cambridge: Cambridge University Press, 2001), 150.

98. Oakes, "Re–Mapping the Universe," 321.

99. N. T. Wright, *Paul in Fresh Perspective* (Minneapolis: Fortress Press, 2005). For an evaluation of Wright's arguments see Kim, *Christ and Caesar*, 13.

100. Wright, *Paul in Fresh Perspective*, 73–74.

101. Ibid., 74.

102. N. T. Wright, "Paul's Gospel and Caesar's Empire," in *Paul and Politics: Ekklesia, Israel, Imperium, Interpretations: Essays in Honor of Krister Stendahl*, ed. Richard A. Horsley (Harrisburg: Trinity Press International, 2000), 160–183. See p. 174.

103. Ibid., 174.

104. Ibid., 174.

105. A more in-depth description of "coded messages" or "hidden transcripts" will be discussed later in this chapter.

106. Wright, "Paul's Gospel and Caesar's Empire," 174–175.

107. Ibid., 177.

108. A more in-depth description on "parallelism" will be discussed later in this chapter.

109. Wright, "Paul's Gospel and Caesar's Empire," 179. See also, Wright, *Paul in Fresh Perspective*, 73–74.

110. Cohick, "Philippians and Empire," 172–173.

111. See Gertrude Grether, "Livia and the Roman Imperial Cult," *AJP* 67 (1946): 222–252; Anthony A. Barrett, *Livia: First Lady of Imperial Rome* (New Haven: Yale University Press, 2002), esp. 215–228.

112. Cohick, "Philippians and Empire," 173–174.

113. That which is to be revealed at the eschaton is both *now* and *not yet*. See Andrew T. Lincoln, *Paradise Now and Not Yet: Studies in the Role of the Heavenly Dimension in Paul's Thought with Special Reference to his Eschatology*, SNTSMS 43 (Cambridge: Cambridge University Press, 1981), 101.

114. I am indebted to the observations of Dorothea H. Bertschmann, *Bowing Before Christ—Nodding to the State? Reading Paul Politically with Oliver O'Donovan and John Howard Yoder*, LNTS 502 (London: Bloomsbury, 2014), 112–114.

115. Ibid., 113.

116. Ibid.

117. Ibid., 116. Bertschmann identifies the "enemies of the cross" in Phil 3:18 which she identifies with defiant Christians and hostile outsiders—though Paul would

not likely cry for outsiders as he would for disobedient believers. Cf. Stephen E. Fowl, *Philippians* (Grand Rapids: Eerdmans, 2005), 170.

118. E.g., Esth 8:12p LXX; 2 Macc 6:1, 11:25; Josephus *Vita* 12. See also Acts 23:1. Cf. Bockmuehl, *The Epistle to the Philippians*, 97.

119. Ibid.

120. Neil Elliott, "Romans 13:1–7 in the Context of Imperial Propaganda," in *Paul and Empire: Religion and Power in the Roman Imperial Society*, ed. Richard A. Horsley (Harrisburg: Trinity Press, 1997), 184–205; Elliott, "Paul and the Politics of Empire," 17–39: Neil Elliott, "The Apostle Paul's Self-Presentation as Anti-Imperial Performance," in *Paul and the Roman Imperial Order*, ed. Richard A. Horsley (Harrisburg: Trinity Press International, 2004), 67–88: Neil Elliott, "The Letter to the Romans," in *A Postcolonial Commentary on the New Testaments Writings*, ed. F. F. Segovia and R. S. Sugirtharajah (New York: T & T Clark, 2007), 194–219; Neil Elliott, *The Arrogance of Nations: Reading Romans in the Shadow of Empire* (Minneapolis: Fortress Press, 2008); Neil Elliott, "Blasphemed Among the Nations': Pursuing an Anti-Imperial 'Intertextuality' in Romans," in *As It Is Written: Studying Paul's Use of Scripture*, ed. Stanley E. Porter and C. D. Stanley, Society of Biblical Literature Symposium Series 50 (Leiden: Brill, 2008), 213–233; Neil Elliott, "Paul's Political Christology: Samples from Romans," in *Reading Paul in Context: Explorations in Identity Formation*, ed. K. Ehrensperger and J. B. Tucker, Library of New Testament Studies 428 (London: T & T Clark, 2010), 39–51.

121. Elliott, *The Arrogance of Nations*, 158.

122. Elliott, "Romans 13:1–7," 190. See also Neil Elliott, *The Rhetoric of Romans: Argumentative Constraint: and Strategy and Paul's Dialogue with Judaism*, JSNT 49 (Sheffield: Sheffield Press, 1990).

123. Elliott, *The Arrogance of Nations*, 158.

124. Elliott, "Paul and the Politics of Empire," 37.

125. Elliott, *The Arrogance of Nations*, 158

126. Elliott, "Paul and the Politics of Empire," 39.

127. Wright, "Paul's Gospel and Caesar's Empire," 167–173.

128. Ibid., 166. Cf. Ps 72:8; 80:11; 89:25–27; 1 Kings 4:21–24; Zech 9:10

129. Wright, "Paul's Gospel and Caesar's Empire," 168.

130. Ibid.

131. Ibid., 171.

132. Ibid., 172.

133. Thomas H. Tobin, *Paul's Rhetoric in Its Contexts: The Argument of Romans* (Peabody: Hendrickson, 2004), 396.

134. Kim, *Christ and Caesar*, 19. Cf. 1 Cor 5:7–8; 6:20; 7:23; 8:11; 11:23–25; 15:3–4; Gal 1:3–4; 2:19–20; 3:13–14; 1 Thess 5:9–10.

135. Ibid.

136. Ibid., 17.

137. Tobin, *Paul's Rhetoric in Its Contexts*, 99.

138. For example, see Joseph A. Fitzmyer, *Romans: A New Translation with Introduction and Commentary*, AB 33 (New Haven: Yale University Press, 1993);

Arland J. Hultgren, *Paul's Letter to the Romans: A Commentary* (Grand Rapids: William B. Eerdmans Publishing Company, 2011). For a contrasting view, see Robert Jewett [*Romans*, Hermeneia (Minneapolis: Fortress Press, 2009), 2, 49], who argues that Romans is an "anti-imperialist letter" which "compromises the antitheses of official propaganda about Rome's superior piety, justice, and honor."

139. Tobin, *Paul's Rhetoric in Its Contexts*, 99.

140. Adolf Deissmann, *Light from the Ancient East: The New Testament Illustrated by Recently Discovered Texts of the Graeco–Roman World*, ed. Gustav Adolf Deissmann, New and completely rev. ed. with eighty-five illustrations from the latest German ed. (London; New York: Harper, 1927). See especially 338–378.

141. Ibid., 342.

142. Ibid., 342–343.

143. Samuel Sandmel, "Parallelomania," *JBL* 81 (1962): 1–13.

144. Ibid., 1.

145. Ibid., 7.

146. Deissmann, *Light from the Ancient East*, 351.

147. Ibid.

148. Sandmel, "Parallelomania," 5.

149. Wright, "Paul's Gospel and Caesar's Empire," 162.

150. Wright draws on the work of R. B. Hays, who lays out seven criteria for detecting Paul's use, or "echoes" of scripture in his letters. Wright, however, uses these criteria to hear "echoes of Caesar" alongside "echoes of scripture" in Paul's letter. See Wright, *Paul in Fresh Perspective*, 61–62. Cf., Richard Hays, *Echoes of Scripture in the Letters of Paul* (New Haven: Yale University Press, 1989).

151. Wright, "Paul's Gospel and Caesar's Empire,"168.

152. Ibid., 174–175.

153. Wright says, "Paul's own self-understanding seeks of radical innovation from within a tradition, and of radical head-on confrontation with other traditions." Ibid., 162. See also Wight, *Paul in Fresh Perspective*, 75–77.

154. Harrison, *Paul and the Imperial Authorities*, 47–62, 88–95.

155. Ibid., 57, n. 47.

156. Ibid., 57–58.

157. Ibid., 62. Helmut Koester makes a similar argument and reaches a similar conclusion about 1 Thess. Koester argues that Paul, by incorporating the "political" term παρουσία into the letter "envisions a role for the eschatological community that presents a utopian alternative to the prevailing eschatological ideology of Rome." See Koester, "Imperial Ideology and Paul's Eschatology, 158–166, esp. 166.

158. Joseph D. Fantin, *The Lord of the Entire World: Lord Jesus, a Challenge to Lord Caesar?* New Testament Monographs 31 (Sheffield: Sheffield Phoenix Press, 2011), 7.

159. Ibid., 210–211, 217. Cf. James D. G. Dunn, *The Theology of the Apostle* (Grand Rapids: Eerdmans, 1998), 247.

160. John M.G. Barclay, "Why the Roman Empire Was Insignificant to Paul," in *Pauline Churches and Diaspora Jews*, WUNT 275 (Tübingen: Mohr Siebeck, 2011), 363–387. See especially, 376–379.

161. Ibid., 376.

162. Ibid.

163. Ibid., 377.

164. Larry W. Hurtado, *Lord Jesus Christ: Devotion to Jesus in Earliest Christianity* (Grand Rapids: William B. Eerdmans Publishing Company, 2003), 101–108.

165. Christopher Bryan, *Render to Caesar: Jesus, the Early Church, and the Roman Superpower* (Oxford: Oxford university Press, 2005), 77–93.

166. Ibid., 90.

167. Ibid., 90–91.

168. Ibid., 91. Cf. Ittai Gradel, *Emperor Worship and Roman Religion* (Oxford: Oxford University Press, 2002), esp. 262–276.

169. Bryan, *Render to Caesar*, 91.

170. Ibid.

171. I am indebted to the work of Seyoon Kim whose logic I closely follow. See Kim, *Christ and Caesar*, 30–32.

172. Cf., Richard A. Horsley, introduction to *Paul and Empire*, 1–4, 10–24.

173. Horsley, "1 Corinthians: A Case Study," 242–252; Horsley, "Rhetoric and Empire," 72–102; Wright, *Paul in Fresh Perspective*, 40–58.

174. Elliott, "The Anti-Imperial Message of the Cross," 167–183.

175. Horsley, "1 Corinthians: A Case Study," 242–252.

176. See, e.g., Efrain Agosto, "Patronage and Commendation, Imperial and Anti-Imperial," in *Paul and the Roman Imperial Order*, ed. Richard A. Horsley (Harrisburg: Trinity Press International, 2004), 103–124.

177. Kim, *Christ and Caesar*, 30–31.

178. Ibid., 32.

179. Ibid., 32.

180. For further examples see: Mark D. Nanos, "The Inter- and Intra-Jewish Political context of Paul's Letter to the Galatians," in *Paul and Politics: Ekklesia, Israel, Imperium, Interpretations: Essays in Honor of Krister Stendahl*, ed. Richard A. Horsley (Harrisburg: Trinity Press International, 2000), 146–159; Harrison, *Paul and the Imperial Authorities at Thessalonica.*; William r. Herzog, II, "Dissembling, a Weapon of the Weak: The Case of Christ and Caesar in Mark 12:13–17 and Romans 13:1–7," *PRSt* 21 (1994): 339–339.

181. Deissmann, *Light from the Ancient East*, 355.

182. Erwin Ramsdell Goodenough, *An Introduction to Philo Judaeus*, 2nd ed. (Oxford: Basil Blackwell, 1962), 55–57.

183. Kenneth Schenck, *A Brief Guide to Philo* (Louisville: Westminster John Knox Press, 2005), 17. See also Goodenough, *An Introduction to Philo Judaeus*, 48.

184. Goodenough, *An Introduction to Philo Judaeus*, 57.

185. "τί δέ; οὐχὶ καὶ ἡμεῖς, ὅταν ἐν ἀγορᾷ διατρίβωμεν, εἰώθαμεν ἐξίστασθαι μὲν τοῖς ἄρχουσιν, ἐξίστασθαι δὲ καὶ τοῖς ὑποζυγίοις; ἀλλ᾽ ἀπ᾽ ἐναντίας γνώμης καὶ οὐχὶ τῆς αὐτῆς· τοῖς μὲν γὰρ ἄρχουσιν ἐν τιμῇ, τοῖς δὲ ὑποζυγίοις διὰ φόβον τοῦ μηδὲν ἀπ᾽ αὐτῶν εἰς ἡμᾶς νεωτερισθῆναι. καὶ διδόντων μὲν τῶν καιρῶν ἐπιτιθεμένους τὴν τῶν ἐχθρῶν βίαν καλὸν καταλῦσαι, μὴ ἐπιτρεπόντων δὲ ἀσφαλὲς ἡσυχάσαι, βουλομένοις

δέ τιν' ὠφέλειαν εὑρίσκεσθαι παρ' αὐτῶν ἁρμόττον τιθασεῦσαι" (Philo, *De Somniis* 2.91–92).

186. Goodenough, *An Introduction to Philo Judaeus*, 57.

187. See also Goodenough's interpretation of Philo's treatment of Joseph in *De Iosepho*. He locates Philo's intentions against Rome in what we could term as "hidden transcript." See Goodenough, *An Introduction to Philo Judaeus*, 60–62. See also, Erwin Ramsdell Goodenough, *The Politics of Philo Judaeus* (New Haven: Yale University Press, 1938). For an argument against Goodenough's interpretation of *De Somniis* 2.81–92 see Arnaldo Momigliano, review of *An Introduction to Philo Judaeus*, by E. R. Goodenough, *JRS* 34 (1944): 163–165. Also, Maren Niehoff, *Philo on Jewish Identity and Culture* (Tübingen: Mohr Siebeck, 2001), 6–7 n.18.

188. Christoph Heilig [*Hidden Criticism? The Methodology and Plausibility of the Search for a Counter-Imperial Subtext in Paul* (Minneapolis: Fortress Press, 2015), 1–20.] analyzes not only Goodenough's argument but also *Somn.* 2. Though Heilig finds political allegory in *Somn.* 2 he rightly suggests that Goodenough overemphasized this aspect.

189. E.g., Elliott, "Paul and the Politics of Empire," 17–39; Elliott, *The Arrogance of Nations*; Elliott, "Romans 13:1–7," 184–204; Harris, *Paul and the Imperial Authorities*, 28.

190. Elliott, "Paul and the Politics of Empire," 33.

191. Ibid.

192. See Neil Elliott, "Disciplining the Hope of the Poor in Ancient Rome," in *Christian Origins*, vol. 1 of *A People's History of Christianity*, ed. R. Horsley (Minneapolis: Fortress Press, 2005), 177–197; Elliott, *Arrogance of Nations*, 36–37; Dieter Georgi, "God Turned Upside Down," in *Paul and Empire: Religion and Power in the Roman Imperial Society*, ed. Richard A. Horsley (Harrisburg: Trinity Press International, 1997), 157; Wright, "Paul's Gospel and Caesar's Empire," 160–183. See also R. L. Parott, *Paul's Political Thought: Rom 13:1–7 in the Light of Hellenistic Political Thought* (PhD diss., The Claremont Graduate School, 1980), 126–155.

The notion that Rome was a police state, actively seeking to persecute dissenters, is much exaggerated. Indeed, prominent citizens and those in the public sphere had to be careful about what they said or did, but Rome did not actively seek out and prosecute dissenters. Even when ancient associations came under the microscope of Julius Caesar and later Augustus, they did not monitor the communique of local associations since these small groups were highly incapable of subverting the authority of the Caesar. See Wendy Cotter, "The Collegia and Roman Law: State Restrictions on Voluntary Associations 60 BCE–200 CE," in *Voluntary Associations in the Graeco–Roman World*, ed., John S. Kloppenborg and S. G. Wilson (London: Routledge, 1996), 74–89.

193. James C. Scott, *Domination and the Arts of Resistance: Hidden Transcripts* (New Haven: Yale University Press, 1990); also James C. Scott, *Weapons of the Weak: Everyday Forms of Peasant Resistance* (New Haven: Yale University Press, 1986). For an extensive and appreciative evaluation of Scott's work with regard to New Testament studies see Richard Horsley, ed., *Hidden Transcripts and the Arts of*

Resistance: Applying the Work of James C. Scott to Jesus and Paul (Atlanta: Society of Biblical Literature, 2004); Harris, *Paul and the Imperial Authorities*, 29.

194. Scott, *Domination and the Arts of Resistance*, 4.

195. Ibid., 4–5.

196. Ibid., 18–19, 136–182.

197. I am indebted to the work of John M.G. Barclay whose critique of Pauline scholars who use Scott's work I closely follow. See Barclay, "Why the Roman Empire Was Insignificant to Paul," 382–383.

198. Ibid., 383.

199. Ibid.

200. Heilig, *Hidden Criticism*, 54–67, esp. 58–65 and 129–138.

201. Heilig's major concern is to rethink how one analyzes data to ascertain whether certain passages in Paul's letters could be understood as counter-imperial. With the application of Bayes Theorem, he is essentially evaluating counter-imperial arguments in relation to explanatory potential and background plausibility. He says [ibid., 155], "We have to determine for each individual case whether the wording we find in the biblical text would 1) evoke a comparison with current concepts described in a similar way and 2) whether there is a subversive potential the author was aware of. For the moment, we can note, quite generally that the denial of a critical potential of lexical parallels cannot be proved easily by noting that an 'antithesis' is not apparent—at least not if we opt for a more modest hypothesis of critical engagement with imperial propaganda."

202. Flavius Josephus, *Against Apion: Translation and Commentary*, ed. and trans. John M. G. Barclay (Leiden: Brill, 2013), 209–210.

203. During the reign of the Emperor Augustus, a decree was issued which stripped Alexandria of their βουλή which meant that Alexandria could no longer function as an autonomous government within the empire. There was also the introduction of the poll-tax, the λαογραφία. In Egypt, the λαογραφία was enforced on the native Egyptians, while Greeks and Jews were liable to pay either a reduced tax or pay no tax at all. The so-called βουλή Papyrus (PSI X 1160: CPJ 150), a document which describes a meeting between an Alexandrian Greek embassy and Augustus, demonstrates not only the frustration of the Alexandrians with their βουλή being taken away but also their frustration with Alexandrian Jews. The βουλή Papyrus has received considerable attention over the years because of the important information it reveals to us in regard to the whole Jewish question in Alexandria. Though "the Jews" are not directly mentioned in the document, scholars presume it is "the Jews" who are directly being mentioned by the embassy as "uncultured and civilized" and as "polluting" the pure Alexandrian society. The βουλή Papyrus shows how the Alexandrian embassy sought not only to reestablish their βουλή but, by reestablishing it, they would also enforce the λαογραφία for Rome. They also sought to cleanse their city of the "pollution" by not allowing outsiders into the gymnasia. Their request for a βουλή was subsequently denied, though the request for the denial of outsiders entering the gymnasia was kept. See the βουλή Papyrus in Victor A. Tcherikover and Alexander Fuks, ed., *Corpus Papyrorum Judaicarum*, 3 vols. (Cambridge: Harvard

University Press, 1957–1964), 2.25–29. Also Herbert Musurillo, ed., *The Acts of the Pagan Martyrs: Acta Alexandrinorum* (New York: Arno Press, 1979). *Yet* as Sandra Gambetti notes, Augustus seems to reinstitute the same rights for the Jews which they had under the Ptolemies. See Sandra Gambetti, *The Alexandrian Riots of 38 CE: A Historical Reconstruction* (Leiden: Brill, 2009) 57–76.

204. Tcherikover and Fuks, *Corpus Papyrorum Judaicarum*, 2.55–107.

205. Tcherikover and Fuks say, "There is far more political and literary fiction in the *AAM* than historical truth. . . . It was not 'classic' work, whose existence was perpetuated by careful copies made by skilled scribes, but a work of no great value circulated in private copies; thus it was possible for anyone to change the text . . . according to his taste or to purpose for which he was copying." See ibid., 2.58–59.

206. Translation, slightly modified, in ibid., 100–105.

Chapter 2

Figured Speech and Pauline Rhetoric

The notion that Paul incorporated "coded speech" into his letters is part of a larger discussion surrounding the use of the rhetorical device known as *figured speech*. The purpose, therefore, of this chapter is twofold. In the first section, I will explain at length figured speech, its different types and methods of use, as discussed in ancient rhetorical handbooks. Part of this section will also detail the methods for creating and detecting figured speech. In the second section, I will examine the most important texts which some counter-imperial interpreters of Paul appeal to in their arguments for Pauline hidden transcripts (1 Thess 2:13–16; Phil 3; Rom 13:1–7). I shall argue that Paul does not undermine the civic authority by incorporating any of the rhetorical devices associated with figured speech in these passages. These passages must be understood with respect to the letter as a whole while not removing Paul from his larger Hellenistic Jewish background.

DEFINING AND UNDERSTANDING FIGURED SPEECH

The rhetorical device commonly referred to as *figured speech* (ἐσχηματισμένος ἐν λόγῳ or *figura*) was taken up by several ancient rhetoricians. As Jason A. Whitlark notes, figured speech is a rhetorical device that seeks to communicate a covert message to the audience.[1] This covert message is conveyed in several ways, but the circumstances and the strategies for creating figured speech will be discussed later in this chapter. With regard to the ancient rhetoricians who describe this rhetorical device, Ps.-Dionysius suggests that figured speech can be used in the three types of rhetoric: deliberative, judicial, and epideictic (*Ars Rhetorica* 8.298.4-5).[2] The *Rhetorica ad Herennium* says that *significatio* "is the figure which leaves more to be suspected than has been actually

43

asserted" (4.53.67 [Caplan, LCL]). Quintilian defines figured speech in a similar way as "*saying one thing and meaning another*" (*Inst.* 9.1.29 [Butler, LCL]. Quintilian also notes that figured speech is not easily detectable, which if it were, it would mean it was never *covert* to begin with. Quintilian says, "If a figure is perfectly obvious, it ceases to be a figure" (*Inst.* 9.2.69 [Butler, LCL]). Simply speaking, figured speech should not be readily detectable but the speech itself, nonetheless, hints at another meaning. Figured speech creates a tacit understanding between the speaker and the audience.

Types of Figured Speech

Ps.- Hermogenes in his *De inv.*, could distinguish three basic types of figured speech or τὰ ἐσχηματισμένα προβλήματα: (1) ἔμφασις—implied meaning, (2) πλάγιον—deflection, and (3) ἐναντίον—saying the opposite (4.13.205–206).[3] Ps.-Dionysius also recognized these three types of figured speaking, though he never uses the term ἔμφασις, in *Ars Rhet.* 8.295.15–296.5.[4] Ps.-Dionysius mentions three more types of figured speaking (297.18–23), but they are dependent on the main categories, which we understand as ἔμφασις, πλάγιον, and ἐναντίον.[5]

Even though there are three types of figured speech, the primary focus for this chapter will be on ἔμφασις. Some counter-imperial interpreters of Paul argue that Paul used figured speech to speak subversively against the empire lest he or his communities incur imperial censure. As we will see, ἔμφασις is incorporated into speeches or letters when one cannot openly speak out of fear. Though not directly cited by these counter-imperial interpretations, they ultimately argue that Paul incorporated ἔμφασις into his letters. We will therefore proceed to discuss figured speech both generally and more specifically focus on the category of ἔμφασις.

Understanding Ἔμφασις

In the strictest sense, ἔμφασις (*implied meaning*)[6] "as a word-trope expresses the more precise meaning of something by means of a less precise semantic content."[7] Ps. -Dionysius explains what he considers the first type of figured speech, which should be understood as a description of ἔμφασις. He explains that this first category of figured speech is when a speaker says what he means but with propriety (εὐπρέπεια), out of respect for his opponent, or out of caution with respect to the audience (ἀσφάλεια) (*Ars Rhet.* 8.295.18f).[8] Quintilian says of ἔμφασις:

> Again, what would eloquence do if deprived of the artifices of amplification and its opposite? Of which the first required the gift of signifying more than we say,

that is *implied meaning* [ἔμφασιν], together with exaggeration and overstatement of the truth, while the latter requires the power to diminish and palliate. (*Inst.* 9.2.3 [Butler, LCL])[9]

In other words, he states that ἔμφασις is when someone says one thing but by means of exaggeration or understatement means something else.

Regarding ἔμφασις and propriety (εὐπρέπειας), Demetrius, in his *De Elocutione*, draws on the example from Plato's *Phaedo* (*Eloc.* 5.298).[10] In *Phaedo* 59B–C, Plato wishes to reproach the friends of Socrates, Aristippus, and Cleambrotus. In this dialogue, Phaedo is narrating the imprisonment and death of Socrates to his friend Echecrates. At one point, Echecrates asks who visited Socrates in prison. After recounting all those who were present, one by one, much to Echecrates's surprise he did not hear of Aristippus or Cleambrotus being at the side of their master. Echecrates says to Phaedo, "What (τί δέ)? Were Aristippus and Cleambrotus there?" and Phaedo responds, "Certainly not (οὐ δῆτα). For they were said to be in Aegina" (Plato, *Phaed.* 59C [Fowler, LCL].[11] Aegina is less than thirty miles from Athens. For them to be so close to Socrates and not at his side is quite embarrassing. As Demetrius says, "Everything that precedes owes its point to the words 'they were in Aegina.' The passage is all the more forcible because its point is conveyed by the fact itself and not by the speaker" (*Eloc.* 5.288). Though Plato wanted to convey his disappointment at Aristippus and Cleambrotus, he did so elegantly by means of a figure (σχῆμα).

Ἔμφασις can also be employed by using an obscure verbal imprecision whose more precise meaning is revealed by context clues which can have the effect of surprise.[12] Of this sort Quintilian says,

> Some, perhaps, may think that words which mean more than they actually say deserve mention in connexion with clearness, since they assist the understanding. I, however, prefer to place *implied meaning* [ἔμφασιν] among the ornaments of oratory, since it does not make a thing intelligible, but merely more intelligible. (*Inst.* 8.2.11 [Butler, LCL])[13]

This form of figured speech is targeting the attentive listener (or reader) who can discover the orator's true intention by means of conjecture. Additionally, there are two types of ἔμφασις which are recognized: the first category is when something said means more than it says (explicitly), and the second type is when something said means something which is not actually said (Quin. *Inst.* 8.3.83).[14]

Quintilian lists two examples of this first type of ἔμφασις, the first from Homer's *Odyssey* and the second from Virgil's *Aeneid* (*Inst.* 8.3.83–84). In the *Odyssey* (11.473–538) Odysseus has made his way into Hades where he is approached by the spirit of his fallen comrade, Achilles. In Odysseus's dialogue with the spirit, he praises the deeds of his friend Achilles while still alive and recalls entering the wooden horse. He says, "And again, when we, the best of the Argives, were about to descend (κατεβαίνομεν) into the horse which Epeius made" (Homer, *Od. 11.*523 [Murray, LCL]).[15] Notice, by means of one verb "to descend" κατεβαίνομεν (first person plural, imperfect active indicative), it indicates the size of the wooden horse. That the wooden horse was so large, it could hold many people. Likewise, recounting the fall of Troy, Vergil in the *Aeneid* states that the Greeks were "sliding down a lowered rope" to exit the wooden horse so they could attack the Trojans (Vergil, *Aen.* 2.262 [Fairclough, LCL]).[16] The phrase indicates the vast height of the wooden horse and its great size.

The second category of ἔμφασις, when something said means something which is not actually said, is expressed in Cicero's *Pro Ligario.* The *Pro Ligario* is Cicero's defense of Quintus Ligarius before Julius Caesar for his alleged attempt to bring arms against Caesar. Cicero says,

> I will speak without reserve what I feel, Caesar. If, in the greatness of your fortunes, the clemency, in which you purposely, yes, purposely persist—and I realize what I am saying—had not been equally great, then your triumph would be overwhelmed in a flood of bitter mourning. How many of the victors would there be who would have you pitiless, since such are found even among the vanquished? How many would be those who, wishing that none should be pardoned by you, would raise barriers against your mercy, when even those whom you yourself have pardoned would have you show no compassion towards others? (Cicero, *Lig.* 15 [Watts, LCL])

Quintilian states that we, the audience, understand that Cicero suppresses "the fact" that Caesar does not lack counsellors who would likely incite him to violence (*Inst.* 8.3.85). But Cicero does not openly suggest this in his speech. The audience, rather, conjectures this by noticing what is not said (Quintilian, *Inst.* 8.3.85).

Understanding Πλάγιον

Πλάγιον (*deflection*) is the second type of figured speech.[17] This figure has the speaker present a set of headings (κεφάλαια) but then develops these headings by seeking out another objective (Ps.-Dionysius, *Ars. Rhet.* 296. 14–20).[18] Demetrius describes πλάγιον as an "indirect expression" which "is more impressive than the direct (εὐθέος)" (*Eloc.* 2.104).[19] In *On Invention* Ps.-Hermogenes says that πλάγιον "is a 'deflected' [πλάγιον] problem whenever, while arguing for the opposite side, the speech also accomplishes something else" (*De inv.* 4.13.205). Πλάγιον can therefore be described as a figured speech that seeks to accomplish one objective overtly while simultaneously accomplishing another covertly.[20]

Ps.-Dionysius gives an example of πλάγιον in *Ars Rhetorica* 325.13–327.18. The example draws from Diomedes's attack on Agamemnon in *Iliad* 9.32–49. The text from the *Iliad* reads,

> Son of Atreus, with you first will I contend in your folly, where it is my right, O king, in the place of assembly: and do not be at all angry. My valor you first reviled among the Danaans, and said that I was no man of war but lacking in valor; and all this know the Achaeans both young and old. But as for you, the son of crooked-counseling Cronos has given you a double endowment: with the scepter he has granted you to be honored above all, but valor he gave you not, in which is the greatest might. Strange man, do you really think that the sons of the Achaeans are so unwarlike and lacking in valor as you proclaim? If your own heart is eager to return home, go; before you lies the way, and your ships stand beside the sea, all the many ships that followed you from Mycenae. But the other long-haired Achaeans will remain here until we have sacked Troy. And if they, too . . . let them flee in their ships to their dear native land; yet will we two, Sthenelus and I, fight on, until we win the goal of Ilios; for with the aid of a god have we come. (*Iliad*, 9.32–49 [Wyatt, LCL])

Ps.-Dionysius rightly suggests that Diomedes's attack of the king seems out of place and quite unsuitable (οὗτος ὁ λόγος, ἂν μή τι ἕτερον διοικῆται ἢ λέγῃ, παντάπασιν ἄτοπός ἐστι καὶ ἀσχήμων). Even Diomedes goes on to acknowledge that his speech is an inappropriate one and even begins to apologize. Ps.-Dionysius suggests that Diomedes is only pretending to be angry with Agamemnon and is essentially speaking in his favor. By giving the impression that he wants Agamemnon to leave, he is actually telling Agamemnon to remain and fight. Though Diomedes begins his speech with an overt objective of suggesting that Agamemnon leave, he accomplishes the covert objective, which is to persuade Agamemnon to remain and do battle.[21]

Malcom Heath states that πλάγιον in speeches, as illustrated in Ps.-Dionysius, highlights "interwoven subjects" which help accomplish multiple purposes.[22] A speech could have multiple covert aims, which could be hidden; Ps.-Dionysius draws on the example from Plato's *Apology* (*Ars. Rhet.* 305.5–309.10). As Jason Whitlark suggests, the aim of the speech is Socrates's defense against his accusers, but the covert aims are many: a condemnation of his Athenian accusers, Plato offering an encomium on Socrates, and teaching one how to be a philosopher.[23]

Understanding Ἐναντίον

Ἐναντίον (*saying the opposite*) is the third type of figured speech.[24] Ps.-Hermogenes defines ἐναντίον as an "opposition." He says, "Problems are opposed [ἐναντίον] whenever we are arguing for the opposite of what we actually say" (*De inv.* 4.13.205). Ἐναντίον is therefore understood to be *irony* in its figured form. Quintilian notes that *saying the opposite* (ἐναντιότης) is disguised *irony* (*Inst.* 9.2.46).

Ἐναντίον is often incorporated into encomia since encomiums are easily adaptable to this form of disguised irony.[25] Blame could be rendered as through praise. Whitlark notes this as a possibility "because virtue was often understood as the mean between two vices. Because virtue is defined relative to the two extremes, virtue can be portrayed as vice and vice as virtue" (cf. Quintilian, *Inst.* 3.7.25). Whitlark draws from the discussion in Plutarch's *De Moralia*. He writes,

> And so in attempts at flattery we should be observant and on our guard against prodigality being called "liberality," cowardice "self-preservation," impulsiveness "quickness," stinginess "frugality," the amorous man "companionable and amiable," the irascible and overbearing "spirited," the insignificant and meek "kindly." (*Adul. am.* 56C [Babbitt, LCL])

The idea presented here is the concealing of one's own opinion. It is important to note here that unlike *implied meaning*, there is no precondition mentioned for the incorporation of ἐναντίον such as fear or propriety. Rather Quintilian notes that "the real orator, the good man, will never do this, unless led into it by the public interest" (*Inst.* 3.7.25 [Russel, LCL]). Ultimately, the aim of ἐναντίον is not to ridicule one's opponent but to achieve a future victory over the opponent, by exposing the opponent's rhetoric as absurd.[26]

CIRCUMSTANCES FOR FIGURED SPEECH

As it has been shown, figured speech had several uses. Considering implied meaning, or ἔμφασις, it is used when a speaker wants to express something but under conditions where the speaker is either unable or unwilling to do so directly. Under this circumstance, the speaker must hint to the audience or reader so that they may find and understand the covert message. Unlike ἐναντίον, the hidden meaning and the real meaning are not opposites but are "like a vessel and its contents, or a shell and its kernel."[27] Quintilian states that there are three circumstances which require the application of ἔμφασις (*Inst.* 9.2.66): fear (*Inst.* 9.2.67–75), respect (*Inst.* 9.2.76–80), and elegance

(*Inst.* 9.2.96–99).[28] Ps.-Demetrius says that are only two conditions: propriety (εὐπρέπεια) and caution (ἀσφάλεια; *Eloc.* 5.287).[29]

Implied Meaning With Regard to Fear and Respect (Caution)

With regard to fear and respect, Quintilian says,

> We imagine conditions laid down by tyrants on abdication and decrees passed … and it a capital offence to accuse a person with what is past. . . . For we may speak against the tyrants in question as openly as we please without loss of effect, provided always that what we say is susceptible of different interpretation, since it is only danger to ourselves, and not offence to them, that we have to avoid. (*Inst.* 9.2.67 [Butler, LCL])

Hence, in instances when a speaker would seek to criticize the ruling elite, especially when the authority may have hindered "free speech," the speaker would employ ἔμφασις. When using the figure under the conditions of fear, the primary task is not to be "too obvious." Quintilian continues,

> And this fault can be avoided, if the *figure* does not depend on the employment of words of doubtful or double meaning as the words which occur in the theme of the suspected daughter-in-law: "I married the wife who pleased my father (Duxi uxorem, quae patri placuit)." (*Inst.* 9.2.69 [Butler, LCL])

On the one hand, Quintilian suggests the avoidance of words with doubtful or double meanings. These words could implicate someone in a court setting where one stands accused of undermining the ruling government. On the other hand, Ps.- Hermogenes states that some situations (though he does not specify which situations) call for words that can have two meanings, "both what is unexceptionable and what is significant" (*De inv.* 4.13.209).

Like Quintilian, Ps.- Demetrius states that at a time when there are despots, the one who seeks to criticize should neither patronize nor offer direct censure of the ruling elite. He says, "It is best to pursue the middle course, that of innuendo (τὸ ἐσχηματισμένον)" (*Eloc.* 5.294).[30] Similarly, Ps.- Hermogenes states that the figure *implied meaning* should be employed, "whenever we are not able to speak (*openly*) because hindered and lacking freedom of speech" (*De inv.* 4.13.206).

Implied Meaning with Regard to Propriety

We have already noted an example of implied meaning in circumstances of propriety with the example of good taste (εὐπρεπείας) in Ps.- Demetrius's

treatment of Phaedo 59B–C; Plato's figured criticism of Aristippus and
Cleambrotus (*Eloc.* 5.288). To reiterate, Aristippus and Cleambrotus are
covertly scorned because they are less than thirty miles away from Athens
where Socrates is imprisoned. They were in Aegina and not at the side of
their master, Socrates. As Ps.- Demetrius explains, everything that leads up to
Phaedo's mention of these friends is done for the sake of mentioning that both
Aristippus and Cleambrotus were close but nowhere to be seen. As Quintilian
notes, the point of *implication* is to give "gentle expression to unpleasing
facts" (*Inst.* 9.2.92 [Butler, LCL]).

STRATEGIES FOR CREATING AND
DETECTING FIGURED SPEECH

Rhetorical Strategies for Creating Implied Meaning

Some ancient Greco-Roman rhetoricians enumerate strategies for creating
figured speech, in particular ἔμφασις. As Whitlark observes, these strategies are not comprehensive but are rather illustrative.[31] The *Rhetorica ad
Herennium* lists five strategies for producing *significatio*, a rhetorical category that corresponds to ἔμφασις (*Rhet. Her.* 4.53.67). The subcategories
of ἔμφασις are hyperbole (*superlatio*), ambiguity (*ambiguum*), logical consequence (*consequentia*), aposiopesis (*abscisio*), and analogy (*similitudo*).[32]

Ps.- Cicero says that hyperbole is "when more is said than the truth
warrants, so as to give greater force to the suspicion" (*Rhet. Her.* 4.53. 67
[Caplan, LCL]). Quintilian suggests that hyperbole can be used in several
ways but is fundamentally "an elegant straining of the truth ... for exaggeration or attenuation" (*Inst.* 8.6.67 [Butler, LCL]). Hyperbole can be employed
by stretching the truth, lavish praise, or by metaphor.

Ambiguity is also a method for creating ἔμφασις. Ps.- Cicero states that
implied meaning is produced by ambiguity "when a word can be taken in
two or more senses, but yet is taken in that sense which the speaker intends"
(*Rhet. Her.* 4.53.67 [Caplan, LCL]). Ambiguity is said to leave one in the
dark with regard to the true meaning of some word, but oftentimes rather
leaves a choice between two meanings.[33] As Ps.- Cicero suggests, "It will be
easy to find them [ambiguities] if we know and pay heed to the double and
multiple meanings of words" (*Rhet. Her.* 4.54.67 [Caplan, LCL]). Quintilian
even suggests that ambiguity is an ingenious play between an obvious and
an underlying meaning (*Inst.* 8.2.21). Ἔμφασις can also be produced by
logical consequence, "when one mentions the things that follow from a given
circumstance, thus leaving the whole matter in distrust" (*Rhet. Her.* 4.54.67
[Caplan, LCL]). In other words, as Jason Whitlark states, logical consequence

is "when either what follows is assumed or the necessary conditions are assumed from resulting circumstances."[34]

Ἔμφασις is also produced through aposiopesis, which is the omission of the expression of an idea, made known by an abrupt stop in the sentence (*Rhet. Her.* 4.54.67).[35] Aposiopesis has several motives which are divided into two groups: the emotive aposiopesis and the calculated aposiopesis. The emotive aposiopesis abruptly stops a sentence due to an increasing emotional outburst. Often, the speaker will realize their emotional outburst and return to their original motive with a transitioning conjunction (Quin. *Inst.* 9.2.54).[36] The calculated aposiopesis is based on a conflict between that which has been omitted. and some opposing force that rejects this omitted utterance.[37] The calculated aposiopesis can occur between a speaker and an audience. The speaker would omit something from their oration, and the audience, in accordance with the speaker's intention, would understand the omitted utterance. This sort of calculated aposiopesis may be called an emphatic aposiopesis (*Rhet. Her.* 4.30.41).

Finally, ἔμφασις is expressed by means of analogy (*similitudo*) which, Ps.-Cicero says, is "when we cite some analogue and do not amplify it, but by its means intimate what we are thinking" (*Rhet. Her.* 4.54.67 [Caplan, LCL]). Elsewhere Ps.-Cicero describes analogy at length, saying, "Comparison (*similitudo*) is a manner of speech that carries over an element of likeness from one thing to a different thing. This is used to embellish or prove or clarify or vivify" (*Rhet. Her.* 4.46.59 [Caplan, LCL]). Analogy is a broad category which includes simile, metaphor, and other types of comparison.[38]

In his *Institutio oratoria*, Quintilian also highlights apostrophe as a means of creating and detecting figured speaking (9.2.38). Apostrophe (ἀποστροφή), literally a "turning away" from the intended audience and the addressing of another audience, is "surprisingly" chosen by the speaker.[39] This figure has an emotive effect on the normal audience. As Heinrich Lausberg observes, apostrophe is "an emotional move of despair on the part of speaker."[40] The figure can also take the form of a question, an *interrogatio*, where the question is asked with no answer given.[41] The answer is supposed to be self-evident. For example, in Vergil's *Aeneid*, Aeneas and his companions land in Thrace and begin to build a settlement. He begins to build and decorate altars to offer sacrifices. When he tears apart myrtle trees for the altars, blood gushes from the branches. The voice of Polydorus is heard from Hades and he speaks to Aeneas telling Aeneas of his demise. The reader learns that Polydorus was sent to Thrace by Troy's king with gold so that the king of Thrace would guard it lest Troy should fall. The Thracian king instead killed Polydorus and kept the gold for himself. Polydorus was killed with spears, which then took root and became the myrtle trees, hence the blood gushing from the branches. Yet in the middle of this speech, Aeneas addresses another audience, and questions them. He says, "To what crime do you not drive the hearts of men, accursed hunger for gold" (*Aen.* 3.56 [Fairclough, LCL])? In this situation, from the point of view of the speaker, the answer is supposed to be self-evident. Often, the apostrophe in the form of a question is meant to humiliate the opposing party (Quint. *Inst.* 9.2.7).

These techniques, in and of themselves, do not necessarily imply figured speaking. Indeed, these rhetorical strategies could function differently under different circumstances (e.g., Quint. *Inst.* 9.2.100). Yet, under what circumstances can we identify a figured speech? Similarly, how can we identify a figured text?

Identifying and Detecting Figured Texts

As Steve Mason suggests, the issue of the "clued-in observer" is crucial for the understanding of figured texts.[42] In his discussion of Josephus, he highlights the importance of inner-textual clues but also, in some cases, the importance of extra-textual historical and literary resources in identifying figured speech. He describes both text-dependent irony and audience-dependent irony.[43]

In our previous discussion of ἔμφασις, we highlighted two types of the figure: when something is said explicitly, and when something said means something which is not actually said. Text-dependent irony corresponds to the former. Text-dependent irony is when the author of a text will ensure that the audience detects the irony and will therefore embed whatever clues are necessary for the audience to hear and understand the irony. The implied audience, therefore, is given certain information which remains unknown to the actual characters in the text.[44]

An example of text-dependent irony can be drawn from the Gospel of Mark.[45] The reader learns from the opening lines that Jesus is the Son of God (Mark 1:1). The reader is also aware of the private revelation between the Father and Jesus, that Jesus is the beloved Son and God is well pleased in him (Mark 1:11). The reader no doubt connects Mark 1:11 to Mark 1:1, and though there is paradox and ambiguity in the gospel, the reader understands the identity of Jesus from the beginning.[46] The disciples of Jesus, though they have seen Jesus exercise authority over evil spirits (cf. Mark 1:21–27; 1:32–34; 5:1–20; 7:24–30; 9:14–29), over nature (cf. Mark 4:35–41; 6:45–52; 11:12–14), over illness (cf. Mark 1:29–31; 1:32–34; 1:40–45; 2:1–12; 3:1–6; 5:25–34; 6:53–56; 7:31–37; 8:22–26; 10:46–52), and over the power of death (cf. Mark 5:21–24, 35–43), still remain ignorant of Jesus's identity (cf. Mark 4:13; 4:40 6:52; 7:18; 8:17; 9:32).[47] Jesus even discloses private information to his disciples (Mark 4:11; 9:2–8), and yet they remain ignorant, even to the point of abandoning him (Mark 14:50). This irony reaches its climax when a pagan centurion at the cross proclaims Jesus's divinity and authority, while those closest to him are nowhere in sight (Mark 15:39).[48] Yet, from the beginning, the audience knows of Jesus's divine origin, which many of the characters in the gospel do not know. This not only helps dramatize the narrative but also generates irony throughout the gospel.

Audience-dependent irony corresponds to ἔμφασις, of the second type; when something said really means something which is not actually said. This type of figured speech is more difficult to detect because hints (of irony) are not embedded in the text itself. Rather, it is the historical context of the text which supplies the reader with information that irony is at play. As Shadi Bartsch notes, this type of figuration, where audience detection is central, became popular in Roman theater in the first century CE.[49] In other words, the audience turned the intentionally ambiguous into the politically allusive.[50]

Ps.-Demetrius highlights this type of figuration in *Eloc.* 1.8. As an instance of concise wording the following may be given, "The Lacedaemonians to Philip: *Dionysius at Corinth.*" This brief expression is felt to be far more forcible than if the Lacedaemonians had said at full length that Dionysius, although once a mighty monarch like yourself, now resides at Corinth in a private station. Once the statement is given in full, it resembles not a rebuke but a narrative; it suggests the instructor rather than the intimidator. The passion and vehemence of the expression are enfeebled when thus extended. As a wild beast gathers itself together for the attack, so should discourse gather itself together as in a coil in order to increase its vigour.

Again, he reiterates in *Eloc.* 5.241, "If they had expanded the thought at full length, saying 'Dionysius has been deposed from his sovereignty and is now a beggarly schoolmaster at Corinth,' the result would have been a bit of narrative rather than a taunt." Notice how the more effective, more ironical, phrase is the shorter one. The force of the phrase is in what is not said. For this reason, this type of irony depends on the knowledge of the audience. For the modern reader, one can only appreciate this irony after a closer study of the historical background of a text.[51]

Summary

In summary, we may conclude that figured speech is a phenomenon in ancient rhetoric that can be detected by means of context clues or by means of inquiry. Three forms of figured speech were commonly recognized among these ancient rhetoricians: implied meaning (ἔμφασις), deflection (πλάγιον), and saying the opposite (ἐναντίον). Inasmuch as figured speech was in vogue in the ancient world, it was used with caution. As mentioned above, Quintilian says that there are three contexts for the use of figured speech: when it was unsafe to speak, in cases of propriety, and for elegance (*Inst.* 9.2.65).

HIDDEN TRANSCRIPTS, IRONY, AND THE LETTERS OF PAUL

In some political readings of Paul, it is argued that Paul wrote in hidden transcripts to avoid persecution by the Roman government. This would suggest that Paul incorporated figured speech into parts of his letters to avoid detection by the civic authority. If these commentators are correct in their observation, that means Paul employs figured speech because it was unsafe to speak. Paul, therefore, used ἔμφασις to convey a hidden message to the followers of Christ lest they should be jailed or even killed.

The argument that Paul incorporates *hidden transcripts* into his letters finds its obstacle, first, in that it lacks a definite body of passages that immediately make an impression on "the contemporary reader as advocating this type of political economy."[52] Rom 13:1–7, however, is the one Pauline text that actually supports a positive reading for the civic authority. The three passages to be discussed, namely, 1 Thess 2:13–16, Phil 3:2–11, and Rom 13:1–7 are not the *standard* texts in discussions of Paul's hidden transcripts.[53] I would argue that there are no standard texts for Pauline hidden transcripts. My attempt in this section is not to be dismissive of what these scholars are attempting to say about Paul's relationship with the civic authority, though I shall be critical of it. As Christoph Heilig observes, it is not a matter of "if" the Roman Empire occupied Paul's thought but how much of it occupied Paul's mind.[54] I am dismissive, however, of their method for ascertaining certain conclusions about Paul's gospel. After analyzing their arguments for hidden transcripts, I will consider these passages in the larger context of the letter.

1 Thessalonians 2:13–16

It must be noted that 1 Thess 2:13–16 has a contentious interpretive history. In more recent scholarship, some have made a good argument that 1 Thess 2:13–16 is an interpolation into the letter.[55] As M. Eugene Boring suggests, much of the argument for this passage being an interpolation arose in a post–World War II era, with sensitivity toward anti-Judaism or perceived anti-Judaism.[56] Ultimately, the dispute revolves around the notion that Paul is claiming all Jews are responsible for the death of Jesus. For instance, many English translations place a comma after verse 14, which introduces a general statement: "for you also endured the same sufferings at the hands of your own countrymen, even as they *did* from the Jews, who both killed the Lord Jesus and the prophets, and drove us out" (1 Thess 2:14–15 NAS; also see the NIV, RSV, etc.). Hence, all Jews were responsible for the death of Jesus. Rather, this should be understood as a restrictive clause since Paul could not have had all Jews in mind, because some Jews, including himself, were believers in Christ. The accusations Paul made against "the Jews" in 2:14–15 should not be understood as Paul's anger toward all Jews but rather against those specific people who were persecuting Paul and the Church.[57] This line of argumentation allows some scholars to maintain that 1 Thess 2:13–16 is not an interpolation into the letter. For the sake of argument, therefore, we will understand 1 Thess 2:13–16 not as an interpolation but as an original part of the letter.

Because of its history, 1 Thess 2:13–16 is often a point of contention when interpreting the larger letter. Some have even ventured to argue that Paul is not actually arguing against the Jews but "the Jews," rather, is code for another enemy, possibly Rome. Abraham Smith is a proponent of this line of argument and understands this passage as coded language meant to undermine the empire.[58]

Smith understands 1 Thess 2:13–16 as Paul's attempt to critique the Roman imperial order by subtle and indirect analogies. Paul's objective in this passage, he argues, is to critique "the dominating pro-Roman elite in Thessalonica through an analogy with pro-Roman priestly aristocracy in Judea."[59] Smith situates his argument on historical and discursive resistances to Roman power.[60] First, he suggests that Paul, who would have spent a long while in Jerusalem, would have been familiar with resistance efforts against Rome by both Judeans and Hellenistic philosophers.

Paul, a Jew, would be aware of the prophetic tradition of resistance and liberation. Most important would be his familiarity with the foundational Passover story, God liberating the Israelites from their bondage in Egypt (Exod 12).[61] Smith also highlights the Jewish uprisings which were instigated by messianic movements in 4 BCE and during the Jewish War of 66–70 CE.[62] These movements even took form in scribal texts, including some among the Dead Sea Scrolls (1QS, CD, etc.), and among the Sicarii movement in the 50s and 60s CE as recounted by Josephus (*B.J.* 7.253–355).[63] Smith says, "Like others before him, Paul drew *discursively* on the Israelite tradition of resistance in his appropriation of Scripture."[64] Paul, who likely drew on the prophetic tradition, especially the Deutero-Isaiah tradition in 1 Thessalonians, would *insure* he is writing a type of resistance literature.[65] The attempt is to restore Paul's ethnic Jewish roots

Furthermore, Paul, who was preaching in the Hellenized Greco-Roman East, would have been acquainted with how the imperial powers described themselves as gods and godlike heroes, benefactors, and saviors. Paul sought to create an alternative community, "a viable, oppositional network of shared value across time and space."[66] Smith goes on to say, "Members of the groups frequently denounced the former honor they received when they achieved wealth and reputation."[67] He therefore argues that Paul's network of communities was a "historical" means of resisting the Roman Empire. Smith concludes that Paul is urging his community at Thessalonica, because of their "brotherhood," to remove themselves from and to refuse to participate in the imperial cultic activities which legitimized the empire.[68]

When Smith reads 1 Thess 2:13–16, he finds "clear evidence" that Paul is criticizing both the Thessalonian aristocracy and the Judean aristocracy, who were both strongly pro-Roman and instruments of Roman imperial authority.[69] We may affirm, however, the strong presence of a pro-Roman sentiment in Thessalonica. Thessalonica, a city of Macedonia, was given the status of a free, immune, and allied city. Though still subject to Rome, their relations were permanently defined if their grant of freedom continued to be recognized.[70] It is interesting to note, that unlike the earlier free cities and colonies of Macedonia, Thessalonica did not adopt Latin as its official language but continued to use Greek, which is seen in their coinage.[71] Nonetheless, Smith argues that 1 Thess 2:13–16 is Paul's analogical attempt at criticizing Rome in three different ways: diction, Paul's worldview, and Paul's specific use of analogy.

Smith understands Paul as setting up a community in direct opposition to Rome and its emperor. Jesus is the true "Lord" and the true "savior" which contrasts the "lordship" and "divine sonship" of the emperor in Thessalonica. Moreover, Paul's use of the technical term of ἐκκλησίαι (assemblies) for his communities "clearly" suggests Paul's intentions at creating oppositional communities.[72] Though we have spoken at length with regard to parallel terminology in chapter 1, it should suffice to reiterate briefly the difficulties with this argument. The mere existence of *parallel* terminology does not necessarily imply an antithetical relationship between Paul and the emperor. What should foremost guide our reading of Paul is his Jewishness. This allows us to take into consideration Paul's use of particular terminology.[73] Greco-Roman society was heavily influenced by notions of the divine and sacred. It is likely that Paul used certain terms not because he wanted to oppose the emperor, but rather certain terms made it easier to communicate his ideas to a particular community. As Christopher Bryan notes, "They all had to use *some* vocabulary and concepts to speak of the things that they held sacred, and if they were to communicate at all, they all had to draw on more or less the same vocabulary and concepts as everyone else. Hence, there were bound to be parallels between them."[74]

Smith further suggests that because Paul is describing persecution in 1 Thess 2:13–16, he is indicating the imminent return of Christ. It is an apocalyptic worldview which Smith proposes has political overtones. Pointing to a tradition of judgment and deliverance (cf. Dan 12:1: Mark 13:19; Matt 24:9–14), Paul is anticipating a new era for his communities. Their persecution indicates the imminence of the *parousia* of Christ wherein they will be delivered from oppression, and God will enact judgment on the old order (Rome). As Smith proposes, this new era is in direct contrast "to the Thessalonian declarations that new eras had begun with the victories of the Roman warlords Antony and Octavian."[75]

Finally, by means of analogy, Paul characterizes the Thessalonian persecutors as relentless and may indicate their "lack of self-control."[76] Their fellow countryfolk, argues Smith, present a lack of "self-mastery" which was a popular philosophical topic in the first century CE.[77] Augustus also adopted this philosophical precept for his empire.[78] This is important because if Paul is arguing against the virtue of the empire, there is irony insofar as the empire claimed self-control "as the basis for its governance of the entire world."[79]

For Smith to claim that Paul uses analogy and irony, subcategories of implied meaning, in 1 Thess 2:13–16 is to suggest that Paul is using figured speech. Smith suggests Paul uses "subtle or indirect ways" to critique the empire because of their "repressive character."[80] This proposes that Paul incorporated implied meaning (ἔμφασις), out of fear of the oppressor. Ἔμφασις is when the speaker must hint to the audience that they may find and understand a covert message. From Smith's description, we may understand that he is describing audience-dependent irony (when something said means something that is not actually said). The notion here is that the historical context of the text supplies the audience with information that irony is at work. This type of irony works by the employment of concise wording or brief expressions, leaving some thoughts to be filled in. The force of this type of ἔμφασις is in what is not said. Smith surmises the audience would understand 1 Thess 2:13–16 as Paul's attempt to critique the lack of self-control of the Roman powers, which the empire adopted as its *official philosophical topos*. Therefore, Paul is trying to delegitimize not only the imperial cultic activities but also those who honor and collaborate with the empire.

Audience-dependent irony, often, depends on short phrases wherein the audience would fill in the gap. As Ps.-Demetrius demonstrated with the short ironical phrase "Dionysius at Corinth," which suggests that this once mighty king is now deposed and lives in exile (*Eloc.* 1.8). If we closely examine 1 Thess 2:13–16, Paul does not seem to clue in his reader to any irony. Even if we venture toward a discussion of self-control, vices and virtues do not seem at issue here as it appears in Paul's other letters (cf. Rom 1:29–32;

13:13–14; 1 Cor 5:9–13; 6:9–11; 2 Cor 6:6–7; 8:7; 12:20–21; Gal 5:19–23; Phil 4:8–9).[81] One must consider Paul's agenda not only in this short passage but also in the entire chapter. Paul is not concerned here to delegitimize the emperor or empire. Instead, Paul is concerned with two things: the defense of his authority and past actions in Thessalonica, and his relationship with the Thessalonian faithful.

First Thessalonians 2:1–12 serves as a defense of Paul's previous work in Thessalonica and abroad.[82] Paul wants to assure the Thessalonian faithful of his continued love and care for them. And in defense of his character, Paul makes many antithetical statements (not *x* but *y*) to provide evidence of his good character and actions when he first founded the community. These antithetical statements seem to suggest that some of the Thessalonian believers were claiming Paul's first visit was "insincere" (κενή; 1 Thess 2:1). Yet Paul makes nine explicit appeals in the letter to their personal experiences with him when he was first among them ("you know," οἴδατε). Four of these appeals occur in 2:1–16 (2:1, 2, 5, 11; see also 1:5, 3:3, 4; 4:2; 5:2).[83] These explicit appeals serve to defend both his moral character and behavior during his first missionary trip to Thessalonica.

After he defends his first missionary "visit" to Thessalonica (2:1–12), he now shifts to their response to his past visit (2:13–16). To reiterate, some scholars contend 2:13–16 is an interpolation but, for the sake of argument, we will understand 1 Thess 2:1–16 as unified composition.[84] 1 Thessalonians 2:13–16 responds to the Thessalonian believers quite positively, that they not only accepted the word of God (2:13) but were also willing to be persecuted for the word, like the faithful believers in Judea (2:14–16).[85] In 2:13, the word which they "received" (παραλαβόντες) and "accepted" (ἐδέξασθε) is not the word of human beings but the word of God. There is no difference between Paul's word and God's word; it is the divine gospel (2:2, 4, 8, 9). And for this reason, their reception and belief in the gospel, Paul "constantly" (ἀδιαλείπτ ως) gives thanks to God. The point is that because they accepted the word of God, this divine message continues to be "at work" (ἐνεργεῖται) in their lives.

For Paul, the evidence that the Thessalonians have accepted the word of God and that is at work in their lives is found in their imitation of the persecuted churches in Judea.[86] They did not intentionally imitate the Judean followers of Christ, but through their belief and circumstance, nonetheless, became imitators (μιμηταὶ ἐγενήθητε; 2:14a) of the Judean believers.[87] Paul's use of the indicative, rather than the imperative, mood further illustrates his satisfaction with the conduct of the Thessalonian believers.[88]

The specific way in which the Thessalonian believers have imitated the churches of Judea is through their suffering, which they have endured for their new beliefs. This theme of persecution runs through the letter (cf. 3:1–5) but the point in 2:13–16 is the affirmation of their beliefs. This in turn is another way in which they have responded positively to Paul's first visit. Both groups, the Thessalonian believers and Judean believers, suffered persecution by their "compatriots" (συμφυλετῶν; 2:14). We should understand "compatriots" geographically, precisely the "compatriots" in Thessalonica, are locals because it stands in direct parallel to "the Jews" who were understood as the persecutors also in a local sense. The emphasis is not on self-control, or some other Stoic virtue, but rather it is the legitimization of the faith of the Thessalonian believers. First, the Thessalonians have received and accepted the divine message, the gospel of God, and it is realized in their life. Their persecution, which is an imitation of the persecution of the Judean Church—the place where the gospel was first received and accepted—certifies the validity of their faith.

It is difficult to see in this passage where Paul is following any of the ancient rhetorical methods for creating figured speech. This passage, rather, is Paul's attempt at defending his first visit. As I. Howard Marshall notes, "These verses [2:13–16] round off the 'apology' by claiming that the Thessalonians themselves accepted Paul's message as God's word and thereby rejected any insinuation that might be made against him."[89] 1 Thess 2:13–16 is Paul's attempt at presenting proof to the Thessalonians that his first visit was neither insincere nor without bearing good fruit.

Philippians 3

I have argued above that in 1 Thessalonians 2:13–16, Paul did not use figured speech to embed a critique of Rome under the guise of "the Jews." In similar fashion, some have understood Paul's critique of the Jews as a coded critique of Rome in Phil 3:2–11. They argue that Paul fears persecution by the imperial forces and therefore speaks overtly about the Jews and covertly about the empire. The method by which they ascertain such a conclusion seems flawed, primarily because Paul is very open about the gospel he preaches claiming he even preached to the praetorian guard (Phil 1:13). The argument for a hidden transcript in Philippians seems to be counterintuitive to the letter itself. Paul, in the wider context of Phil 2–3, is making an anthropological argument wherein he exhorts his community to live a transformed life in the Spirit and not in the flesh. They live their life in the Spirit, but are to live in the world "in a manner worthy of the gospel of Christ" (Phil 1:27). This is not a life of subversion and dismay, but a life of love and harmony.

One of the most prominent advocates for Pauline *hidden transcripts* is N. T. Wright. In his essay *Paul's Gospel and Caesar's Empire*, he argues that Paul encodes in some of his letters the message "Jesus is Lord, Caesar is not."[90] For example, Wright understands Paul's critique of the Jews in Phil 3:2–7, "beware of the dogs, beware of the evildoers, beware of the mutilators

of the flesh" (Phil 3:2), as such, a coded message against the Roman
imperial order which correlates with Paul's claim that their true "citizenship"
(πολίτευμα) is in heaven (Phil 3:20). He proposes that Paul, in his critiques,
has both Judaism and Paganism in mind. Regarding Philippians, the emperor
cult takes center stage. Wright says:

> Paul's main concern here is not to warn the Philippians against Judaism or an
> anti-Pauline Jewish-Christian mission. . . . His concern is to warn them against
> the Caesar-cult and the entire panoply of pagan empire. But his method of
> warning them, and of encouraging them to take a stand for the counterempire of
> Jesus, is given for the most part in code.[91]

This message of subversion is primarily found in 3:2–11. This passage, suggests Wright, has both an overt and a covert message.

The overt meaning is Paul making a direct claim against the Jews, not
Jewish Christians.[92] But the covert aim are the pagans. Wright argues that
the Jews can also be categorized as pagans. The first two epithets in 3:2 can
be applied to the pagans, namely, "the dogs" and the "workers of evil." But
the third suggests that Paul had Jews in mind, "mutilators [of the flesh]."
Wright notes that Paul does something similar in Galatians 4:1–11, where
Paul reminds the Galatian churches that if they submit to circumcision it is
as if they are reverting to paganism, back to the "beggarly elemental spirits"
that are not gods (Gal 4:9). In other words, the realm of the flesh is paganism,
whether Jewish or otherwise. Wright even goes so far as to note the different types of Judaism which arose during the Second Temple period (e.g.,
Pharisees, "Qumran"). These groups recognized their Judaism as true while
all others were false, "this move was a standard way in which many Jewish
groups in the Second Temple period would define themselves over against one
another."[93] By employing this "inner Jewish rhetorical strategy" Paul is setting
up a polemic which helps him build up an "anti-Caesar message" as well as a
counter-imperial community.[94]

Paul is making the argument that in the same manner he has rethought his
Judaism with regard to the Christ-event, so too must the Philippians rethink
their relationship to Paganism and the Roman Empire. The final coded message for Wright appears in Phil 3:17–21. He says,

> [Paul] is building up to saying: do not go along with the Caesar-cult that is
> currently sweeping the Eastern Mediterranean. You have one Lord and Savior,
> and he will vindicate and glorify you, if you hold firm to him, just as the Father
> vindicated and glorified him after he had obeyed.[95]

Philippi, which was re-founded as a colony by Augustus, was proud of its status as a Roman colony.[96] Yet, for Wright, Paul is admonishing his community not to compromise their new faith in Jesus by taking part in the imperial cultic activities. They must not be leery of the emperor since their citizenship (πολίτευμα) is in heaven and not in the empire.

Wright understands Philippians to contain an anti-Roman polemic by means of hidden code. Though previously mentioned in chapter 1, it should suffice to number here the inconsistencies in Wright's argument: (1) Wright argues that Paul makes an explicit challenge to the Roman emperor in Phil 2:5–11 only to suggest that Paul makes a similar message in code in Phil 3.[97] (2) He argues that Paul is creating a striking contrast between loyalty to Christ and loyalty to Caesar in 2:5–11 and in 3:20–21 but then he contradicts himself saying Phil 3 makes this same message but in "subtle" coded language.[98] (3) If Paul sought to remain safe because of the subversive character of the gospel of God, why would he openly preach Christ in the letter and admit that praetorian guard even heard the gospel (Phil 1:13)?

Though not specified by Wright, he is suggesting that Paul incorporated both ἔμφασις (implied meaning) and πλάγιον (saying the opposite). Recall that ἔμφασις, which may be used in situations of fear and respect, can be created and detected by several rhetorical techniques including hyperbole, ambiguity, logical consequence, aposiopesis, analogy, or apostrophe. The method by which he ascertains a Pauline hidden transcript has gaps. Analyzing Phil 3, Paul does not incorporate any of the rhetorical devices associated with ἔμφασις. Moreover, Wright says that Paul has an overt aim while seeking out a covert aim. As previously noted, πλάγιον is a figure that seeks to accomplish an objective overtly while simultaneously accomplishing another covertly. Indeed, Paul wanted to criticize the Jews overtly and he did so quite blatantly! But, is Wright's claim that Paul's covert aim is to criticize the emperor and the imperial cults correct? When Ps.-Dionysius illustrates πλάγιον in Diomede's speech to Agamemnon (*Il.*9.32–49), he says that the speech seems out of place (*Ars Rhetorica* 325.13–327.18). Not only does the speech seem out of place but also within the speech itself, Diomedes insinuates exactly what he wants. He wants Agamemnon and his troops to remain and fight in Troy. In the context of Phil 3, Paul's message seems more straightforward than coded; a life defined by faith in Christ rather than the Law of Moses.[99]

Paul exhorts the Philippians to be steadfast in their character as followers of Christ. He also commands them to be unified giving them Christ as the prime example of this accord (Phil 2:1–12). Furthermore, the Philippians belonged to a Greek colony of Rome and belonged to its citizenship. Though the term πολίτευμα may call to mind a place, Paul here is emphasizing a people.

They will await Christ the Lord and Savior who will ultimately subdue all things, including the flesh, and transform them into this new citizenship. The emperor does not seem to be at issue here. Rather, it is Christ's transformative power that will bring all believers into himself [Christ] (3:21).

Indeed, the focus in Phil 3 is the church as the eschatological hope of believers. The church becomes a paradigm for the heavenly *politeuma*, and believers live firmly in a hostile world. As Dorothea H. Bertschmann observes some counter-imperial readings of Phil 3 almost advocate for a kind of "free-state of Christianity," or even a revolutionary movement against the current political structures. It is as if Paul is implying an antagonistic stance toward the Roman Empire.[100] But as noted by Clifford Ando there was a general appreciation in the Greek east for the political and economic stability the civic authority endowed upon its peoples.[101] I would think Paul had this general appreciation as well, taking Rom 13:1–7 at face value.

I understand that Paul is making an anthropological argument in Phil 3:21. Ultimately, humanity is mortal and the flesh will be subjected to decay. Yet by Christ's transformative powers, their bodies will be metamorphized like his, by that same power that subdues all things to Christ (ὃς μετασχηματίσει τὸ σῶμα τῆς ταπεινώσεως ἡμῶν σύμμορφον τῷ σώματι τῆς δόξης αὐτοῦ κατὰ τὴν ἐνέργειαν τοῦ δύνασθαι αὐτὸν καὶ ὑποτάξαι αὐτῷ τὰ πάντα; Phil. 3:21). Though in a different key from his other letters, Paul is exhorting his community at Philippi to live a life in the Spirit and not in the flesh (Phil 3:3; cf. Rom 8:1–14; 13:11–14; Gal 5:4–6, 16–25; 6:7–10), while simultaneously maintaining good conduct in their daily lives (Phil 1:27). I will return to these themes in chapter 5. There, I will expand and more fully develop Paul's anthropological argument in his letter to the Philippians.

Romans 13:1–7

Romans 13:1–7 is the crux of many counter-imperial interpretations of Paul.[102] This apparent, unqualifiedly, positive view of the civic authority has led some to question Paul's *true* intention. These *true* intentions are often characterized as covertly counter-imperial. Yet, after careful inquiry, the method employed for establishing figured speech in Rom 13:1–7 does not bear scrutiny. Rather, Rom 13:1–7 should be understood within its wider context. Namely, Rom 13:1–7 is part of Paul's larger exhortation in Rom 12–15 to live a moral life apart from the Mosaic Law, a life that is also free from divisiveness. In this section, I will primarily critique the approaches some counter-imperial scholars employ in their exegesis of Rom 13:1–7.

One of the fuller treatments of *hidden transcripts* in Romans is taken up by William Herzog. He understands Paul's positive view of the authority as "coded speech" for resistance to the empire.[103] For Herzog, Paul's political speech seems to support the dominant political powers but is actually subverting it. The technical term Herzog applies to Paul's rhetorical technique is "dissembling," which is Paul's attempt at disguising the hidden transcript in submissive language. "Dissembling," then, is comparable to a kind of rhetorical subcategory of ἔμφασις, namely, aposiopesis. Recall that one can create and detect ἔμφασις by means of aposiopesis, or by the omission of the expression of an idea, made known by an abrupt stop in the sentence. Developing Ernst Käsemann's and Stanley Porter's observations of Paul's *apparent omission*, Herzog suggests that Paul's silence about the limits of the Roman imperial order is intentional and is part of his coded speech.[104] Herzog suggests that Paul is not necessarily defining a just or an unjust government. Herzog, using the sociological study of James C. Scott, says that Paul's letter (a public transcript) used coded speech in case the letter should be intercepted by the imperial authority.[105] Herzog argues that because the letter is a public transcript, Paul would criticize the empire in a figured way so that he may remain incognito and avoid persecution.

Romans 13:1 begins with a command and two assertions. First, all people (Πᾶσα ψυχή) are to be subject (ὑποτασσέσθω) to the governing authorities (ἐξουσίαις ὑπερεχούσαις). They should be subject because all power comes from God, and those with authority are ordained by God. Romans 13:1 is then reinforced through a negative restatement were the focus becomes three groups of people, authorities, subjects, and rebels with descriptors for each.[106] Herzog notes, "Thus far, Paul seems to be writing a piece that . . . 'could have been written by the emperor himself!' All responsibility is on the subjects, and all legitimation falls on the authorities, including the right to crush rebellion."[107]

In Romans 13:4, Paul uses the term διάκονος to describe the rulers. Paul's intention, according to Herzog, "comes like a surgical strike."[108] The root meaning of the verbal cognate for διάκονος is "to wait at table" (cf. Luke 17:8).[109] Herein lies part of the hidden transcript. "Serving" was a menial form of service and for Paul to say that these imperial authorities are mere *servants* of God is antithetical to their actual positions. Immediately, though, Paul continues this figured speech by hiding his intentions with what follows in the remainder of the verse. His attention shifts to the retributive powers of the authority. But even this contains coded speech, "because it specifies that the military be used solely to suppress anarchy and wrong behavior. That the use of the military was hardly ever limited to these purposes was obvious."[110]

Romans 13:5 gathers together all the previous verses, including their figured speech, into a single sentence. At face value, the verse is clear that because all these things previously mentioned (διό), one should respect the authority because its source is ultimately God. But again, suggests Herzog, Paul's declaring that the rulers are mere servants of God is denying their divine origins.[111] They are not gods by any means but humans, servants of the God of Israel. Furthermore, he suggests that Rom 13:1–7 is a recollection of Roman propaganda, "a public transcript of the elites."[112] Herzog states, "Paul has produced an ambiguous and coded version of the hidden transcript and described an empire that does not exist."[113] This Roman state, expressed in Rom 13:1–7, does not exist because those who obey do not do so out of good conscience but out of fear of punishment. He claims that Paul's community in Rome knew that the imperial authority was abusive of their military and judicial powers, and they recognized the irony in Paul's words. They knew, on the one hand, the authority punished not only the evil while rewarding the good but also, on the other hand, the good while rewarding the evil.[114]

In the remaining verses of this passage Paul shifts his attention to the question of taxes (φόρος). As Herzog suggests, Paul continues to undermine the deity of the imperial authority by referring to them as λειτουργοί ("servants"), "a variant of *diakonoi*."[115] The role of λειτουργοί was to carry out the work of the state, that is those public works like the collection of taxes.[116] He categorizes the Roman Empire as a "police state," and police states have three primary areas of concern which are military, financial, and ecclesiastical.[117] So when Paul says to "pay to all people their dues" (ἀπόδοτε πᾶσιν τὰς ὀφειλάς), he is saying just that; give them their due "but no more." As Herzog says, "This implies resistance to conceding to the finance ministers more than is their due. Give no more than absolutely necessary."[118] Romans 13:7 summarizes Paul's position, "Pay to all people their dues, tax to whom tax is due, revenue to whom revenue is due, respect to whom respect is due, honor to whom honor is due." But then again, what does Paul mean by respect and honor? Herzog conjectures, "[Paul] means that Christians should always display the public deference that the oppressed show their masters."[119] But Herzog suggests that Paul, ultimately, is advising the Roman Christians to practice resistance in ways that will not place the community at danger. Paul's seemingly loyal statement about the Roman authority in Rom 13:1–7 is *actually* a hidden transcript for the Roman Christians to understand how they are to live and survive in an authoritarian state.[120]

Herzog's argument is notable because he sees in Rom 13:1–7 a hidden transcript created by means of omission and double meaning. Like the arguments made previously for 1 Thessalonians and Philippians, Herzog argues that Paul created hidden transcripts out of fear of persecution by the "police state."[121] Again, Paul would be incorporating ἔμφασις by means of aposiopesis (omission), a subcategory of ἔμφασις, and words with double meanings (διάκονος and λειτουργοί).

Ἔμφασις is produced by aposiopesis when an expression is omitted. The omission is made known by an abrupt stop in the sentence (Quint. *Inst.* 4.54.67). Herzog, as well as others, may conjecture that Paul is omitting a discussion on other aspects of the Roman government only for the audience to fill in what is missing. For example, Herzog states that Paul's community will understand that they are only to appear to be conforming to the authority. Instead Paul is encouraging them, by means of omission, "to practice the art of resistance" in a way that would not jeopardize their community.[122] But the text of Rom 13:1–7 does not indicate such. Omission, or aposiopesis, would suggest that there is some type of abrupt stop or syntactical oddity in the text (Quint. *Inst.* 9.2.54–57). There are none. Rather it is a smooth pericope both grammatically and syntactically.

With regard to ἔμφασις produced by double meanings of words, Quintilian suggests avoiding such strategies because it could possibly implicate you in a court (*Inst.* 9.2.69). Ps.-Hermogenes, however, says that some situations do call for the incorporation of double meanings but does not specify which situations (*De inv.* 4.13.209). Nonetheless, Herzog comments that διάκονος and its "variant" λειτουργός contain a double meaning. Whereas the emperor and his authorities may sometimes be recognized as divinities, Paul recognizes them as mere "servants" of God undermining their authority.

Why would Paul, or any Jew for that matter, regard the emperor or any civil authority as a deity? It would not be shocking to the emperor, or any other Greco-Roman person for that matter, that a Jew would not recognize the divinity of the emperor. In fact the emperor Claudius, renewing the decrees of Augustus, decreed that the Alexandrian Jews should be left alone to worship their own god according to their own customs (P.Lond.1912).[123] A Jewish text which helps contextualize Paul's place in the Greco-Roman world comes from Josephus's *Contra Apionem*, a contemporary of Paul.

> He [Moses] did not prohibit that good men be paid homage with other honors, secondary to God: with such expressions of respect we give glory to the emperors and to the Roman people. We offer on their behalf perpetual sacrifices, and not only do we conduct such rites every day at the common expense of all Judeans, but we perform no other sacrifices on a common basis, not even for children; it is only for the emperors that we collectively exhibit this exceptional honor, which we render to no (other) human being. (Josephus, *C. Ap.* 2.75–76 [Barclay])[124]

Josephus claims that the Jewish people honor not only the emperor but all the Roman people, second only to their God. They even offer daily sacrifices on behalf of the emperor, an honor which they do not offer to any other person.

Paul's view of the relationship of believers to the Greco-Roman civil authority is emphasized in the greater Jewish tradition as well. For example, Prov 8:15–16 shows his views are not out of the ordinary:

> By me [God] kings reign, and sovereigns prescribe what is just; by me nobles are exalted and by me autocrats control the earth. [LXX][125]

This same attitude is found in other Jewish and Hellenistic Jewish texts where the emperor and the Roman people are treated in similar fashion.[126] So is Paul dishonoring the Roman imperial order? Not at all. Paul declaring them "servants" equates them to the other "servants" he mentions in his letters (e.g., Rom 16:1; 1 Cor 3:5.).[127] All serve God, in Paul's Jewish understanding, for this is what God has ordained.[128] This was a religiously grounded point of view held not only by Paul but also by the larger Jewish population in the Greco-Roman world.[129] Indeed, Paul is relativizing the role of the authority but how else could a Hellenized Jew describe the authority?[130] As Thomas H. Tobin observes,

> There was nothing absolute about either political power or submission to it. Rather, it was a religiously grounded attitude on the part of a minority group in the Roman empire toward the overwhelming reality of Roman power. It also included a recognition of the value of the relative social and political stability Roman power provided.[131]

Therefore, Romans 13:1–7 must first be understood within the context of the letter as well as its *Sitz im Leben*.

Romans 13:1–7 is often said to be a discussion of the "state" or of Rome, but there is mention neither of the "state" nor of Rome. Rather, Romans 13:1–7 is not a stand-alone passage, as some have suggested, but is part of Paul's larger exhortation in 12:1–15:7.[132] This passage may seem out of place because of its subject matter.[133] Yet there are verbal links to what precedes 13:1–17 and what follows it, such as the contrast between "good" (ἀγαθόν) and "evil" (κακόν) (e.g., 12:2, 9, 17, 21; 13:3, 4; 13:10).[134] Moreover, the vocabulary of "justice" in Rom 12–13 serves as a verbal link uniting Paul's thought on the civil authority to the wider context of Paul's theology. Both in the LXX and in the New Testament, the vocabulary of "justice" (ἐκδικ-) is "contextually linked to and intertwined with God's justice, his saving the righteous, his wrath, his judging and his punishing evildoers who oppress those who trust in him and cry to him for their salvation and vindication."[135] One also notices the link between God's divine wrath in Rom 12:19 and in 13:4. In 12:19, it is God's wrath which will be wrought against evildoers both in the present and in the future.[136] Yet, in Rom 13:4 it is the civil authority that embody and imitate God's prerogative to reward the good and punish the evil. For Paul, Christ followers live in a new reality which is expressed in terms of God's Spirit. Yet, this new life in Christ does not necessarily usurp the civil order of the world. Bertschmann observes that the political authorities are not against God since they are carrying out God's justice. She says,

> they [the civil authority] are God's servants precisely by judging evil and condemning it and to a lesser degree through praising good . . . even after God's deeply *counter intuitive* and asymmetrical approach to good and evil in Christ the moral structure of the universe stays firmly in place and judgment is to be expected.[137]

The civil authority is, therefore, an extension of God's justice in the sphere of the temporal/corporeal. They are there to help preserve the good of all people (13:4; cf. Rom 12:2,9,21; 13:3). They are to reward the good while punishing evildoers (13:4), which is the task of God (12:19–20).[138]

In his forthcoming commentary on 1 Peter, Troy W. Martin shows how Peter relies upon a general theory of government whose purpose is to reward good conduct and promote public morality.[139] This general theory was widely held and can be located among several authors. In Aristotle's *Politica*, for example, he provides a detailed description of this theory. He suggests that the *polis* exists for the good life (*Politica* 1.1.8 1252b) and that justice is expressed by judicial procedure, in regulating what is right and wrong (*Politica* 1.1.12 1253a–b). In his *Legatio ad Gaium*, Philo of Alexandria not only affirms this theory of government but states that "no law can be complete unless it includes two provisions—honours for things good and punishments for things evil. . . . For penalties are good for the morals of the multitude, who fear to suffer the like" (*Legat.* 1.7 [Colson, LCL]). When Paul says that "rulers are not a terror to good conduct, but to bad" (Rom 13:3a), he is only affirming a positive theory of civil authority that ancient society already subscribed to.

In Romans 13:1–5, Paul exhorts all people (πᾶσα ψυχή) to be subject (ὑποτασσέσθω) to the governing authorities (ἐξουσίαις ὑπερεχούσαις). He is not speaking about supernatural forces but about the civil authorities of the empire.[140] Paul here is not trying to emphasize disharmony. Paul calls the Roman followers of Christ to be "subject" because all authority is ordained by God. Rom 12:1–2 clarifies the type of subjection. They are not to be "conformed" (συσχηματίζω) to this world, so that they may demonstrate the "will of God." It may be necessary for a Christ follower, who lives in the world, to speak when necessary against an immoral ethic. Yet the acceptance of the authority is consistent with their faith in Christ, and to revolt against their civil authority is to go against the will of God. That is why ὑποτάσσεσθαι is not just a request for followers of Christ but to all people (πᾶσα ψυχή).[141] And because these rulers are ordained by God, they are God's servants who are there to administer God's wrath to the evildoer. This subjection, which Paul reiterates and emphasizes in 13:5, is not only because of fear of punishment but it is a matter of good conscience.

Paul is ultimately doing two things in this passage within the context of the larger passage in 12:1–15:7. He is first exhorting the Roman followers of Christ to live a life of morality and harmony, which is emphasized in their freedom from the observance of the Law of Moses. Indeed, this section in Romans is highlighted by what has preceded it, namely, God's redemptive work in Christ. Though their old life has ended, a new and more profound life, characterized by the cessation of aspects of the Law of Moses, now begins in Christ (Rom 7:1–6). Now that they are in Christ through baptism (Rom 6:1–14), Paul now lays out for the believers how to live a life in Christ. This life includes, but is not limited to, the commandments (Rom 13:9), the call to love one another (Rom 13:8–10), and living by the example of Christ (Rom 15:7–8).[142]

Second, he wants to curtail any divisiveness in the community at large and so admonishes them simply to pay their taxes or revenues. Paul, who is writing in the immediate context of Claudius's exile of the Jews in 41, admonishes the believers that their new life in Christ does not necessarily mean their withdrawal from their civic obligations.[143] As Thomas M. Coleman observes, Paul is emphasizing that the Roman faithful have ethical obligations to a wider sphere of binding commitments, not just to their immediate faith community but to the larger world.[144]

In Romans 13:6–7, Paul seems to switch gears to discuss ethical obligations, particularly tangible obligations (taxes and revenues) and intangible obligations (reverence and honor). Paul is emphasizing that the Roman faithful have ethical obligations to a wider sphere of binding commitments, commitments not just to their immediate faith community but to the larger world. First Corinthians may help clarify the previous statement. Notice how Paul suggests that the Corinthian believers are sanctified "in Christ" (1Cor 6:11) and that they must not associate with the unrighteous (1Cor 6:9–10), especially in matters relating to their community. But this notion of separation seems to regard internal relationships as opposed to external relationships.

The passage in Rom 13:1–7 emphasizes proper engagement in the world; believers, as well as all people, are to recognize that authority derives from God. The civil leaders are servants of God. They are administrators of God's powers of rewarding the good and punishing the evil, an idea that is not foreign within Judaism. Furthermore, the believer lives within this world, which is under the control of a civic government. Their new life in Christ does not exempt them from their civic responsibilities.[145] This relationship between Paul's community and their wider Greco-Roman environment will be further developed in chapter 4 of this study.

CONCLUSION

A method in empire critical interpretations of the Pauline corpus rests on the notion that Paul may write in *hidden transcripts*. This idea hinges on several presuppositions; Paul, a follower of Christ, wrote amid a dominant Greco-Roman culture and if he speaks against it, he will be persecuted. Therefore, under certain circumstances, Paul must incorporate figured speech not only to encourage faithfulness but to avoid detection by the Roman authority when he criticizes them. This interpretation has produced many studies which deserve careful analysis. But they seem to overlook two very important aspects of Pauline studies: Paul's use of Greco-Roman rhetoric and Paul's Jewishness.

As Hans Dieter Betz explains in his commentary on Galatians, Paul is indebted to the ancient schools of Greco-Roman rhetoric.[146] Therefore, if one is arguing that Paul has incorporated figured speech into his letters, we must test this claim against the ancient rhetorical strategies for creating and utilizing figured speech. I have shown that ancient rhetoricians like Quintilian, Ps.-Cicero, Ps.-Hermogenes, and Ps.-Dionysius recognize three types of figured speech: ἔμφασις, πλάγιον, and ἐναντίον. Each of these rhetorical categories was used in particular situations. Of the three, our primary focus was on ἔμφασις since it is the only category of figured speech that ancient rhetoricians suggested to be used in situations when it was unsafe to freely speak.

Some interpreters argued that because Paul could not speak openly against the Roman authority, he had to incorporate figured speech into his letters. However, the outcome of some of their research has been in question. I conjecture this issue is primarily due to their methodology. A method for locating hidden transcript, or subtext, must first take into consideration Paul's Hellenistic Jewish background and consider Paul's use of rhetorical devices. Second, a method must also consider the immediate context of author, community, and church as has been successfully done with, I think, the book of Revelation.[147]

Moreover, in these instances, it would be difficult to reconcile Paul with coded messages of subversion. The Roman Empire recognized the Jews as having a long-standing tradition and understood that the Jews did not recognize the emperor as a god.[148] It was a mutual understanding, though their relationship was far from perfect.[149] That did not mean they did not honor or respect the emperor, or the civil authority. With regard to Romans 13:1–7, Palestinian Jewish literature as well as Hellenistic Jewish literature only bolsters Paul's claims in this passage. To honor a pagan king, or emperor, is not out of the ordinary for the Jewish people but is encouraged due to God's role in this respect. It is God who ordained these people to positions of power. Therefore, by revering their civil authorities they are ultimately honoring God.

We should not be surprised that counter-imperial readings of Paul, as well as other parts of the New Testament, have been a more recent phenomenon in biblical exegesis. Cold War tensions and the fall of the Soviet Union in 1989 have led to a restructuring of the world's authoritative powers. This includes the formation of many new democracies as well as the emergence of human rights groups in countries where human rights were promised to only one group of people (e.g., the United States and South Africa).[150] I contend that a secondary objective of a counter-imperial reading is to potentially offer interpretations that open pathways of enhancing human freedom and dignity.[151] Yet much of counter-imperial Pauline scholarship does not place weight on human dignity and freedom, but rather on the subversion of radical political powers. If Paul seeks to restructure the empire, what would the alternative be? If his hidden transcript is one of radical subversion, then how should the contemporary reader understand their relationship with contemporary *oppressive* authorities? On the contrary, Paul structured his communities in such a way that complemented Greco-Roman society, while remaining distinct in its call to all peoples, regardless of their race, sex, or creed. Most especially is his call to follow Jesus Christ in the midst of the world. This study will proceed to situate Paul in his proper Greco-Roman context. Particularly, in what ways did the Roman Empire emerge in the eastern Hellenic provinces and in what ways did the empire express its relationship with the local populations?

NOTES

1. I am indebted to the work of Jason A. Whitlark [*Resisting Empire: Rethinking the Purpose of the Letter to "The Hebrews"* (London: Bloomsbury/T&T Clark, 2014)], whose discussion of figured speech I closely follow. Whitlark's analysis of figured speech, to my knowledge, is the most recent discussion on this topic. See idem., 21–48. He obverses that the Greek phrase ἐσχηματισμένος ἐν λόγῳ is found in Ps.-Demetrius (*Eloc.* 5.287), Ps.-Dionysius of Halicarnassus (*Ars Rhetorica* 8-9), and Ps.-Hermogenes (*On Invention* 4.11). The Latin rhetorical term (*significatio*) as well as the Greek σχήματα appears in Quintilian (*Inst.* 9.1.1). Figured speech is also referred to as *significatio* in *Rhet. Her.* 4.53.57. See idem., 21 n.1.

2. The Greek text of *Ars Rhetorica* consulted and referred to is from Ps.-Dionigi di Alicarnasso, *I discorsi fiurati I e II* (*Ars Rhet. VIII e IX Us. Rad*): *Introduzione, Traduzione e Commento a cura di Stefano Dentice di Acadia*, trans. Stefano Dentice di Acadia (Pisa: Fabrizio Serra Editore, 2010). See also Hermann Usener and Ludwig Radermacher, ed., *Dionnysii Halicarnasei quae exstant,* vol. 6; Bibliotheca scriptorum graecorum et romanorum teubneriana (Stuttgart: B. G. Teubner, 1967–1985).

3. Whitlark, *Resisting Empire*, 23. The Greek text used and consulted and referenced for Ps.-Hermogenes's *Invention* and *Method* is from George A. Kennedy trans., *Invention and Method: Two Rhetorical Treatises from the Hermogenic Corpus* (Atlanta: Society of Biblical Literature, 2005).

4. Malcolm Heath, "Pseudo-Dionysius 'Art of Rhetoric' 8-11: Figured Speech, Declamation, and criticism," *AJP* 124 (2003): 81–105, 82. See also Whitlark, *Resisting Empire*, 23 n. 8.

5. Cf. D. A. Russell, "Figured Speeches: 'Dionysius,' Art of Rhetoric VIII-IX," in *The Orator in Action and Theory in Greece and Rome: Essays in Honor of George A. Kennedy*, ed. Cecil W. Wooten (Brill: Leiden, 2001), 156–168.

6. Though there are other ways of translating ἔμφασις, in these contexts "implied meaning" best captures the meaning of this term.

7. Heinrich Lausberg, *Handbook of Literary Rhetoric: A Foundation for Literary Study*, ed. David E. Orton and R. Dean Anderson, trans. Matthew T. Bliss et al. (Brill: Leiden, 1998), 407.

8. Heath, "Pseudo-Dionysius," 82. Also Whitlark, *Resisting Empire*, 23.

9. Slightly modified translation.

10. The Greek text consulted and referenced from *De Elocutione* is from W. Rhys Roberts trans., *Demetrius on Style* (Cambridge: University Press, 1902).

11. Slightly modified translation.

12. Lausberg, *Handbook of Literary Rhetoric*, 262–263.

13. Translation slightly modified.

14. Lausberg, *Handbook of Literary Rhetoric*, 407.

15. Slightly modified translation.

16. For other examples of *significatio* in Virgil see Richard F. Thomas, "A Trope by Any Other Name: "Polysemy," Ambiguity, and Significatio in Virgil," *HSCP* 100 (2000): 381–407.

17. Though there are other ways of translating πλάγιον, in these contexts "deflection" best captures the meaning of this term.

18. Whitlark, *Resisting Empire*, 26. See also Heath, "Pseudo-Dionysius," 82.

19. See also Lausberg, *Handbook of Literary Rhetoric*, 408.

20. Whitlark, *Resisting Empire*, 26.

21. Whitlark highlights another example of πλάγιον in Aeschylus's play *Agamemnon*. See Ibid., 26–27.

22. Heath, "Pseudo-Dionysius," 83. Also, Whitlark, *Resisting Empire*, 27.

23. Whitlark, *Resisting Empire*, 27, 27 n.20.

24. Though there are other ways of translating ἐναντίον, in these contexts, "saying the opposite" best captures the meaning of this term.

25. Whitlark, *Resisting Empire*, 28.

26. Lausberg, *Handbook of Literary Rhetoric*, 405.

27. Ibid., 408.

28. There is not much to discuss with regard to ἔμφασις and elegance. Quintilian states that it is merely an artistic device used to indicate something by allusion (*Inst.* 9.2.97).

29. Frederick Ahl ["The Art of Safe Criticism in Greece and Rome," *AJP* 105 (1984): 174–208; esp. 187–192] accounts for their difference in terminology by

suggesting that these texts are products of their time. Quintilian writes not out of politeness or decency but rather is trying to survive as a rhetorician in a post-Julio-Claudian Empire which was riddled with civil war and other political problems. Ps.-Demetrius, writing almost two centuries after Quintilian, does not seem to worry much about "survival" possibly because of his "Greekness." Also, Whitlark, *Resisting Empire*, 29–31.

30. Slightly modified translation.

31. Whitlark, *Resisting Empire*, 33. See also pgs. 33–35.

32. In his *Institutio oratoria*, Quintilian also highlights other methods for the creation and detection of figured speech: ellipses (*detractio*) (9.2.37), suggestion (*suggestio*) (9.2.15), anticipation (*praesumptio*) (9.2.17), impersonation (*persona*) (9.2.30-37), and apostrophe (*aversus*) (9.2.38).

33. Lausberg, *Handbook of Literary Rhetoric*, 1070.

34. Whitlark, *Resisting Empire*, 33.

35. Lausberg, *Handbook of Literary Rhetoric*, 394. Aposiopesis is also called *reticentia* (Ps. Cicero, *Rhet. Her.* 4.54.67), *obticentia* (Celsus, *De oratore* 3.205), and *interruptio* (Quintilian, *Inst.* 9.2.54).

36. Lausberg, *Handbook of Literary Rhetoric*, 395.

37. Ibid.

38. Thomas, "A Trope by Any Other Name," 404.

39. Lausberg, *Handbook of Literary Rhetoric*, 338.

40. Ibid.

41. Ibid., 339–340.

42. Mason, "Figured Speech and Irony in Josephus," 249–250.

43. Ibid., 249–251.

44. Ibid., 250.

45. See Steve Mason's treatment of the gospel of John in, ibid. See also Jason Whitlark's more detailed treatment of Mason's argument in Whitlark, *Resisting Empire*, 34–35.

46. R. T. France, *The Gospel of Mark*, NIGTC (Grand Rapids: William B. Eerdmans Publishing Company, 2002), 79.

47. On the ignorance of the disciples in the Gospel of Mark see Eduard Schweizer, *The Good News According to Mark*, trans. Donald H. Madvig (Richmond: John Knox Press, 1970), 162–225; Adela Yarbro Collins, *Mark*, Hermeneia, ed. Harold W. Attridge (Minneapolis: Fortress Press, 2007), 441; France, *The Gospel of Mark*, 27–29.

48. On irony in the Gospel of Mark, see Jerry Camery-Hogatt, *Irony in Mark's Gospel: Text and Subtext*, SNTSMS (Cambridge: Cambridge University Press, 1992).

49. Shadi Bartsch, *Actors in the Audience: Theatricality and Doublespeak from Nero to Hadrian* (Cambridge: Harvard University Press, 1994), 75–82.

50. Ibid., 78.

51. Ahl, "The Art of Safe Criticism," 176.

52. Oudshoorn, *Pauline Politics*, 64.

53. E.g. [1 Thess 2:13–6] Abraham Smith, ""Unmasking the Powers": Toward a Postcolonial Analysis of 1 Thessalonians," in *Paul and the Roman Imperial Order*, ed. Richard A. Horsley (Harrisburg: Trinity Press International, 2004), 47–66: [Phil

3] N. T. Wright, "Paul's Gospel and Caesar's Empire," in *Paul and Politics*, ed. Richard A. Horsley (Harrisburg: Trinity Press International, 2000), 160–183; [Rom 13:1–7] Herzog II, "Dissembling, A Weapon of the Weak," 339–360.

54. Heilig, *Hidden Criticism?*, 134.

55. E.g. see Birger Pearson, "1 Thessalonians 2:13-16: A Deutero-Pauline Interpolation," *HTR* 64 (1971): 79–94; Daryl Dean Schmidt, "1 Thess 2:13-16: Linguistic Evidence for an Interpolation," *JBL* 102 (1983): 269–279. For arguments against an interpolation see J. W. Simpson, "The Problems Posed by 1Thessalonians 2.15-16 and a Solution," *HBT* 12 (1990): 42–72; Jon Allen Weatherly, "The Authenticity of 1 Thessalonians 2.13-16: Additional Evidence," *JSNT* 42 (1991): 79–98; Bruce C. Johanson, *To all the Brethren: A Text-Linguistic and Rhetorical Approach to 1 Thessalonians*, ConBNT (Stockholm: Almqvist & Wiksell International, 1991).

56. Boring, *I & II Thessalonians*, NTL, 91. See his fuller discussion in defense of a unified composition of 1 Thessalonians 2:13-16 on pages 91–95.

57. See Jefferey A. D. Weima, *1-2 Thessalonians*, BECNT (Grand Rapids: Baker Academic, 2014), 168. Also, Frank D. Gilliard, "The Problem of the Antisemitic Comma Between 1 Thessalonians 2.14 and 15," *NTS* 35 (1989): 481–502; C. B. Amphoux, "1 Th 2, 14-16: Quel Juifs sont-ils mis en cause par Paul?" *Filologia neo-testamentaria* 16 (2003): 85–101.

58. Smith, "Unmasking the Powers," 47–66. See also Donfried, "The Imperial Cults, 215–223. Also, Harrison, *Paul and the Imperial Authorities*.

59. Smith, "'Unmasking the Powers,'" 49–50.

60. Ibid., 50–51.

61. Ibid., 51. Also Richard A. Horsley, *Jesus and Empire: The Kingdom of God and the New World Disorder* (Minneapolis: Fortress, 2002), 38.

62. Smith, "'Unmasking the Powers,'" 51. Also, Stephen L. Dyson, "Native Revolt Patterns in the Roman Empire," *ANRW* (1975): 138–175.

63. Smith, "'Unmasking the Powers,'" 51.

64. Smith, "'Unmasking the Powers,'" 52. For a general introduction to the Dead Sea Scrolls and 1QS see James H. Charlesworth, ed., *The Dead Sea Scrolls: Hebrew, Aramaic, and Greek Texts with English Translations: Volume 1: Rule of the Community and Related Documents* (Tübingen: J. C. V. Mohr Paul Siebeck, 1994); and Michael A. Knibb, "Rule of the Community," in *Encyclopedia of the Dead Sea Scrolls,* ed., Lawrence H. Shiffman and James C. VanderKam, Vol. 2 (Oxford: Oxford University Press, 2000), 793–797.

65. Smith, "'Unmasking the Powers,'" 23. Emphasis mine.

66. Ibid., 54.

67. Ibid.

68. Ibid. See also Neil Elliott, *Liberating Paul: The Justice of God and the Politics of the Apostle* (Maryknoll: Orbis, 1994), esp. 195.

69. Smith, "'Unmasking the Powers,'" 58–62.

70. J. A. O. Larsen, "Roman Greece," in *An Economic Survey of Ancient Rome*, ed. Tenney Frank (Baltimore: The John Hopkins Press, 1938), 4:259–498; esp. 4.445, 449.

71. Ibid., 449.

72. Smith, "'Unmasking the Powers,'" 60–61.

73. Barclay, "Why the Roman Empire Was Insignificant to Paul," 363–387.

74. Bryan, *Render to Caesar*, 90.

75. Smith, "'Unmasking the Powers,'" 61.

76. Ibid.

77. For more information on Stoicism and Middle-Platonism, especially on the topic of self-control in the first century CE, see Hans Svebakken, *Philo of Alexandria's Exposition on the Tenth Commandment* (Atlanta: Society of Biblical Literature Press, 2012).

78. Catherine Edwards, *The Politics of Immorality in Ancient Rome* (Cambridge: Cambridge University Press, 1993), 25.

79. Smith, "Unmasking the Powers," 62.

80. Ibid., 54.

81. On the ethical lists in the New Testament, see B. S. Easton, "New Testament Ethical Lists," *JBL* 51 (1932): 1–12; Neil J. McEleney, "Vice Lists of the Pastoral Epistles," *CBQ* (1974): 203–229; John T. Fitzgerald, *Cracks in an Earthen Vessel: An Examination of the Catalogues of Hardships in the Corinthian Correspondence* (Atlanta: Scholars Press, 1988); Bj Oropeza, "Situational Immorality—Paul's 'Vice Lists' at Corinth," *ExpTim* 110 (1998): 9–10: Jennifer Wright Knust, "Paul and the Politics of Virtue and Vice," in *Paul and the Roman Imperial Order*, ed. Richard A. Horsley (Harrisburg: Trinity Press International, 2004), 155–173. On the stoic virtues see A. A. Long and D. N. Sedley, *The Hellenistic Philosophers*, 2 vols. (Cambridge: Cambridge University Press, 1987); Christoph Jedan, *Stoic Virtues: Chrysippus and the Religious Foundations of Stoic Ethics* (New York: Continuum, 2009).

82. Weima, *1-2 Thessalonians*, 121–25. Also, Jefferey A. D. Weima, "An Apology for the Apologetic Function of 1 Thessalonians 2.1-12," *JSNT* 68 (1997): 73–99; Traugott Holtz, "On the Background of 1 Thessalonians 2:1–12," in *The Thessalonians Debate: Methodological Discord or Methodological Synthesis?*, ed. Karl P. Donfried and Johannes Beutler (Grand Rapids: Eerdmans, 2000), 69–80; Kim, *Christ and Caesar*, 37–47. For an opposing view that 1 Thess 2:1-12 functions primarily as a parenesis see A. J. Malherbe, "'Gentle as a Nurse:' The Cynic Background to 1 Thess ii," *NovT* 12 (1970): 203–217; George Lyons, *Pauline Autobiography: Toward a New Understanding*, SBLDS 73 (Atlanta: Scholars Press, 1985); W. Stegemann, "Anlass und Hintergrun der Abfassung von 1 Th 2, 1-12," in *Theologische Brosamen für Lother Steiger*, DBAT 5, ed., G. Freund and E. Stegemann (Heidelberg: Esprint, 1985), 397–416; Richard, *First and Second*, 87–89; G. S. Shogren, *1 & 2 Thessalonians*, Zondervan Exegetical Commentary on the New Testament (Grand Rapids: Zondervan, 2012), 81–83.

83. Weima, *1-2 Thessalonians*, 124.

84. See n. 54.

85. Weima, *1-2 Thessalonians*, 159.

86. Ibid., 165.

87. Wanamaker, *The Epistles to the Thessalonians*, 112.

88. Weima, *1-2 Thessalonians*, 165.

89. I. Howard Marshall, *1 and 2 Thessalonians: Based on the Revised Standard Version*, NCB (Grand Rapids: Eerdmans), 9.

90. Wright, "Paul's Gospel and Caesar's Empire," 160–183. See also N. T. Wright, *Paul: In Fresh Perspective* (Minneapolis: Fortress Press), 40–58, 69–78. For a more extensive treatment of N. T. Wright and his postcolonial interpretation of Paul, see my chapter 1.

91. Wright, "Paul's Gospel and Caesar's Empire," 175.

92. Ibid., 176.

93. Ibid., 177.

94. Ibid.

95. Ibid., 178. See also Oakes, *Philippians*.

96. Philippi was later named *Colonia Iulia Augusta Phillipensium*. See Larsen, "Roman Greece," 449.

97. Wright, "Paul's Gospel and Caesar's Empire," 174.

98. Ibid., 174–75.

99. Fee, *Paul's Letter*, 289. Also, Richard R. Melick Jr., *"Philippians, Colossians and Philemon*, NAC 32 (Nashville: Broadman Press, 1991), 126.

100. Bertschmann, *Bowing Before Christ—Nodding to the State?*, 104.

101. Ando, *Imperial Ideology and Provincial*, 49–70.

102. E.g., Elliott, *The Rhetoric of Romans*; Elliott, "Romans 13:1-7, 184–205; Georgi, "God Turned Upside Down,", 148–57; E. G. Singgih, "Towards a Postcolonial Interpretation of Romans 13:1-7: Karl Barth, Robert Jewett and the Context of Reformation in Present-Day Indonesia," *AsJT* 23 (2009): 111–22; Robert Jewett, *Romans: A Commentary*, Hermeneia (Minneapolis; Fortress Press, 2007), 780–803; R. Cassidy, "The Politization of Paul: Romans 13:1-7 in Recent Discussion," *ExpTim* 121 (2010): 383–389; M. Forman, *The Politics of Inheritance in Rome* (Cambridge: Cambridge University Press, 2011); Bernard Lategan, "Romans 13:1-7: A Review of Post-1989 Readings," *Scriptura* 110 (2012): 259–272; Wright, "Paul's Gospel and Caesar's Empire," 167–173.

103. Herzog, "Dissembling, A Weapon of the Weak," 339–360.

104. Herzog, "Dissembling, A Weapon of the Weak," 354. Cf. Ernst Käsemann, *Commentary on Romans*, trans. and ed. G. W. Bromiley (Grand Rapids: Eerdmans 1980), esp. 354; S. E. Porter, "Romans 13:1-7 as Pauline Political Rhetoric," *FNT* 3 (1990): 115–139.

105. Scott, *Domination and the Arts of Resistance*. In chapter 1 of this study, I made the argument that Paul's letters are not public transcripts but are rather private transcripts written specifically to the followers of Christ. Paul is quite open about faith in Christ and is not hesitant to speak out against those which may hinder the gospel he is preaching. Scott's argument, rather, speaks against the interpretations of many counter-imperial scholars of Paul. See the argument of John M.G. Barclay that I closely followed; Barclay, "Why the Roman Empire Was Insignificant to Paul," 363–387. See especially 376–379.

106. Cf. James H. McDonald, "Romans 13:1-7: A Test Case for New Testament Interpretation," *NTS* 35 (1989): 540–543.

107. Herzog, "Dissembling, A Weapon of the Weak," 355. Herzog quotes R. David Kaylor, *Paul's Covenant Community: Jew and Gentile in Romans* (Atlanta: John Knox, 1988), 204.

108. Herzog, "Dissembling, A Weapon of the Weak," 356.

109. Cf. H. W. Beyer, "διακονέω, διακονία, κτλ," *TDNT* 2:81–93.

110. Herzog, "Dissembling, A Weapon of the Weak," 356.

111. Ibid., 357.

112. Ibid.

113. Ibid.

114. Ibid.

115. Ibid.

116. Ibid., 357–58. Cf. C. K. Barrett, *A Commentary on the Epistle to the Romans*, HNTC (New York: Harper & Brothers, 1932), 247.

117. Cf. Tom Carney, *The Shape of the Past* (Lawrence: Coronado Press, 1975), 62.

118. Herzog, "Dissembling, A Weapon of the Weak," 358.

119. Ibid., 359.

120. Ibid., 359.

121. The notion that Rome was a police state, actively seeking to persecute dissenters, is much exaggerated. Indeed, prominent citizens and those in the public sphere had to be careful about what they said or did, but Rome did not actively seek out and prosecute dissenters. Even when ancient associations came under the microscope of Julius Caesar and later Augustus, they did not monitor the communique of local associations since these small groups were highly incapable of subverting the authority of the Caesar. See Wendy Cotter, "The Collegia and Roman Law, 74–89.

122. Herzog, "Dissembling, A Weapon of the Weak," 359.

123. "With regard to the responsibility for the disturbances and rioting, or rather to speak the truth, the war, against the Jews, although your ambassadors, particularly Dionysius the son of Theon, argued vigorously and at length in the disputation, I have not wished to make an exact inquiry, but I harbor within me a store of immutable indignation against those renewed the conflict. I merely say that, unless you stop this destructive and obstinate mutual enmity, I shall be forced to show what a benevolent ruler can be when he is turned to righteous indignation. Even now, therefore, I conjure the Alexandrians to behave gently and kindly toward the Jews who have inhabited the same city for many years, and not to dishonor any of their customs in their worship of their god, but to allow them to keep their own ways, as they did in the time of the god Augustus and as I too, having heard both sides, have confirmed. The Jews, on the other hand, I Order not to aim at more than they have previously had and not in future to send two embassies as if they lived in two cities, a thing which has never been done before, and not to intrude themselves into the games presided over by the *gymnasiarchoi* and the *kosmetai*, since they enjoy what is their own, and in a city which is not their own they possess an abundance of all good things." Translation of P.Lond.1912 from Tcherikover and Fuks, *Corpus Papyrorum Judaicarum*, 2.43.

124. Josephus, *Against Apion*.

125. The Greek text of the Septuagint is from Alfred Rahlf's (ed.) *Septuaginta* (2006). All translations are mine unless otherwise noted.

126. Cf. Jer 29:7 (36:7 [LXX]); Ezra 6:10; 1 Macc 7:33. Also, *Let. Aris.*45; Philo, *Legat.* 157; Josephus, *B.J.* 2.197; *C. Ap.* 2.76-77). See Tobin, *Paul's Rhetoric in Its Contexts*, 397–398.

127. Notice the unique ascription of this title to Christ as a "servant of the Jews" in Rom 15:8.

128. Cf. Prov 8:15-16; Jer 27:5-7 (34:5-7 [LXX]); Isa 45:1-3; Dan 2:21, 36-38; 4:17; Sir 10:4. Also, *Let. Aris.* 224; Wis 6:3; Josephus, *B.J.* 2.140; *A.J.* 15.374; *C. Ap.* 2.76-77. Tobin, *Paul's Rhetoric in Context*, 396. Also, Hultgren, *Paul's Letter to the Romans*, 467.

129. Tobin, *Paul's Rhetoric in Context*, 398.

130. Hultgren, *Paul's Letter to the Romans*, 472.

131. Tobin, *Paul's Rhetoric in Context*, 398.

132. E.g. Rom 13 as an interpolation: James Kallas, "Romans xiii. 1–7: An Interpolation," *NTS* 11 (1964–1965): 365–374; Joseph C. O'Neil, *Paul's Letter to the Romans* (Middlesex: Penguin Books, 1975), 207–209; Winsome Munro, *Authority in Paul and Peter: The Identification of a Pastoral Stratum in the Pauline Corpus and 1 Peter*, SNTSMS 45 (Cambridge: Cambridge University Press, 1983), 15–19. On studies that argue for authenticity Rom 13, which I ascribe to, see e.g. J. Freidrich, W. Puhlmann, and P. Stuhlmacher, "Zur historischen Situation und Intention von Rom. 13.1–7," *ZTK* 73 (1976): 131–166, esp. 134–135; Käsemann, *Commentary on Romans*, 351; Thomas R. Schreiner, *Paul, Apostle of God's Glory in Christ: A Pauline Theology* (Downers Grove: InterVarsity Press, 2006), 447.

133. Joseph A. Fitzmyer, *Romans*, Anchor Yale Bible, 662.

134. Tobin, *"Paul's Rhetoric in Context,"* 396–97, esp. 397 n. 40.

135. See Exod 7,4. 12,2; Jer 51,11; (LXX) Ps 17,47–50; Wis 12,12; Ezek 7,24–25.16,38; Luke 18,3–8; 1 Thess 4,6; Heb 10,30; 1Pet 2,13–16; Rev 6:10. Cf. Erwin Ochsenmeier, "Romans 12,17–13,7 and the Justice of God: Two Neglected Features of Paul's Argument," *ETL* 89 (2013): 361–82, esp. 365.

136. Heinrich Schlier, *Der Römerbrief*, HThKNT 6 (Freiburg: Herder, 1977), 382; James D. G. Dunn, *Romans*, WBC 38A-B (Dallas: Word, 1988), 2.749; Jewett, *Romans*, 775–776.

137. Dorothea H. Bertschmann, "The Good, the Bad and the State—Romans 13.1–7 and the Dynamics of Love," *NTS* 60 (2014): 232–249, esp. 244. On the positive aspects of authority in Rom 13:1-7, see Paul Valadier, *Des versets encombrants. « Toute autorité vient di Dieu » (Epître aux Romains, 13,1) Théophilyon* 20 (2015): 99–113.

138. Vengeance as expressed in Rom 12, 19–20, which paraphrases Duet 32:33, is a divine prerogative which does not require human vindictiveness. See Jewett, *Romans*, 777.

139. My thanks to Troy W. Martin, who pointed out to me how this theory concerning the civil authority was relevant not only to 1 Peter but also to Paul. See Troy W. Martin, *Apostolic Confirmation and Legitimation in an Early Christian Faith Document: A Commentary on the First Epistle of the Apostle Peter*, NIGTC (Grand Rapids: Eerdmans, forthcoming).

140. Hultgren, *Paul's Letter to the Romans*, 471. Also, Tobin, *Paul's Rhetoric*, 395.

141. Cf. Gerhard Delling, "ὑποτάσσω," *TDNT* 8: 39–46.

142. Hultgren, *Paul's Letter to the Romans*, 436.

143. Cf. Marcus Borg, "A New Context for Romans 13," *NTS* 19 (1972); 205–218: J. Friedrich, W. Puhlmann, and P. Stuhlmacher, "Zur historischen Situation und Intention von Rom. 13.1-7," *ZTK* 73 (1976): 131–166; A. J. M. Wedderburn, *The Reason for Romans* (Minneapolis: Fortress Press, 1991), 62.

144. Thomas H. Coleman, "Binding Obligations in Romans 13:7: A Semantic Field and Social Context," *TynBul* 48 (1997): 307–327.

145. Ibid., 475.

146. Hans Dieter Betz, *Galatians: A Commentary on Paul's Letter to the Churches in Galatia*, Hermeneia (Philadelphia: Fortress Press, 1979), 14–15, 24–25.

147. E.g. Edmondo F. Lupieri, *A Commentary on the Apocalypse of John*, trans. Maria Poggi Johnson and Adam Kamesar (Grand Rapids: Eerdmans, 2006).

148. Victor Tcherikover, *Hellenistic Civilization and the Jews* (Grand Rapids: Baker Academic Press, 1999), 296–332; John M. G. Barclay, *Jews in the Mediterranean Diaspora: From Alexander to Trajan (323 BCE–117 CE)* (Berkley: University of California Press, 1996), 55–60.

149. E.g., see Gambetti, *The Alexandrian Riots of 38 CE.*

150. Bernard C. Lategan, "The Quality of Young Democracies from a Constitutional Perspective," in *Democracy under Scrutiny: Elites, Citizens, Cultures*, ed. U. J. Van Beck (Opladen: Barbara Budrich, 2010), 95–114.

151. The primary objective of counter-imperial readings is to understand Paul's relationship with the larger civic authority by focusing on Paul's immediate political and economic context.

Chapter 3

Roman Imperialism and Foreign Cults

Conceptions of the expansionist periods of Roman Republic/Empire, at one time, drew on nineteenth- and twentieth-century models of Western European imperialism. In the nineteenth century, Theodor Mommsen considered Republican Rome's expansionism as defensive imperialism.[1] Mommsen's theory found strong supporters in the twentieth century with scholars like Tenney Frank, Maurice Holleaux, and R. M. Errington.[2] Several proposals have been offered to explain why Republican Rome often fought in wars: they had a drive for domination; they fought only in defense of themselves and their allies; they fought for economic reasons.[3]

Indeed, there were certainly definite economic and military advantages on conquering a new territory, but evidence from the middle to late Republic (264–30 BCE), and early Principate (27 BCE–14 CE) reveals conquest for the sake of military honorifics. An honorific is a title that confers or conveys esteem and respect for a position of rank when addressing a person. In the Republican era, military honorifics were requisites for an aristocrat if he sought political power. A year without war could potentially hinder a Roman aristocrat from seeking political office. Military campaigns were, therefore, necessary because they were the main contributing factors for an aristocrat to secure political power. But when the Principate was inaugurated, Rome's drive for conquest dramatically decreased, eventually seeing a major change in military policy at the end of Augustus's reign (14 CE).

The expansionary policies and militaristic model of Rome see a significant change during the transition from the Republic to the early Principate especially post Augustus. This transition is, ultimately, a reconfiguration of the political system. During the Republic, wars were fought for imperialism and booty. In the Principate wars were fought to consolidate existing powers and to settle internal rebellions. This change also had a direct effect on Rome's relationship with foreign cults. Because the empire understood itself as a benevolent guardian, Rome suggested that its rule was in the best interest of all people (see, e.g., Vergil, *Aen.* 6.851-853). But if foreign peoples, or their cults, try to undermine or subvert Roman power, they would be swiftly, sometimes violently, dealt with.

In this chapter, we will inquire into how Rome transitioned from a senatorial Republic to a total autocracy. This inquiry will allow us to better understand how, over a period of several centuries, Rome reconsidered its relationship to foreign nations and peoples. By the time of the Principate, the city of Rome and the surrounding communities in the rest of Italy were a multiethnic state unified under Roman authority. Each group of people brought with them their own cults and traditions. Some cults would often come under suspicion, such as the cult of Bacchus, because of their late-night ceremonies. Others were overtly targeted because of the cult's political ties with an enemy state, such as the cult of Isis because of its connections to Egypt. I shall therefore survey Rome's relationship to several foreign cults: the cult of Bacchus; the cult of Isis; the cult of Yahweh (Judaism). What this investigation will reveal is that a foreign cult would be tolerated, insofar as it did not undermine Roman authority, cause civic unrest, or undermine the ancient gods of Rome. If a foreign cult should rouse the suspicion of the authorities, it would be mercilessly targeted until it was no longer considered a threat.

ROMAN IMPERIALISM: REPUBLIC TO EMPIRE

During the age of the Roman Republic, war was an annual ritualized event. War, to a great extent, was enmeshed in the Republic's civic life. Due to almost four centuries of constant war the Republic gained power, wealth, and new territories. Arguments have been offered to explain why they actively sought combat. Some have argued economically for their drive to war, suggesting that Rome was in many ways dependent on plunder.[4] Others have offered a defensive model, suggesting that Rome fought only when the city or its allies were under threat of attack.[5] In some situations, these arguments are quite valid, but they cannot alone explain Rome's warfare ethos and their drive for power (*imperium*). Rather, as I will attempt to show, Rome's desire for war was a combination of these models. Moreover, it will be shown how military campaigns were crucial for the election to public office, but this eventually begins to dissipate in the third century BCE and onward. In the Republic, aristocrats who sought public office were required to have served in (numerous) military campaigns. Yet, when the emperor Augustus inaugurates the Principate, *imperium* becomes the sole prerogative of the imperial family.

What follows is a description of these models, including a minor inquiry into the *Res Gestae Divi Augusti*.

Economy and War

In the last century, scholarship on the Roman Empire was influenced by modern political consciousness, and by historically recent forces of imperialism.[6] But did Rome necessarily conceive of "empire" as we do, that is to say, as a direct control by the state over other peoples and lands which were acquired by means of annexation, occupation, and exploitation? Erich Gruen observes,

> Romans threw their weight around in certain places and at certain times; on occasion they exercised firm authority, barked commands, carried off the wealth of a state. On other occasions and under other circumstances, they shunned involvement or decision, showed little interest in tangible gain, and shrank even from anything that can be characterized as "hegemony."[7]

So, in some ways ancient Rome did reflect our contemporary notions of "empire," but in some other ways it did not. Considering the Greek cities of Asia Minor under Roman rule, it was a rare occurrence to see Rome interfere in the internal affairs of those Hellenized communities.

During the middle Republic (264–133 CE), Rome preserved or granted free status to certain Greek cities in return for their loyalty in wars against Rome's adversaries.[8] These cities had administrative independence, but this was not necessarily accompanied by political independence.[9] If these free cities were politically and socially stable, paid their taxes, and contributed to the needs of Rome's military, Rome refrained from interfering in their internal politics and administration.[10] As P. A. Brunt observes, "It was not the practice of the Romans to govern much. The governor had only a small staff, and he did little more than defend his province, ensure the collection of the taxes and decide the most important criminal and civil cases. The local communities were left in the main to run their own affairs."[11]

Regarding annexed territories, Rome's ultimate concern was how these territories could support Rome's military. Among Rome's allies, the need for troops was the only obligation of their alliance.[12] But these foreign troops, *socii*, although they could not be expected to be automatically loyal to Rome, were essential. Arnaldo Momigliano comments,

> As military obligations were the only visible tie between Rome and the allies, Rome had to make the most of these obligations lest they became meaningless or, worse, lest the allied armies turn against Rome . . . the organization of the

Italian alliance had its own logic—no tribute and therefore maximum military partnership.[13]

Among the provinces loyalty to Rome was encouraged externally, by the Roman officers, and internally, by the allied aristocracy.[14] In exchange for their loyalty, the *socii* were rewarded with glory, plunder, and land. This structure of alliance, which included the possible benefits of war, was a means for encouraging continued military campaigns. War led to more alliances, and the allies benefited from booty. In this manner, the Roman Republic conquered the Italian and Greek lands while, simultaneously, creating an infrastructure of power.[15] By the end of the fourth century BCE, Rome became the dominant power in Italy and had conquered the peninsula by 264 BCE.

William V. Harris notes that by the early years of the first century BCE there was a shift in the location of power in Roman society. He was the first scholar to challenge a defensive warfare model. He argues that Rome was an aggressor, led by the aristocrats, and sought land, wealth, and plunder. He says, "Foreign wars and expansion gradually ceased to be preoccupations of the Roman aristocracy and the citizen body, and became instead the specialized policy of certain 'great men' and their followers."[16] Tim Cornell suggests that Harris does not go far enough in his assessment.[17] He notes that the Roman warfare model in the first century BC sees a gradual change from its frequency, intensity and duration, nature, and function within society. Moreover, the change is a gradual one beginning in the latter years of the third century CE.[18]

Expansionist Rome

The defensive imperialism model was championed in the mid-twentieth century, when countries like Britain and France took possession of overseas territories, which helped spin a positive view on ancient Roman *imperialism*.[19] Simply put, Rome unintentionally became an imperialist force. Erskine observes that American scholarship of the last century supported this defensive model as well, possibly a consequence of both world wars and the Cold War.[20]

The first scholar to challenge the defensive model was William V. Harris, who, in 1979, suggested that the defensive model is argued based on particular wars rather than the whole history of the Middle Republic.[21] Harris concludes saying, "We have encountered little evidence of wars which the Romans fought primarily to ward off a long-range strategic danger to their empire as a whole . . . the only war which might fit easily into this category is the war against Hannibal."[22] As Harris shows, the defensive imperialism model is argued on notions of Roman just law and fetial law.[23]

The *fetiales*, as explained in ancient literature,[24] was a college of twenty priests who were concerned with the procedures of declaring war.[25] The priests are said to have overseen the religious aspects during transitional times between peace and war.[26] Ultimately, the actions performed by the *fetiales* were primarily intended to shift the blame for war to the enemy, thus allowing the Roman declaration of war to be both pious and just.[27] Then the enemy would be given the opportunity to make amends for their non-compliance with Rome or its allies. If their demands were not met, the *fetiales* would perform the proper ritual for declaring war. Some scholars, therefore, recognize the fetial laws as Rome's unwillingness to fight wars unless the war itself was perceived as defensive.[28]

The fetial laws were therefore instruments for setting a war into action. Erskine suggests that the primary function of the fetial laws was religious in nature and had the potential of promoting peace. But it also became a means of "self-righteous aggression."[29] The defensive model argued that Rome was reluctant to pursue war and to annex territory, but did so only when their hand was forced. Harris's detailed investigation of the Republican wars from 327 to 70 BCE shows that some battles, such as when the Gauls in 284/283 BCE and in 225 BCE attacked Rome at Arretium and Telamon respectively, were fought in pure defense of Rome and its citizens. But, as it will be shown in the following section, most wars were fought to serve the interest of the aristocracy. Rome was eager to annex territory but did so only when it was practical.

Rome eventually gained a vast empire, but to base this acquisition on a lust for imperium or because of self-defense does not necessarily explain why Rome so often sought wars. Critics of defensive imperialism stress the importance of *praise* and *glory*. In the early and middle Republic (458–133 BCE), warfare was formative in the lives of Romans. From the age of seventeen, a young Roman aristocrat would begin schooling which was heavily focused in war and military command.[30] To become a man of renown, one had to achieve praise and glory (*laus* and *gloria*), the pre-eminent source of which was victory in battle and other military achievements.[31]

Praise, Glory, and the Res Gestae Divi Augusti

War was built into the fabric of the Roman Republic, so much so that it became an essential part of the aristocrat's life. The greatest distinction a young aristocrat could obtain was accessible only by means of warfare. Military achievement was the pre-eminent source of praise and glory. Yet, as Harris observes, there was a shift of power within Roman society as the Republic transitioned into the Principate. Ultimately, he says, "foreign wars and expansion gradually ceased to be the preoccupations of the Roman aristocracy and the citizen body, and became instead specialized policy of certain 'great men' and their followers."[32] As noted earlier Cornell expands on this observation and suggests that the entire institution of war-making, "its frequency, intensity, and duration, and its nature and function within society," were significantly different in the first century BCE than it was previously in the Republic. Furthermore, Cornell suggests that the transformation was not sudden but was a gradual change which did not take full effect until the death of the emperor Augustus.[33]

The central importance of glory and military honorifics during the Republican era is evident in sources of first century BCE. Cicero, in *De off.*, recalls the traditional Roman ethos surrounding "great men." He says that men of renown are recognized in three ways, which are to make a career of defending lawsuits, leading an assembly, and to make war (*De off.* 1.121).[34] Indeed, as reflected in Cicero, the most notable thing a Roman could do in the Republic was to seek success and glory, which were primarily secured through military campaigns.[35] In one of his rhetorical works, Cicero suggests that the greatest men are judged by their achievements in war. He says,

> Who, for instance, in seeking to measure the understanding possessed by illustrious men, whether by the usefulness or the grandeur of their achievements, would not place the general above the orator? Yet who could doubt that, from this country alone, we could cite almost innumerable examples of leaders in war of the greatest distinction, but of men excelling in oratory a mere handful? (*De or.* 1.7 [Sutton, LCL])

Cicero states here that the pre-eminent sources of fame are military achievements.[36] Though the first century BCE saw a change in the nature of war and imperialism, it was still understood that the greatest men of Rome were the military heroes of old (Cicero, *Mur.* 19–30).[37]

Competition among the aristocracy, as well as the warfare ethos, in early Republican society drove Roman imperialism by an almost continuous demand for war, wherein the elite could obtain praise and glory. Harris has shown that after 327 BCE it was rare that Rome did not engage in a yearly battle.[38] Stephen Oakley observes that from 415 to 265 BCE Rome did not commit to war for only thirteen years.[39] Also, Polybius reports that in order for one to hold political office in Rome, he must have completed ten military campaigns (*Hist.* 6.19.4).[40] Even if one regards Polybius's observation as an exaggeration, it is likely that many years of military service were still a prerequisite to hold political office in Rome. However, Harris shows signs that by the second century BCE, military service was no longer an essential requirement for political office.[41]

The early Republic had high regard for military service. Military service was an indispensable qualification for public office and was the mark of success of a Roman aristocrat. Yet, the first century BCE shows a shift in aristocratic life. As Cornell correctly observes, the educated classes of Rome had no experience of war. War, as seen in Cicero, was only read about.[42] So by the early Principate, most senators and other public officials had very little to no military experience. Aristocrats could no longer depended on *laus* and *gloria* of war for booty or to hold some civic position. They depended, rather, on the direct benefaction of the emperor.[43] Elites who did have some level of militaristic expertise would likely not take part in any combat.[44] Combat seemed to be something in far off lands and provinces. This is not to say that Rome did not engage in military activity in the late first century BCE or the first century CE. At that time, however, expansion slowed down, and the military was almost exclusively positioned in the provinces, in distant places away from most Romans. Cornell observes, "The effect of these developments was that Italy and the inner provinces of the empire were gradually demilitarized, and the warlike tradition of the Roman people faded out of existence."[45] What was left of this warfare ethos remained in reconstructions of past battles in the writings of ancient historians and orators, as well as in gladiatorial spectacles.[46]

Aristocratic competition for *laus* and *gloria* in the military field became redundant once Augustus inaugurated the Principate. The achievements of the emperor Augustus, which are recalled in *Res Gestae Divi Augusti*, demonstrate the emperor as the greatest of all men past and present. In many ways, Augustus sought to revive the early Republic warfare mentality but military glory became the prerogative of the imperial family and, after 19 BCE, the celebration of the *triumph* was reserved only for them.[47] In the *Res gest. divi Aug.*, no one could surpass the emperor, whether it be in honorifics, military achievements, or benefaction.

The *Res gest. divi Aug.* is an autobiographical aretalogy of the emperor Augustus.[48] The document, written primarily in the first person, is an account of how Augustus balances honors and his position in Rome, along with his achievements and his role as benefactor.[49] The *Res gest. divi Aug.* serves as a summary of Augustus's public life. Originally, it was engraved on two bronze tablets and placed in front of his mausoleum. These bronze tablets have yet to be discovered. However, the text itself was preserved in Latin, as well as being translated into Greek. Extant text comes from inscriptions on monuments from eastern Galatia. The *Monumentum Ancyranum* is the largest inscription of the *Res gest. divi Aug.* and was found on the walls of a mosque, located in Ankara, Turkey, which had formerly served as a temple to the goddess Roma and Augustus.[50]

It is important to note that Augustus does not maintain his rule over the empire by appeal to some divine right. Rather, it was Rome, the senate, and the people who acknowledged Augustus's authority on account of the superior benefits he conferred upon them.[51] Though much can be said about the *Res gest. divi Aug.*, I shall highlight only a few points that relate directly to the notions of imperium, *laus* and *gloria*.

The *Res gest. divi Aug.* is an autobiographical story of how Augustus came to acquire complete dominance, *imperium,* over the empire. The first sentence begins with, then, Octavian having no power and how he begins to acquire it by means of his virtues. The honors that he immediately receives on account of his virtue shows his power growing.[52] His authority was also increased by his military conquests. Chapters twenty-five through thirty recount some of his greatest military triumphs. He says,

> I cleared the sea of pirates, and in that same war I handed over to their masters for punishment nearly 30,000 slaves who had run away from their owners and had taken up arms against the Republic (5.25.1–3) . . . I extended the frontiers of all Rome's provinces that were bounded by peoples who were not under our imperial sway . . . I ended hostilities in the Alps—from the region that is closest to the Adriatic Sea to the lands bordering the Tuscan Sea—without a single tribe suffering exposure to unjust war. (5.26.9–10, 13) . . . Egypt I added to the domain of the Roman people . . . (5.27.24) . . . Before my Principate no army of the Roman people had ever advanced as far as the Pannonian Tribes, but through Tiberius Nero, who was then my stepson and legate, I conquered them and made them subjects of the Empire of the Roman people; and I extended the frontiers of Illyricum to the banks of the Danube River. (5.30.44–46)[53]

What one notices here and throughout the *Res gest. divi Aug.* is Augustus does not share his authority. Even the victory won by Tiberius Nero was Augustus's to claim since he commanded the military. These wars served a purpose of legitimization, ultimately securing him as emperor par excellence and his heirs. No one else had achieved what he had, and no one succeeded in military campaigns as much as he had. Furthermore, the *Res gest. divi Aug.* presents both the senate and the people going about their daily lives in normal Republican manner while Augustus moves through the document as the supreme ruler who displays his supreme authority.[54]

In the transition from senatorial Republic to the imperial system of the Principate, and as is reflected in the *Res gest. divi Aug.*, one's political office was dependent more on the patronage of the emperor than on military triumphs. Though some major military campaigns were still conducted during Augustus's reign, these were conducted by the emperor himself or one of his legates in remote areas of the empire. Augustus conducted war, as did his successors, when it suited his personal (dynastic) reasons. With regard to battles fought during the Principate Cornell observes that "military commands gave prestige and public recognition to members of the imperial family, helped to secure the loyalty of the armies to Caesar's heirs, and served to legitimize dynastic succession."[55] During the Republic, foreign policy was fashioned by the generals in the midst of their battles.[56] During the age of the Principate, however, there was a strong centralized authority in the person of the emperor. The *Res gest. divi Aug.* ultimately expresses how glory and triumph belonged to the emperor and the imperial family alone.

Summary

The early Roman Republic depended on war to keep its social order intact. War brought in money, slaves, territory, and gave them *imperium*. War also brought with it honors, praise, and glory for the victorious commanders. A competition ensued among the aristocrats with regard to *laus* and *gloria*, that were primarily obtained by successful military campaigns. In numerous ways in the early Republic, the driving force for *imperium* was initiated by a search for military honorifics to hold public office. A year without war meant a year without a *triumph*, which could hinder one's political success. However, during the late empire and early Principate imperium became more of means to maintain power and regional stability.

The *Res ges. divi Aug.* reveals Augustus to be the ultimate consul who no one could ever surpass. Augustus transforms the *laus* and *gloria* given to a commander in the Republic, to an unsurpassable *laus* and *gloria* attributed only to the emperor and the imperial family. For these reasons, no military leader of the past could ever compare to Augustus. What emerges because of Augustus's rise to power is a major decline in frequency of major military campaigns. Though major wars of expansion still occurred under emperors who had personal or dynastic concerns. However, the boundaries of the Roman Empire remained much of what they were at Augustus's death in 14 CE (though Britain and Dacia were later added).

What remains to be discussed is Rome's attitudes toward its foreign neighbors. The *Res ges. divi Aug.* suggests that when it was safe, policy would allow conquered peoples to remain in or return to their territory under the imperium of Rome (*Res Ges.* 1.3). Many of these peoples brought their foreign deities and cultic practices to Rome. What was Rome's attitude toward foreign cults in Rome and across the eastern provinces of the empire? The following section will inquire into Rome's relationship with the cult of Bacchus, the cult of Isis, and the cult of Yahweh (Judaism) to better understand how Rome conceived of its relationship to these foreign cults.

ROME AND THE CULTS OF BACCHUS,
ISIS, AND YAHWEH

In their conquests the Roman Republic/Empire did not systematically replace native cults with what we can call *Roman religion*. Instead, there was an integration of Roman religion with those of the native peoples.[57] In the third century CE, Minucius Felix, a Christian writer, suggests that the reason the Roman Empire was so successful in the past was because of its receptivity to foreign cults. He writes,

> When they have captured a town, even in the fierceness of victory, the Romans respect the deities of the conquered people. They invite to Rome gods from all over the world and make them their own, raising altars even to unknown gods and to the shades of the dead. And thus, while the Romans were adopting the religious rites of all the nations, they also earned for themselves dominion. (*Oct.* 6.2–3)[58]

Minucius Felix alludes to the fact that Rome, as well as the rest of Italy, became a multiethnic state unified by Roman citizenship. Rome was able to unite the people by means of religious commonalities. Furthermore, the city of Rome adopted foreign deities and assimilated foreign festivals with their Roman customs.

In the late first century BCE, Dionysius of Halicarnassus reflects on Rome's relationship to foreign peoples and their gods. He writes,

> And, the thing which I myself have marveled at most, the innumerable nations which have come into Rome who are compelled to worship the gods of their fathers according to their own customs, yet the city has never officially adopted any of those foreign practices, as has been the experience of many cities in the past; but, even though she has, in pursuance of oracles, brought in rites beside her rites, she celebrates them in accordance with her own traditions, after casting-out the legendary pedantry. (*Ant. rom.* 2.19.3[Cary, LCL])[59]

By the first century BCE, Rome was a multiethnic city. Though foreign peoples brought with them their religious rights and practices, Rome did not forbid or ostracize the foreigners because of their customs. Notice how Rome was not only open to foreign cults but also incorporated foreign deities into their festivals. In fact, the Roman Republic and Empire adopted foreign cults in times of crises, especially plagues and disasters in war.[60] One may conjecture that if some foreign deity became popular among the native inhabitants of Rome, Romans would honor that foreign deity according to their own cultic practices. Clifford Ando observes that the Roman imperial government incorporated foreign deities because they "sought to advertise to its subjects the existence of a shared history and a common political theology: the history was that of Rome in the era of her empire and the one constant in the religious firmament was the emperor."[61] Rome did not seek to subvert local peoples' customs, in so far as they posed no threat to the Roman order, but rather incorporated local peoples and their customs to those of the wider empire.

To help illustrate Rome's affiliation with foreign cults, this chapter will proceed to analyze Rome's relationship to the cult of Bacchus, the cult of Isis, and the cult of Yahweh. Each of these cults shows, in different ways, how Rome engages foreign peoples and their gods. Rome tolerated foreign cults insofar as they did not come under suspicion of seeking to disrupt Rome's political and religious systems. It should be noted that the purpose of the following section is not to give a detailed account of the myth and development of these cults. Instead, it will give a brief description of the cult, noting the ways in which Rome reacted to them.

Bacchus and the Bacchanalia

Rome greatly expanded its imperium from the time of the middle Republic to the beginnings of the Principate. During this expansionist movement, Rome did not place pressures on subjugated peoples to *convert*. This sentiment was not because of Rome's unlikely respect of diversity or religious freedom, but because there was no *religion* to which a subjugated people could convert. James Rives explains, "The Graeco-Roman tradition was not a cohesive system of integrated practices and beliefs, but instead involved overlapping sects of cult practices, myths, iconographic conventions, and philosophical propositions."[62] When Rome began annexing foreign lands, they not only absorbed the local populations but also, to some extent, their local traditions and deities.

The Greek god Dionysus, also known as Bacchus, took center stage in Rome in 186 BCE. At that time, the senate issued a decree forbidding certain religious cultic practices associated with Bacchus. Those who disobeyed the senatorial decree were liable to capital punishment. But who was Bacchus and how is this decree important to our understanding of Rome's relationship to this foreign cult?

Dionysus is often associated with wine and with theater, which were often brought together in ancient Athenian festivals. Athens had two major festivals commemorating the god: the Dionysia and the Lenaea.[63] At the Dionysia, Pausanias reports that the ancient statue of Dionysus was carried from Eleutherae, northern Attica, and enshrined at the Academy in Athens (*Descr.* 1.29.2). On the eve of the festival of his epiphany, the image of Dionysus would be ceremoniously processed to the god's temple in Athens.[64] At the Lenaea, Athenians would attend theatrical plays and dithyrambic events in honor of the god's birthday.[65] Included in these Athenian festivals were rites of initiating young women into society, which celebrated a woman's intrinsic and mysterious link to the forces of life and death.[66]

By the fifth century BCE, there were already connections between Dionysus and mystery cults. A mystery cult denotes that admission and participation in the cult depends on a personal ritual performed on the initiand. In most cases, secrecy and nocturnal ceremonies gave precedence to the cult's *mystery*.[67] Euripides's *Bacchae*, composed toward the end of the fifth century BCE, tells the myth of Dionysus. In a telling of this myth, Euripides reveals that the cultic practice contains elements of secrecy.[68] In a conversation between Pentheus, king of Thebes, and Dionysus we learn that certain elements in the rites (τελεταί), as well as the efficacy of initiation, are to be revealed only to the initiated. Euripides writes,

Pentheus: What is the source of these rites (τελετὰς) you bring to Greece?
Dionysus: Dionysus himself initiated me, Zeus's son . . .
Pentheus: Did he compel you by night, or by your sight?
Dionysus: Seeing me just as I saw him, he gave me rites (ὄργια).
Pentheus: These rites (ὄργι')—what is their nature?
Dionysus: They may not be told to the uninitiated (ἀβακχεύτοισιν).
Pentheus: But those who perform them—what kind of benefit do they get?
Dionysus: You are not allowed to hear—though they are well worth knowing.
Pentheus: This is a clever counterfeit, so that I desire to hear.
Dionysus: The rites (ὄργι') of the god are hostile to whomsoever
    practices impiety. (*Bacch.* 465–66, 469–76 [Kovacs, LCL])[69]

The rites of the cult of Dionysus includes elements of secrecy. The rites themselves are said to come from the god himself. They take place in the night, when you come face to face with the person who is leading the ceremony of initiation. Since the rite is performed in secret, the initiand is set apart from the rest of society. Furthermore, the rite and the efficacy of the initiation are not to be told to those who are outside of the group. Therefore, the initiated would be punished by the god if they should ever reveal the mysteries of the cult to an outsider.

Pentheus was drawn to the cult of Bacchus because he desired to hear the mystery. This draw, in part, led many of the inhabitants of Rome and many across the regions of Italy to join this cult. What erupted in 186 BCE was a consequence of what the Roman senate considered a possible subversive group. Livy's account of the cult of Bacchus, written during the end of the first century BCE, gives some insight to the issue surrounding this controversy.

Demoralized by the longevity of the Second Punic War, Livy reports that Romans became dejected and began joining foreign cults (*Ad urbe condita*, 25.1.6). Livy writes that this cult led people to perform many acts that were contrary to both Roman piety and civility. In his first account of the cult of Bacchus, the *Bacchanalia*, he says that a nameless itinerant Greek, a humble man, initiated several men and women into the Bacchanalia in Etruria. What was only a few initiates had become a large number who were attracted to the festivals of wine and impropriety. Livy suggests that they met nocturnally, and their meetings were occasions for debauchery and offenses of all kinds, as they danced and frolicked to a cacophony of cymbals, drums, and screams of human victims offered up (*Ad urbe condita*, 39.8.1–8).

Livy's second account recalls a Roman consul discovering a Bacchanalia. A prostitute named Hispala, the mistress of this Roman consul, describes how the cult developed. Hispala suggests that the cult was first restricted to women. The rites of initiation occurred only three times a year during the day, and a married woman would officiate as priestess.[70] Hispala goes on to explain that the rites changed under the direction of a woman from Campania named Paculla Annia. Paculla Annia began to initiate men and performed the rites nocturnally five nights per month.

Under Paculla Annia, the Bacchanalia became a nocturnal cult highlighted by sexual promiscuity of all kinds that occurred in excess, as well as all forms of debauchery. Livy writes,

There were more lustful practices among men with one another than among women. If any of them were disinclined to endure abuse or reluctant to commit crime, they were sacrificed as victims. To consider nothing wrong, she continued, was the highest form of religious devotion among them. Men, as if insane, with fanatical tossings of their bodies, would utter prophecies. Matrons in the dress of Bacchantes, with dishevelled hair and carrying blazing torches, would run down to the Tiber, and plunging their torches in the water (because they contained live sulphur mixed with calcium) would bring them out still burning. Men were alleged to have been carried off by the gods who had been bound to a machine and borne away out of sight to hidden caves: they were those who had refused either to conspire or to join in the crimes or to suffer abuse. Their number, she said, was very great, almost constituting a second state; among them were certain men and women of high rank. Within the last two years it had been ordained that no one beyond the age of twenty years should be initiated: boys of such age were sought for as admitted both vice and corruption. (*Ad urbe condita* 39.13.11–12 [Sage, LCL])

If we take Livy at his word, Rome was oblivious to the cult until 186 BCE. But if the Bacchanalia were active in Rome since, at least, the Second Punic War (218–201 BCE) their nocturnal gatherings should have made enough noise that Romans would have become aware of their existence sometime before 186 BCE.[71] As Hugh Bowden suggests, Livy's accounts read like a piece of drama, as if Livy borrowed it from a comic play.[72] But what truth can be drawn from Livy's accounts can be seen against the backdrop of the senatorial decree against the Bacchanalia, the *Senatus Consultum de Bacchanalibus*.

The *Senatus Consultm de Bacchanalibus* survives in a bronze copy, currently housed in the Kunsthistorisches Museum Wien, in Vienna Austria, and is accurately summarized by Livy (CIL 1.2.581 = ILS 18.511). The decree demanded that all Bacchic shrines, except where an ancient altar or image had been consecrated, must be destroyed. Furthermore, no new Bacchic shrine may be installed. Those for whom the worship of Bacchus was traditional or necessary had to bring their plea to the urban praetor, who would then consult the senate (at least 100 senators had to be present). If the senate agreed, the supplicant would offer a sacrifice with no more than five people present. A common fund for the cult was denied, and no official priest could preside at the ceremonies (Livy, *Ad urbe condita* 39.9). The decree led to special trials as well as several thousand charges and sentences.[73] Ultimately, the Bacchanalia survived only sporadically, for example, at Pompeii, but was eradicated in Rome.

We learn that the repression of the Bacchanalia was merciless. This quelling was the first instance of Roman religious intolerance, but it is significant to understand why Rome suppressed this cult. It was not an attack on religion since established cultic centers of Dionysus were protected.[74] Only the newly created Bacchic shrines and cultic associations were targeted, likely because of their great numbers and nighttime ceremonies. Livy reports that there were over 7000 Bacchants in Rome, their ceremonies were at night, and their rites were secret (*Ad urbe candita* 39.17.6).

The Roman political authority did not have direct control over the cult or its practices. This suppresion was Rome's response to sources of authority not associated with the ruling elite. Roman rule largely consisted of collecting taxes, maintaining peace and social stability, and resolving disputes. Roman officials were not in the business of intervening in matters of religion unless public peace and order were at stake. As James Rives observes, "Claims to religious authority made on a basis other than socio-economic status were thus potentially subversive of the entire social and political system . . . and could elicit a sharp response from Roman authorities."[75] Indeed, because of its stand-alone nature, its mysterious nocturnal ecstatic meetings, and its popularity, the Roman authority considered the Bacchanalia and its secret rites a disguise for their plotting against Rome.

Though extant evidence is not clear as to whether there was a legitimate threat against Rome at that time or not, the aroma of conspiracy was enough to draw the attention of the authorities. Ultimately, any organization or meeting outside the direct control of the authority was considered, at least potentially, politically subversive. Consequently, the Bacchanalia were suppressed to near extinction.

Cult of Isis

The goddess Isis, of Egyptian provenance, was one of the more popular cults during the Hellenistic period (323–31 BCE). Her worship was multifaceted, and she was praised as the goddess, "mistress of life," protectress of women and marriage, protectress of maternity and the new-born, she who guarantees the grain harvest and abundance of the harvest, and protectress of travelers by both land and sea.[76] Because of the plurality of Isis's power, she was easily assimilated to the many different aspects of Greco-Egyptian and, toward the end of the second-century BCE Greco-Roman religiosity.[77]

By the Hellenistic period, the worship of Isis and, to a large extent, her male counterpart Osiris was widely popular both among the Greeks and, later, among the Romans. This is attested by the four hymns of Isidorus to the goddess Isis, which are dated to the very early first century BCE.[78] These hymns were found at the south gate of an ancient temple near the modern Egyptian village of Medinet Madi. The hymns are particularly important to understanding the development and characterization of the cult of Isis in Greco-Egyptian and in Greco-Roman culture. In the hymns of Isidorus, Isis's plasticity is quickly recognized by her three main titles: Hermouthis, Demeter, and *Good Fortune* (Τύχη Ἀγαθή). Importantly, Isidorus suggests that Isis is also known throughout the world by many other names. The inscription reads,

All mortals who live on the boundless earth,
Thracians, Greeks and Barbarians,
Express Your fair Name, a Name greatly honoured among all, (but)
Each (speaks) in his own language, in his own land.
The Syrians call You: Astarte, Artemis, Nanaia,
The Lycian tribes call You: Leto, the Lady,
The Thracians also name You as Mother of the gods,
And the Greeks (call you) Hera of the Great Throne, Aphrodite,
Hestia the goodly, Rheia and Demeter.
But the Egyptians call you 'Thiouis' [Θιοῦιν] (because
    they know) that You, being One, are all
Other goddesses invoked by the races of men (Isidorus,
    Hymns to Isis 1.14–24 [Vanderlip]).

Isis is equated to many female deities of the ancient world. This syncretism would lead to the popularity and spread of the Isianic cult across vast areas of the Greek world.[79] It was primarily spread "by means of merchants, Greeks who served in the Egyptian military or civilian capacities, travelers, sailors, and priests."[80]

The earliest surviving and most complete myth of Isis is found in Plutarch's *de Iside et Osiride*, which is likely derived from earlier Egyptian sources.[81] Plutarch's *Is. Os.* is considered to be one of his more philosophical works written toward the end of his life (120 CE).[82] The text, though highly philosophical, gives a glimpse into the life of Greco-Romans in the early second century CE. Importantly, it conveys to us that by this time the myth of Isis has reached a greater level of popularity across the Mediterranean, so much so that *Is. Os.* was accepted by Plutarch's contemporaries as both desirable and needful.[83]

The cult of Isis reached Rome during the late Republic, roughly in the late second century BCE. Her first temples were erected in Puteoli, a region of Campania, in 105 BCE and in Pompeii in 80 BCE.[84] Notice that both Puteoli and Pompeii were two important trading centers for Rome. The reception of the Isianic cult in Italy is likely a consequence of trading between Rome and Egypt.[85] Egypt provided Rome with large quantities of grain yearly and so a cult to Isis, who is often associated with the harvest, should not strike one as odd.[86] The cult came to Rome and flourished during a time of great political unrest. Opposition to the cult first appeared during the period known as the first *triumvirate*: when political power was equally shared between Julius Caesar, Pompey, and Crassus in 60 BCE.[87] The temples and shrines of Isis were ordered to be destroyed in 59, 58, 53, 50, and 48 BCE. There are two overarching reasons why the cult was understood to be hostile toward Rome. First, as seen with the cult of Bacchus, any cult or organization that may possibly threaten the civic order was understood to be subversive. The cult of Isis was perceived to infiltrate Roman culture; hence, Rome removed Isianic shrines and temples from the city of Rome. And second, because the cult was associated with the Ptolemaic rulers, tensions between Rome and Egypt could be manifested by means of the cult.

In the middle of the first century BCE, Cleopatra ruled her native Egypt by virtue of Rome (51–31 BCE). Rome was ultimately threatened by her success since it would possibly jeopardize Rome's position in the world.[88] Rome was an established patriarchal society, so for a woman to have control over Roman territory and Roman legions could be seen to threaten the patriarchal society of Rome. At the time of the second *triumvirate*, when Roman authority was shared between Octavian, Marcus Antony, and Marcus Lepidus, there was a declaration among the three to establish a temple of Isis (Cass. Dio. *Roman History*, 47.15.4). Among the *triumvirate*, there was a struggle for power that ultimately led Antony to marry his longtime mistress, Cleopatra, and escape to Egypt.[89] At the defeat of Antony by Octavian, at the battle of Actium in 31 BCE, Cassius Dio describes Rome's distaste with Cleopatra; a foreign woman with power.

> For that we who are Romans and lords of the greatest and best portion of the world should be despised and trodden under foot by an Egyptian woman is unworthy of our fathers, who overthrew Pyrrhus, Philip, Perseus, and Antiochus, who drove the Numantians and the Carthaginians from their homes, who cut down the Cimbri and the Ambrones . . . Should we not be acting most disgracefully if, after surpassing all men everywhere in valour, we should then meekly bear the insults of this throng, who, oh heavens, are Alexandrians and Egyptians (what worse or what truer name could one apply to them?), who worship reptiles and beasts as gods, who embalm their own bodies to give them the semblance of immortality, who are most reckless in effrontery but most feeble in courage, and who, worst of all, are slaves to a woman and not to a man. (*Historia Romana*, 50.24.1–7 [Cary, LCL])

Because Octavian, as well as the rest of Rome, believed that Cleopatra seduced and manipulated Antony, there was a public outcry against the Egyptian gods. Three years after the battle of Actium, Octavian forbade the worship of the Egyptian gods in Rome. But because of its popularity the Isianic cult was not resisted outside of Rome.[90]

It could be argued that the cult of Isis was disruptive to society and its foreignness could come under some suspicion as a subversive group.[91] Furthermore, because of Antony's betrayal, devotion to an Egyptian deity could be regarded as a conflict of interest. Simply put, the goddess Isis is understood to be doing battle with the ancient gods of Rome.[92] Octavian's religious attitude was expressed in his prohibition of foreign cults and rites, as well as his support for the traditional Roman cults.[93] It was understood that those who joined the Isianic cult took on an Egyptian identity. Because Egypt was associated with Antony's betrayal, Egyptian identity was perceived to be a threat to Rome's stability.

Thus far, both the cults of Bacchus and Isis were understood as subversive. The cult of Bacchus was outside of the direct control of the elite. Because of its popularity and nighttime activities, the senate considered it a subversive group and mercilessly extinguished the Bacchanalia in Rome and throughout the regions of Italy. In similar fashion, the cult of Isis was understood as subversive insofar as Egypt was an enemy of Rome. Hence to be an adherent of Isis meant to be an enemy of the ancient gods of Rome. Yet, as I have attempted to show, Plutarch in the first century CE gives a detailed account of the myth of Isis showing the popularity of the cult outside of Rome. Moreover, Apuleius in the second century CE writes about Isis and her mysteries in his *Metamorphoses* (11.23–25), showing how Romans had a great interest in her mysteries. We may infer that while tensions were high between Rome and Egypt, the Isianic cult was understood to be subversive and an attack on Roman society. It was not until the reign of Gaius Caligula, that the Isianic cult was decriminalized in Rome and allowed to flourish once again.[94]

Yahweh and Judaism

Judaism's place in the Greco-Roman world is unique. In the ancient world they were a people defined by their own laws, worshipping their own god, and having their own traditions within a predominantly Greco-Roman, non-Jewish, society. The topic of Judaism in the ancient world is important, but the enormity of this subject is well beyond the scope of this chapter.[95] Instead, what follows is a general description of the relationship between Greco-Romans and diasporic Jews during the Hellenistic period into the very early Principate.[96]

Jews who lived outside of Palestine organized themselves into communities where they could live a public life while remaining distinctly Jewish in their practice. The "civic" situation of the Jews in antiquity was one of the larger looming issues we find in the Hellenistic world, especially during the rise of the Roman Empire. The main concern of many Jews who existed outside of Palestine was the issue of civic rights and, often, citizenship. For example, Victor Tcherikover notes that in Hierapolis in Phrygia, the Jewish community there were organized as a κατοικία.[97] This term refers to a colony of people who are of foreign birth but enjoyed privileges of self-administration.[98] The Jews were also categorized as a πολίτευμα, an organization of foreign-born inhabitants of a city where they have a right of residence in that city.[99] To classify the Jews as κατοικία or πολίτευμα allows for two further considerations. Even though the Greeks acknowledged the Jews as foreigners in their territories, they recognized the autonomy of Jewish assemblies within their communities.[100]

The Jewish Roman historian Josephus recounts a letter sent from the Hellenistic Greek king Antiochus III to his governor Ptolemy. In it, Antiochus III decreed that the Jews had the right to live "according to their ancestral laws" (Josephus, *A.J.* 12.138–141, 151; 16:168 [Marcus, LCL]).[101] This meant that as a πολίτευμα, the Jews were privileged to receive complete freedom in all matters of religion. Though they received these privileges, their exclusivity as a distinct religious group made them quite unpopular.[102] Nonetheless, Antiochus III allowed the Jews several privileges that were carried over in some fashion into the Roman period.[103]

Likely the most important privilege of existing as a πολίτευμα was that Jews were not obliged to worship in the traditional cults. As it has been shown, Roman attitude to foreign cults was one of toleration, as long as the cult was not hindering the traditional cults of Rome or causing suspicion of subversion. Judaism was significant in that it recognized no other god before the God of Israel. Tcherikover observes,

> The God of Israel acknowledged no rivals, nor could one pray to Him and simultaneously offer sacrifices to another deity. The cult of the gods was in Jewish eyes the complete negation of Judaism. The existence of the Jewish communities was therefore bound up with the exemption of the Jews by the authorities from participation in the cult of the Greek deities, and this was its negative condition.[104]

Even with Judaism's denial of the worship of the gods, which was tied to the civic well-being of the larger community, Judaism's interest in morality allowed them to exist in thriving communities without hindrance by the Republican/imperial authority (for the most part). It is important to note that there is no official document that precisely lists this privilege, namely, that the Jews were exempt from the worship of the Greco-Roman gods. Though it may be the case that such a document did not survive, it is more likely that such a document could not be drafted out of piety. As Tcherikover suggests, "For could anyone—whether Greek king, Roman governor or Greek city— write the words: 'I permit the Jews not to respect the gods?'"[105] Diaspora Jews had to petition each new emperor for their rights to worship. In their petition they were likely to refer to the previous emperor's benevolence in allowing their worship (e.g., Philo, *Legat.* 143–49), in order to show precedence for their request. But even when an emperor approved the rights of Jews to freely worship according to their customs, they would never specify that they could not worship the gods of empire (e.g., P. Lond. 1912). This lack of documentation would be a major point of contention for Jews as they sought to obtain civic rights throughout the Hellenistic and Roman periods.

As a πολίτευμα, the Jews were given rights to congregate as an association. A common feature of the Jewish associations in the diaspora was the synagogue, also known as a "house of prayer."[106] The Jewish synagogue functioned as a meeting house in which Jews would gather for worship. The assembly had a number of functions granted to it: it allowed for regular assembly on the Sabbath for religious and educational purposes, a right to collect funds for maintaining the grounds, and keeping a collection to be sent to the temple in Jerusalem.[107] It was under Julius Caesar that Jewish synagogues received their most important recognition, when he publicly emphasized Jewish rights.[108] Josephus records one of Caesar's edicts written to Parium. In it he says that the Jews of the Delos may live according to "their national customs and sacred rites" since they are "friends and allies." Furthermore, they would be allowed to "contribute money to common meals and sacred rites" and he points to the fact that "they are not forbidden" of these rights even in Rome (*A.J.* 14.213–214 [Marcus, LCL]).

These concessions are quite important when one considers that many *collegia* (θίασοι), or ancient associations, and foreign cults were dissolved three times: by the Roman senate in 64 BCE, again in 58 BCE, and during the Roman civil war during the consulship of Octavian.[109] Though collegia were dissolved, Jewish associations were exempt from these laws. Again, Josephus recounts the benefaction of Julius Caesar.

> Similarly do I forbid other religious societies but permit these people alone to assemble and feast in accordance with their native customs and ordinances. And if you have made any statutes against our friends and allies, you will do well to revoke them because of their worthy deeds on our behalf and their goodwill toward us. (*A.J.* 14.216 [Marcus, LCL])[110]

John Barclay links this passage to Caesar's decree as recorded by Suetonius that dissolved all collegia "except those of ancient foundation" (Cuncta collegia praeter antiquitus constituta distraxit) (*Iul.* 42.3 [Rolfe, LCL]).[111] Thus one can understand that Caesar recognized the Jewish synagogues as an apolitical ancient collegium, permitting them to exist and function in full capacity.[112]

As was Julius Caesar, Augustus was suspicious of foreign cults and collegia and reissued the edict of their dissolution. Augustus sustained the privileges promised to the Jews by his father and even ordered that whenever gifts were distributed to the people of Rome, if it coincided with the Jewish Sabbath, allowed the Jews to receive their share sometime after the Sabbath. Philo says,

> He [Augustus] never put the Jews at a disadvantage in sharing the bounty, but even if the distributions happened to come during the sabbath when no one is permitted to receive or give anything or to transact any part of the business of ordinary life, particularly of a lucrative kind, he ordered the dispensers to reserve for the Jews till the morrow the charity which fell to all. (*Legat.* 158 [Colson, LCL])

In the longer passage of Philo's *Legat.*, he shows how Augustus maintained the status quo of the Jews in the empire (*Legat.* 156–58). But these distributions show an extension of Augustus's benefaction to the Jews insofar as a concession is made for Jewish Sabbath worship.[113] Evidence shows that Jews flourished in Rome during the Principate of Augustus; their population grew and their significance as a social group was widely recognized.[114] There were many accusations made against the Jews during the period of Julius Caesar's dictatorship and Augustus's Principate, but these allegations were never made by the imperator. As previously seen in Josephus's *Antiquities*, Julius Caesar admonishes the authorities in Parium to revoke any laws made against the Jews in Delos (*A.J.* 14.216).

This seemingly friendly attitude toward the Jews from Julius Caesar and Augustus seemed to fade somewhat during the Principates of Tiberius (14–37 CE), Gaius Caligula (37–41 CE), and Claudius (41–54 CE). I am persuaded by John Barclay's thesis, wherein he argues that aspects of Judaism were becoming popular among the inhabitants of Rome. For example, some Romans began to "observe" the Sabbath insofar as they closed their shops. In Horace's *Sermones* (e.g., 1.9.60–78) and in Ovid's *Ars amatoria* (e.g., 1.75–76), they both mock Jewish religious and social customs. Though Horace and Ovid wrote before Tiberius's Principate, their perception of Judaism may indicate that Romans had a general understanding of some Jewish customs. These customs were gaining popularity among the lower classes in Rome, but it was not yet considered a threat to Roman society.

Cassius Dio says that the expulsion of Jews under Tiberius in 19 CE was a consequence of many Romans being converted to certain Jewish customs. Dio writes,

> As the Jews had flocked to Rome in great numbers and were converting many of the natives to their ways, he banished most of them. (*Historia Romana*, 57.18.5a [Cary, LCL])

Josephus also narrates the story of Fulvia, the wife of a Roman senator, who adopted certain Jewish customs because of four Jews in Rome who eventually stole her donations made to the Jerusalem temple (*A.J.* 18.81–84). Tiberius's actions against the Jews came simultaneously with his actions against the cult of Isis; he therefore viewed both the cult of Isis and Judaism as suspicious. We have seen actions taken against the cults of Bacchus and Isis, but this was the first-time action was taken to limit the influence of Judaism in Rome.

At this point, I think it is important to make a few remarks on Paul and the early Pauline communities. I would like to consider how Roman attitudes on Judaism may have affected Paul and the communities he founded. Though this topic is well beyond the scope of this study, I think it important to consider several points. Paul is on the cusp of forming a new religious identity, which is not completely Jewish and not completely Greco-Roman. Paul understands himself as a Jewish follower of Jesus Christ (Gal 1:13–14; 2:15 Phil 3:4–6). But faith in Jesus Christ means that he is no longer obligated to observe certain aspects of Mosaic Law, like circumcision and kashrut (Rom 2:16–29; 3:31;

8:3-4; 13:8-10; 1 Cor 7:19; Gal 5:13, 22–24). It is probably the case that Paul saw his communities under the umbrella of Judaism. This interpretation could mean that Roman attitudes toward early Christ groups were indistinguishable from their attitudes toward other Jewish groups. If this notion is the case, then it is likely that Roman attitudes toward Jews in middle of the first century CE had major ramifications on the organization of Pauline communities.

Summary

In summary, we notice that the rights of Jews during the Hellenistic and Roman periods were dependent on the benefaction of the ruler. There was no set law regarding the status of Judaism. Their rights to worship their God were dependent on the support of the ruler. Under Julius Caesar and Augustus, Jews were understood to be a threat neither to the civic society nor to the Roman way of life. At one time, they were even considered "allies and friends" of Rome. But like the Roman response to the cults of Bacchus and Isis, when Judaism began to threaten a Roman way of life the empire answered antagonistically. Jewish rights became a point of contention for many years following the Augustan Principate. It led to several uprisings including the Judean War in 66–73 CE, two revolts in Alexandria in 66 CE and in 115–17 CE, as well as another Judaean revolt led by Bar Kochba in 132–35 CE.[115] The Roman Empire allowed the Jewish cult to practice their religion in Rome because of their patronage of the emperor. When Rome perceived a threat to their way of life, on account of acculturation (Romans adopting Jewish customs), they restricted the rights of Jews. In other words, Judaism was tolerated until it was perceived as a civic threat.

CONCLUSION

The Roman Republic actively sought war and conquest. This drive for power was legitimized by economic and defensive justifications, but underlying these reasons was a political motivation. In the age of the early Republic, war was an integral part of society which even made up a large part of a young aristocrat's education. A year without war in Rome was an anomaly. Underlying this warfare ethos was a competition among the elite for military honors. Military honors allowed one the ability to obtain political office. For a Roman to be qualified for political office, he must have served in numerous military campaigns. Yet this drive for war began to decline in the late Republic in the Principate. The *Res Gestae Divi Augusti* presents the emperor Augustus as the greatest military leader who had ever come to power. His authority is unrivaled. Therefore, all military honorifics applied only to emperor and the imperial family. If one sought political office, he became reliant on the bene-faction of the emperor rather than on military campaigns.

As a consequence of Rome's politicking, the city became a multiethnic metropolis welcoming foreign peoples and their cults. Some foreign cults were first welcomed until they aroused suspicion of political subversion. With the cult of Bacchus and the Bacchanalia, their nighttime rituals, their popularity, as well as their being outside of the direct authority of the elite provoked suspicion of political subversion. This Greek cult was mercilessly targeted by the Republican authorities. Bacchic temples were destroyed, peoples arrested and executed, and sacrifices to Bacchus became a rare and non-publicized event. The cult of Isis was widely popular for almost two cen-turies in Rome until Antony's betrayal of Octavian. To worship Isis meant, in some way, that one was taking on an Egyptian identity. Considering the Ptolemaic rulers and Antony's betrayal, this identification threatened Roman civic society. Not only could Isis worship undermine Rome's imperium, but it could also undermine the ancient gods of Rome. The cult was suppressed by Octavian/Augustus and Tiberius because it was considered subversive and threatened the civic stability of Rome.

The cult of Yahweh, like Bacchus and Isis, was largely tolerated by Rome. Julius Caesar as well as Augustus considered the Jews to be "friends and allies," an apolitical and morally respectable people. They were considered a πολίτευμα by the Greeks and Romans, foreign-born inhabitants of a city where they have a right of residence in that city. Under Julius Caesar and Augustus, the Jews were considered a collegium with an "ancient founda-tion" allowing them certain privileges: permission to gather weekly at their prayer houses (synagogues), permission to collect money, and permission to send money to the Jerusalem temple. It was not until the reign of Tiberius that Judaism came under suspicion of being politically subversive. As noted, Jewish practices like Sabbath "observance" became popular among lower-working-class Romans. Hence, Jews were understood to be proselytizing Romans. This meant they were undermining the Roman religion as well as creating civil unrest. What began as an apolitical "collegia" eventually became a subversive organization that roused the attention of Tiberius and the emperors who followed him. What the cults of Bacchus, Isis, and Yahweh have in common is that they were tolerated by the authority until they stirred the suspicion of the elite.

Regarding Paul, he considered himself a Jewish follower of Christ. If that holds true, then his communities of Christ followers were likely considered in the same light. But literary evidence suggests Paul's "prayer houses" were not recognized with the synagogues of the Jews. Paul never calls his communities of Christ believers collegia (θίασοι). Nor does he establish "synagogues" for gathering for worship. However, he does call his communities *churches* (ἐκκλησίαι). Therefore, in the following chapter we must consider Paul's relationship to the larger Greco-Roman ancient association, and how this shaped his call to follow Christ as an ἐκκλησία.

NOTES

1. Theodor Mommsen, *The History of Rome*, trans. W.P. Dickson, 5 vols. (London: Richard Bentley & Sons, 1894).

2. Tenney Frank, *Roman Imperialism* (New York: MacMillan, 1914); Maurice Holleaux, *Rome, la Grèce et les monarchies hellénistiques au IIIe siècle avant J. C. (273-205)*, BEFAR 124 (Paris: E.de Boeeard, 1921); R. M. Harrington, *The Dawn of Empire: Rome's Rise to World Power* (Ithaca: Cornell University Press, 1971).

3. E.g., Joseph Schumpter, *The Economics and Sociology of Capitalism* (Princeton: Princeton University Press, 1991).

4. Cf. Tenney Frank, "Mercantilism and Rome's Foreign Policy," *AHR* 18 (1912–1913): 233–252; Frank, *Roman Imperialism* (New York: Macmillan, 1914), 277–297.

5. See n.2. Cf. William V. Harris, *War and Imperialism in Republican Rome: 327–70 B.C.* (Oxford: Clarendon Press, 1985), 163–166.

6. Andrew Erskine, *Roman Imperialism* (Edinburgh: Edinburgh University Press, 2010), 3. See also Erich S. Gruen, *The Hellenistic World and the Coming of Rome*, 2 vols. (Berkley: University of California Press, 1984), 1.1–12.

7. Gruen, *The Hellenistic World*, 1.273.

8. With regard to Philip V of Macedon see Polybius, *Hist.* 18.47.10–13; Livy, *Ad urbe condita* 7.12.4. Antiochus III; *Syll.3* 618.10–12; Polybius, *Hist.* 21.46.1-2; Livy, *Ad urbe condita* 38.39.7–17. The Achaean League: Pausanias, *Descr.* 7.16.9. Mithradates: *Syll.3* 785 (=*IGR* IV943). See Sviatoslav Dmitriev, *City Government in Hellenistic and Roman Asia Minor* (Oxford: Oxford University Press, 2005), 308. Especially 308 n. 90.

9. Dmitriev, *City Government*, 310.

10. Stephen Mitchell, *Anatolia: Land, Men, and Gods in Asia Minor*, 2 vols. (Oxford: Clarendon Press, 1993), 1.210. Also, Dmitriev, *City Government*, 310.

11. P. A. Brunt, *Roman Imperial Themes* (Oxford: Clarendon Press, 1990), 116–117.

12. Compare to the Athenian empire, whose allies paid tribute. See Erskine, *Roman Imperialism*, 15. On tribute in the Athenian empire, see Adalberto Giovanni "The Parthenon, the Treasury of Athena, and the Tribute of the Allies," in *The Athenian Empire*, ed. Polly Low (Edinburgh: Edinburgh University Press 2008), 164–184.

13. Arnaldo Momigliano, *Alien Wisdom: The Limits of Hellenization* (London: Cambridge University Press, 1975), 45.

14. Ibid.

15. Erskine, *Roman Imperialism*, 15–16.

16. Harris, *War and Imperialism in Republican Rome*, 5.

17. Tim Cornell, "The End of Roman Imperial Expansion," in *War and Society in the Roman World*, ed. John Rich and Graham Shipley (London: Routledge, 1993), 139–170, at 142.

18. Ibid., 155–156. Also, Harry Sidebottom, "Imperialism: The Changed Outward Trajectory of the Roman Empire," *Historia* (2005): 315–330.

19. Erskine, *Roman Imperialism*, 37.

20. Ibid.

21. Harris, *War and Imperialism in Republican Rome*, 110–111, esp.163–166. Cf. Moses I. Finley, "Empire in the Greco-Roman World," *GR* 25 (1978): 1–15; Keith Hopkins, *Conquerors and Slaves,* Sociological Studies in Roman History 1 (Cambridge: Cambridge University Press, 1978).

22. Harris, *War and Imperialism in Republican Rome*, 253.

23. Cf. J. W. Rich, *Declaring War in the Roman Republic in the Period of Transmarine Expansion* (Brussels: Latomus, 1976); Sigrid Albert, *Bellum iustum: die Theorie des "gerechten Krieges" und ihre praktische Bedeutung für die auswärtigen Auseinandersetzungen Roms in republikanischer Zeit*, Frankfurter althistorische Studien 10 (Kallmünz: Lassleben, 1980).

24. E.g. Livy, *Ad urbe condita*, 1.32.5-10; Cicero, *Off.*, 1.34–36.

25. Federico Santangelo [The Fetials and Their 'Ius,'" *BIHR* 51 (2008): 63–93, at 66] makes an important comment on the *fetiales* suggesting, "What matters most is that the institution of the fetials is said to have served in the development of the early expansion of Rome . . . [the fetials] were a religious institution that could also have a political function, by negotiating with the neighbouring populations the circumstances that could potentially lead to war . . . the fetials could act as 'peace-makers': one of their tasks was to explore the ways that could solve a controversy and avoid the war."

26. Erskine, *Roman Imperialism*, 38. Also Harris, *War and Imperialism in Republican Rome*, 166.

27. Walter Moskalew, "Fetial Rituals and the Rhetoric of the Just War," *Classical Outlook* 67 (1990): 105–110, esp. 107.

28. Frank, *Roman Imperialism*, 9. Harris, *War and Imperialism in Republican Rome*, 166.

29. Erskine, *Roman Imperialism*, 39.

30. Harris, *War and Imperialism in Republican Rome*, 14.

31. Ibid., 20.

32. Ibid., 5.

33. Cornell, "The End of Roman Imperial Expansion," 154. See also Erskine, *Roman Imperialism*, 40.

34. si igitur non poterit sive causas defensitare sive populum contionibus tenere sive bella gerer . . . (Cicero, *De off.* 1.121).

35. John Rich, "Fear, Greed, and Glory: The Causes of Roman War-Making in the Middle Republic," in *War and Society in the Roman World*, ed. John Rich and Graham Shipley (London: Routledge, 1993), 38–69, esp. 49–54.

36. Harris, *War and Imperialism in Republican Rome*, 22.

37. Cf. Claude Nicolet, "'Consul Togatus:' Remarques sur le Vocabulaire Politique de Cicéron et de Tite-Live," *REL* 38: 236–254.

38. Harris, *War and Imperialism in Republican Rome*, 9–10.

39. Stephen Oakley, "The Roman Conquest of Italy," in *War and Society in the Roman World*, ed. John Rich and Graham Shipley (London: Routledge, 1993), 9–37, esp. 15–16.

40. πολιτικὴν δὲ λαβεῖν ἀρχὴν οὐκ ἔξεστιν οὐδενὶ πρότερον, ἐὰν μὴ δέκα στρατείας ἐνιαυσίους ᾖ τετελεκώς (Polybius, *Hist.* 6.19.4).

41. Harris, *War and Imperialism in Republican Rome*, 257. Cf. Cornell, "The End of Roman Imperial Expansion," 166.

42. Cornell, "The End of Roman Imperial Expansion," 166.

43. Sidebottom, "Imperialism: The Changed Outward Trajectory," *passim*.

44. Cornell, "The End of Roman Imperial Expansion," 165.

45. Ibid., 165.

46. On the gladiatorial games see Keith Hopkins, *Death and Renewal* (Cambridge: Cambridge University Press, 1983), 1–30. For a discussion on the possible non-literary sources for the interpretation of the New Testament, see Alan Cadwallader, "Assessing the Potential of Archaeological Discoveries for the Interpretation of New Testament Texts: The Case of a Gladiator Fragment from Colossae and the Letter to the Colossians," in *The First Urban Churches 1: Methodological Foundations*, ed. James R. Harrison and L. L. Welborn (Atlanta: SBL Press, 2015), 41–66.

47. The most visible and striking manifestation of Roman honors and militaristic victories was the Republican *triumphal procession* (*pompa triumphalis*). The *pompa triumphalis* was a procession of sorts. The military commander, being granted a triumph, crossed back into Rome where he was preceded by his army, his plunder, his prisoners of war, up to the Capitolium, where he would offer a victim to Jupiter Optimus Maximus—the chief god of the triumph. Ultimately, the *pompa triumphalis* was a ritual wherein all commanders were celebrated as "great men," no matter the amount of plunder or slaves recovered. Every victorious commander was permitted to enjoy this position. But once the ritual ended, the commander would lay aside his role and return to his normal life. See Tanja Itgenshorst, "Roman Commanders and Hellenistic Kings: On the 'Hellenization' of the Republican Triumph," *AncSoc* 36 (2006): 51–68; Larissa Bonfante Warren, "Roman Triumphs and Etruscan Kings: The Changing Face of the Triumph," *JRS* 60 (1970): 49–66. Also, Roger Antaya, "The Etymology of Pomerium," *AJP* (1980): 184–189; M. T. Boatwright, "The Pomerial Extension of Augustus," *Hist* (1986): 13–27.

48. Cf., Ronald T. Riley, *The Emperor's Retrospect: Augustus' Res Gestae in Epigraphy, Historiography, and Commentary*, StHell 39 (Leuven: Peeters, 2003).

49. P. A. Brunt and J. M. Moore, Introduction to *Res Gestae Divi Augusti*, by Augustus, trans. P. A. Brunt and J. M. Moore (Oxford: Oxford University Press, 1967), 4.

50. Cynthia Damon, ed., *Res Gestae Divi Augusti* (Bryn Mawr: Bryn Mawr Commentaries, 1995), 1. Also, Frederick W. Danker, *Benefactor: Epigraphic Study of a Graeco-Roman and New Testament Semantic Field* (St. Louis: Clayton Publishing House, 1982), 257.

51. Danker, *Benefactor: Epigraphic Study*, 256–257.

52. Edwin S. Ramage, *The Nature and Purpose of Augustus' "Res Gestae"* (Stuttgart: Franz Steiner Verlag Wiesbaden GMBH, 1987), 48.

53. Translation of *Res Gestae Divi Augustus* is from Danker, *Epigraphic Study Benefactor*, 258–269.

54. Ramage, *The Nature and Purpose*, 52.

55. Cornell, "The End of Roman Imperial Expansion," 162.

56. J. S. Richardson, *Hispaniae: Spain and the Development of Roman Imperialism* (Cambridge: Cambridge University Press, 1986), 172–180.

57. J. S. Richardson, "Imperium Romanum: Empire and the Language of Power," *JRS* 81 (1990): 1–9.

58. Translation in Valerie M. Warrior, ed., *Roman Religion: A Sourcebook* (Newburyport: Focus Publishing, 2002), 84.

59. Modified translation.

60. E.g. a temple to Apollo was built in Rome in 431 BCE during a plague (Livy, *Ad urbe condita*, 4.25). See Valerie M. Warrior, *Roman Religion* (Cambridge: Cambridge University Press, 2006), 80–86.

61. Ando, *Imperial Ideology and Provincial*, 23.

62. James B. Rives, *Religion in the Roman Empire* (Oxford: Blackwell Publishing, 2007), 182.

63. Hugh Bowden, *Mystery Cults of the Ancient World* (Princeton: Princeton University Press, 2010), 106.

64. Walter F. Otto, *Dionysus: Myth and Cult*, trans. Robert B. Palmer (Bloomington: Indiana University Press, 1965), 83. Also Bowden, *Mystery Cults*, 106.

65. Rosemarie Taylor-Perry, *The God Who Comes: Dionysian Mysteries Revisited* (New York: Algora Publishing, 2003), 55.

66. Ibid. On the relationship between the theater and the Dionysian rites of initiation, see Richard Seaford, "Dionysiac Drama and the Dionysiac Mysteries," *ClQ* 31 (1981): 252–275. On the Dionysian Athenian festivals, see Carl Kerényi, *Dionysos: Archetypal Image of Indestructible Life*, vol.2 of *Archetypal Images in Greek Religion*, trans. Ralph Manheim (Routledge: London, 1976), 290–315.

67. Walter Burkert, *Ancient Mystery Cults* (Cambridge: Harvard University Press, 1987), 1–11, esp. 7–8.

68. I am indebted to Bowden for his insights. See Bowden, *Mystery Cults*, 108–109.

69. Slightly modified translation.

70. Erich Gruen, *Studies in Greek Culture and Roman Policy* (Leiden: Brill, 1990), 34–78. Also, Bowden, *Mystery Cults*, 126.

71. Robert Turcan, *The Cults of the Roman Empire*, trans. Antonia Nevill (Oxford: Blackwell, 1996), 305.

72. Bowden, *Mystery Cults*, 127. Cf., P. G. Walsh, "Making a Drama out of a Crisis: Livy on the Bacchanalia," *GR* 43 (1996): 188–203.

73. Turcan, *The Cults of the Roman Empire*, 305.

74. Robert Turcan, *The Gods of Ancient Rome: Religion in Everyday Life from Archaic to Imperial Times*, trans. Antonia Nevill (Edinburgh: Edinburgh University Press, 2000), 119.

75. Rives, *Religion in the Roman*, 187.

76. Warrior, *Roman Religion*, 107.

77. On the significance of Isianic aretalogies and syncretism in Greco-Egyptian religions, see François Dunand, "Le syncrétisme isiaque à la fin de l'époque hellénistique in *Les syncrétismes dans les religions grecque et romaine: Colloque de Strasbourg (9-11 join 1971)*, eds. Françoise Dunand and Pierre Levêque (Paris: Presses Universitaires, 1973), 79–93.

78. On dating the hymns of Isidorus, see Vera Frederika Vanderlip, *The Four Greek Hymns of Isidorus and the Cult of Isis*, ASP 12 (Toronto: A.M. Hakkert LTD, 1972), 9–13.

79. Ibid., 75–83. On the anthropology of syncretism, see Charles Steward, "Syncretism and its Synonyms: Reflections on Cultural Mixture," *Diacritics* 29 (1999): 40–62; Charles Stewart and Rosalind Shaw, ed., *Syncretism/Anti-syncretism: The Politics of Religious Synthesis* (London: Routledge, 1994). See also Robert Wild, *Water in the Cultic Worship of Isis and Serapis* (Leiden: Brill, 1981).

80. Sharon Kelly Heyob, *The Cult of Isis Among Women in the Graeco-Roman World* (Leiden: Brill, 1975), 8–9. Also, Thomas A. Brady, *The Reception of the Egyptian Cults by the Greeks (330–30 B.C)*, University of Missouri Studies, vol. 10 (Columbia: Universit of Missouri, 1935).

81. James Alvar, *Romanising Oriental Gods: Myth, Salvation and Ethics in the Cults of Cybele, Isis, and Mithras*, ed. and trans. Richard Gordon (Leiden: Brill, 2008), 39. For commentaries on Plutarch's *Is. Os.* see Theodore Hopfner, *Plutarch über Isis und Osiris* (Darmstadt: Wissenchaftliche Buchgesellschaft, 1967): J. Gwyn Griffiths, *Plutarch's de Iside et Osiride* (Cardiff: University of Wales Press, 1970); Hans Dieter Betz and E. W. Smith, "De Iside et Osiride (Moralia 351c–384c)," in *Plutarch's Theological Writings and Early Christian Literature* (Leiden: Brill, 1975), 36–84.

82. On the dating of this work see Griffiths, *Plutarch's de Iside et Osiride*, 16. On the Middle-Platonic implications of Plutarch's work and his choosing of an Egyptian myth to convey such philosophy, see Daniel S. Richter, "Plutarch on Isis and Osiris: Text, Cult, and Cultural Appropriation," *TAPS* 131 (2001): 191–216.

83. Alvar, *Romanising Oriental Gods*, 40.

84. Bowden, *Mystery Cults*, 161. Also Franz Cumont, *Oriental Religions in Roman Paganism* (New York: Dover, 1956), 79.

85. Brady, *The Reception of the Egyptian Cults*, 32. On Roman economy see Walter Scheidel, ed., *The Cambridge Companion to the Roman Economy* (Cambridge: Cambridge University Press, 2012), esp. 133–320.

86. The first hymn of Isidorus reads, "By Your power the channels of Nile are filled, everyone,/ at the harvest season and its most turbulent water is poured/ on the whole land that produce may be unfailing" (1.11–13 [Vanderlip]). Also, Bowden, *Mystery Cults*, 161. And, Michel Malaise, *Les conditions de pénétration et de diffusion des cultes Egyptiens en Italie* (Leiden: Brill, 1972).

87. Warrior, *Roman Religion*, 107.

88. Elizabeth A. McCabe, *An Examination of the Isis Cult with Preliminary Exploration into New Testament Studies* (Lanham: University Press of America, 2008), 35.

89. It is interesting to note that ancient authors suggest Marcus Antony disguised himself as a priest of Isis to escape from Rome (E.g., Appian, *Bella Civilia* 4.4.7). Cf. John M. Carter, *The Battle of Actium: The Rise & Triumph of Augustus Caesar* (London: Hamilton, 1970).

90. Bowden, *Mystery Cults*, 163.

91. Howard Clark Kee, *Miracle in the Early Christian World: A Study in Sociohistorical Method* (New Haven: Yale University Press, 1983), 129.

92. Cyril Bailey, *Phases in the Religion of Ancient Rome* (Westport: Greenwood Press, 1972), 186. Also, McCabe, *An Examination*, 36.

93. Horst R. Moehring, "The Persecution of the Jews and the Adherents of the Isis Cult at Rome A.D. 19," *NovT* 3 (1959): 293–304, esp. 294.

94. R. E. Witt, *Isis in the Graeco-Roman World* (Ithaca: Cornell University Press, 1971), 224.

95. For more detailed discussions on Judaism in the Greco-Roman world see these important and helpful studies: Shimon Applebaum, *Jews and Christians in Ancient Cyrene,* SJLA 28 (Leiden: Brill, 1979); Barclay, *Jews in the Mediterranean Diaspora*; Elias J. Bickerman, *The Jews in the Greek Age* (Cambridge: Harvard University, 1988); John J. Collins, *Between Athens and Jerusalem: Jewish Identity in the Hellenistic Diaspora,* 2nd ed. (Grand Rapids: Eerdmans, 2000); John J. Collins, *Jewish Wisdom in the Hellenistic Age* (Louisville: Westminster John Knox, 1997); Louis H. Feldman, *Jew and Gentile in the Ancient World: Attitudes and Interactions from Alexander to Justinian* (Princeton: Princeton University, 1993); Martin Goodman, *Rome and Jerusalem: The Clash of Ancient Civilizations* (London: Allen Lane, 2007); Erich S. Gruen, *Diaspora: Jews amidst Greeks and Romans* (Cambridge: Harvard University Press, 2002); Erich S. Gruen, *Heritage and Hellenism: The Reinvention of Jewish Tradition,* HCS 30 (Berkeley: University of California Press, 1998); Aryeh Kasher, *The Jews in Hellenistic and Roman Egypt: The Struggle for Equal Rights* (Tübingen: Mohr Siebeck, 1985); D. S. Russell, *The Jews from Alexander to Herod* (London: Oxford University Press, 1947); Leonard V Rutgers, *The Hidden Heritage of Diaspora Judaism: Essays on Jewish Cultural Identity in the Roman World,* CBET 20 (Leiden: Brill, 1998); Leonard V. Rutger, *The Jews in Late Ancient Rome* (Leiden: Brill, 1995); Shemuel Safrai, and Malcom Stern, ed., *The Jewish People in the First Century: Historical Geography, Political History, Social, Cultural and Religious Life and Institutions,* 2 vols. CRINT 1/1–2 (Philadelphia: Fortress, 1974–1976); E. Mary Smallwood, *The Jews under Roman Rule,* SJLA 20 (Leiden: Brill, 1976); Victor Tcherikover, *Hellenistic Civilization.*

96. For a detailed study of Hellenism and its effects on Palestinian Jews see Martin Hengel, *Judaism and Hellenism: Studies in their Encounter in Palestine During the Early Hellenistic Period,* 2 vols., trans. John Bowden (London: SCM Press LTD, 1974).

97. Tcherikover, *Hellenistic Civilization,* 298.

98. Ibid., 25, 298. See also Sandra Gambetti for her discussion of κατοικία and Alexandrian Jews; Gambetti, *The Alexandrian Riots of 38 C.E.,* 57–76.

99. Smallwood [*The Jews under Roman Rule,* 139] observes that "such a corporation was a quasi-autonomous civic unit with administrative and judicial powers over its own members, distinct from and independent of the Greek citizen body and

its local government." Victor Tcherikover suggests that the term κατοικία better describes the position of the diaspora Jews. See Tcherikover, *Hellenistic Civilization,* 297–298.

100. Tcherikover, *Hellenistic Civilization,* 298.

101. Slightly modified translation.

102. Smallwood, *The Jews under Roman Rule,* 123 n.15, 16, 17.

103. On Antiochus III and the conquering of Judea, see Collins, *Between Athens and Jerusalem,* 64–69.

104. Tcherikover, *Hellenistic Civilization,* 305.

105. Ibid., 306.

106. ἡ προσευχή, e.g., Philo, *Legat.* 132, 134, 137, 138, 148, 152, 156, 157, 165, 191, 346,371; *Flacc.* 41, 45, 47, 48, 49, 53; Acts of the Apostles 16:3. See also Smallwood, *The Jews under Roman Rule,* 133.

107. Smallwood, *The Jews under Roman Rule,* 133.

108. Philip Harland [*Associations, Synagogues, and Congregations: Claiming a Place in Ancient Mediterranean Society* (Minneapolis: Fortress Press, 2003), 223] notes, "The notion that 'each cult in the Empire was either a *religio licita* or a *religio illicita*' is not supported by any ancient source. The benefits granted were part of the exchanges involved in conventions of friendship and patronage, part of the benefactor-beneficiary relationship in which . . . many other associations of Asia were also participants." For arguments suggesting the Jews were a *religio licita,* see Smallwood, *The Jews under Roman Rule,* 135; Cotter, "The Collegia and Roman Law, 74–89, 77.

109. Peter Richardson, "Early Synagogues as Collegia in the Diaspora and Palestine," in *Voluntary Associations in the Graeco-Roman World,* ed., John S. Kloppenborg and Stephen G. Wilson (London: Routledge, 1996), 90–109. Also, Cotter, "The Collegia and Roman Law," 75.

110. With exactitude, one is unsure why Caesar calls the Jews "friends and allies." Barclay [*Jews in the Mediterranean Diaspora,* 291] conjectures, "What benefit Caesar derived from the support of the Roman Jews we cannot tell, but his policy in the East was dependent to an important degree on the co-operation of the Judaean rulers, and its appears that the Roman Jews were able to benefit from this alliance on the basis of their common nationality. . . . Their support proved to be crucial for Caesar's campaigns in the East."

111. Ibid.

112. Ibid., 292. See also Zvi Yavets, *Julius Caesar and His Public Image* (London: Thames & Hudson, 1983), 85–96.

113. Smallwood, *The Jews under Roman Rule,* 136.

114. Barclay, *Jews in the Mediterranean Diaspora,* 295–298.

115. Rives, *Religion in the Roman,* 195–196.

Chapter 4

Pauline Christ Assemblies

Considering Greco-Roman Associations

In chapter 1, I argued if Paul does critique the empire it is much more nuanced than what some counter-imperial scholars have thus put forward. Chapter 2 attempted to show, by means of a rhetorical critical investigation of particular Pauline passages, that Paul does not incorporate *coded speech* in them to subvert the empire. Rather, what should first inform the reader about Paul's writings is his Hellenistic Jewish background. Paul lived in a culture where he could not avoid daily interactions with the spiritual and political. His interactions, nevertheless, with civic society were multifaceted. When Paul wrote his letters and preached his gospel, he did so within a framework that depended on the commonalities between his Christ assemblies and the wider Greco-Roman civic environment.[1]

The Pauline Christ assemblies were a small minority group in the first century. Though these assemblies are distinctive in the first century, they should not be studied in isolation from analogous social structures of that time.[2] Since they all developed in similar contexts Philip Harland observes that Greco-Roman associations, Christian assemblies, and Jewish assemblies have significant parallels.[3] The Pauline epistles and other early Christian documents employ the terms ἐκκλησία and συναγωγή to describe the early Christ assemblies.[4] It is important to note that "*voluntary* association" is a contemporary term. Such a term did not exist in the ancient world. As John S. Kloppenborg correctly observes, "It is fatuous to object to classifying the emic term *ekklēsiai* or *synagōgai* as 'associations' on the grounds that they did not think of themselves as associations."[5] Such a classification did not exist in the ancient world. But "association" is used as a "subordinate term for small face-to-face groups that *we* see as similar in *certain specific respects* and to mobilize those similarities in the service of our understanding."[6]

This chapter will, therefore, explore Paul's relationship to the wider civic community, particularly the relationship between his assemblies and Greco-Roman ancient associations. First, this chapter will discuss the ancient Greco-Roman association: its general functions, its loyalties, and other socioreligious demands. Then, I will describe Paul's assemblies, that are both similar and dissimilar to the ancient association. Paul's assemblies not only have several parallels to ancient associations, but also have distinctive features. Though Paul draws on Septuagintal language and from his immediate context to describe his communities, his assemblies were different insofar as he calls them to live in a *new reality*. This new reality does not exclude their life in the world that must be lived in a manner of the gospel of Christ. Finally, each of Paul's assemblies had unique relationships to their wider Greco-Roman communities.[7] One will begin to see how Paul's ethic and gospel were translocal. But it was Paul's gospel that was a unifying aspect of his theology among his assembles.

THE ANCIENT GRECO-ROMAN ASSOCIATION

The term "association" is a catch-all term that some scholars use in their discussion of ancient "clubs" or "guilds."[8] These groups had multiple functions in the ancient world but their purposes included socialization, and were more often connected to some cultic activity as well.[9] Associations would honor their patron deity through oblations and rituals in a group setting. In the Hellenized eastern empire, there were a variety of terms that were used to describe these associations, terms that were shared within broader civic or imperial institutional contexts. Common group designations included κοινόν ("association"); σύνοδος ("synod"); θίασος ("society"); συνέδριον ("sanhedrin"); ἔρανος ("festal-gathering"); συνεργασία ("guild"); συμβιωταί ("companions"); ἑταῖροι ("associates"); μύσται ("initiates"); συναγωγή ("synagogue"); σπεῖρα ("company").[10] Other associations took on names that were reflective of their resident city, or the god whom the group worshipped.[11]

To give a complete historical overview of the ancient association is beyond the scope of this study.[12] Since our concerns are with Paul in his sociohistorical context, I shall remark on the history, societal roles, and societal function of ancient associations in Paul's immediate setting, particularly in the late Republic, the triumvirates, to early Principate (53 BCE–68 CE).

Greco-Roman Associations from the Late Republic to Early Principate

At the beginning of the Hellenistic period (late fourth century BCE), associations in the east became widely popular as a consequence of wars, trade, and displaced peoples. There were "significant populations of slaves, former slaves, resident aliens, foreign traders, merchants, and other non-citizens" who joined associations to share their common ethnic and/or religious identities.[13] During the age of the Republic (458–30 BCE), Roman associations, just like Hellenistic associations in the east, had organized rather freely; they organized meetings, collected funds, and honored their patronal deities without direct interference by the state.[14] As the Republic grew so did membership in these associations. In this section, I will offer a summary of the Greco-Roman association from the late Republic to the early Principate.

When civil war broke out in Rome, it was revealed that revolutionaries used the associations as fronts for their agenda of political subversion. Therefore, in 64 BCE, a *senatus consultum* decreed that all *collegia*, the Latin equivalent of "associations," that were suspected of sedition were dissolved. The ban seems to have affected only certain associations and should not be understood as a general prohibition of all *collegia*.[15] In 58 BCE Clodius, after becoming the tribune of the people, lifted the ban (*Lex Clodia de collegiis*) on the associations.[16] Clodius's use of the *collegia*, for his plans of political upheaval, led the senate to renew its strict regulations on associations.[17] In 55 BCE, after the Catiline affair, the *Lex Licinia de sodaliciis* was directed against political associations for their unfair practices of supporting a candidate for a magistracy during the electoral period (cf. Cicero, *Quint. fratr.* 2.3.2; 2.3.4-5).[18]

At the beginning of Julius Caesar's dictatorship in 49 BCE, a decree was issued that permitted only the most ancient *collegia* to exist. Though the precise wording of this decree is no longer extant, we surmise from existing evidence that Julius Caesar dissolved all associations except for the most ancient ones (Suetonius, *Jul.* 42.3; Josephus, *A.J.* 14.10.8).[19] It must be noted that it is not clear how Julius Caesar's decree defined an ancient association. Nonetheless, this law fell out of use during the turmoil of the Republican civil war (49–45 BCE), but was later reinstated by the emperor Augustus with new provisions.[20] The *Lex Iulia de collegiis* is attested to in a funerary inscription attributed to the *Collegium symphoniacorum* in Rome. The inscription has a *terminus post quem* of 27 BCE. It says that their association received approval from Augustus and that they accepted responsibility for providing public service:

> Dedicated to the *manes* gods. The guild of musicians who are at hand for the sacred public [rites?], for whom the senate permitted to come together, to be assembled [and] to be convoked by the Julian law for the sake of the [public] games by the authority of Augustus (*CIL* VI 2193 = *ILS* 4966). (Translation mine)[21]

That under Augustus, there were three requisites for an association to exist: association must be of considerable age; to exist, it must have direct approval by the emperor by means of the senate; it must meet its obligations for public service (see Suetonius, *Aug.* 32.2-3).[22] These requisites ensured the loyalty of associations to the empire.

Likely during the second-half of Augustus's Principate, a *senatus consultum (de collegiis tenuiorum)* was issued, that allowed the people of lesser means (*tenuiores*) to convene together once a month and to contribute to a common fund.[23] An inscription from the city of Lanuvium, dated to 136 CE, attests to the *senatus consultum de collegiis tenuiorum* of Augustus:

> Chapter from a senatorial decree of the Roman people: It is allowed to persons of lesser means to meet and assemble a *collegium*. People wishing to contribute on a monthly basis an amount of money for sacral purposes, they can meet for this purpose as a *collegium*, and not under the guise of an existing *collegium*, unless they gather once a month in order to contribute to a fund, at the expenses of which they are going to bury the deceased (*CIL* XIV 2112 = *ILS* 7212).[24]

The inscription suggests that Julius Caesar's prohibition of associations had been relaxed under Augustus. Augustus allowed for the formation of *collegia tenuiorum*, provided they assembled only once a month, limited the associations to funerary activities, and allowed for a common fund for funerals.[25] That Augustus limits the associations to funerary activities suggests that prior to the *Lex Iulia*, associations were social in nature meeting frequently rather than monthly.[26] The reason why the provision exists for the common fund is to emphasize that even this sacred rite of burial does not warrant a valid excuse for meeting more than once a month.[27] As Arnaoutoglou notes, this *senatus consultum* "may have effectively opened the floodgates for the formation of *collegia*" since the vast majority of associations from the late Hellenistic period to the early Roman Republic had sacred obligations or funerary rites related to their association.[28]

Despite the bans on *collegia* in Rome during the reigns of Caesar and Augustus, associations in Asia Minor continued to exist. Arnaoutoglou observes that inscriptions from Attica and the Peloponnese, dated to the period of Julius Caesar, indicate that Roman laws had little to no effect in the Greek east.[29]

The emperor Tiberius sought to extinguish the presence of any foreign association in Rome. As I argued in chapter 3 of this study, this persecution was likely due to the acculturation of the native Romans.[30] Romans began observing foreign practices that may have threatened the integrity of a Roman *ethos*. Suetonius writes:

He abolished foreign cults, especially the Egyptian and the Jewish rites, compelling all who were addicted to such superstitions to burn their religious vestments and all their paraphernalia. (*Tib.* 36 [Rolfe, LCL])

Like his predecessors, Tiberius issued no law against associations in the provinces. There are claims that Tiberius sought strict control of the associations in Egypt, but primary evidence suggests that no such concern was ever voiced by the emperor.[31] Yet, as Arnaoutoglou shows, Flaccus's ban and dissolution of associations was in response to rising tensions in Alexandria.[32] Philo of Alexandria recounts:

The sodalities and clubs, which were constantly holding feasts under pretext of sacrifice behaved in matters generally like drunkards, he dissolved and dealt sternly and vigorously all who resisted his command. (*Flacc.* 4 [Colson, LCL])[33]

Within the historical context, Flaccus is not responding to the emperor's *distrust* of associations but responding to increased pressures in Alexandria. Neither Philo nor epigraphical evidence maintains that there was ever a general ban on the formation of associations in Egypt.[34]

Regarding the legal status of associations in Rome, extant evidence for associations after Augustus's Principate is ambiguous. In 41 CE, Cassius Dio reports Claudius disbanded the *collegia* of Rome: "He also disbanded the clubs (τε ἑταιρείας), which had been reintroduced by Gaius (*Hist.* 60.6-7 [Cary, LCL])." Anthony A. Barrett understands this passage as referring to Gaius Caligula's lax position on associations in Rome.[35] It is more likely, however, that Claudius's disbandment of the *collegia* was a temporary measure that was lifted when such civil disturbances subsided. Cassius Dio groups the dissolution of *collegia* with Claudius's temporary closure of Jewish assemblies, and with restrictions on taverns in Rome. E. Mary Smallwood observes, "All three rulings can be seen as a police measure issued in answer to recent disorders."[36] That Claudius affirms the religious rights of Jews, while simultaneously forbidding their activity in Rome is no contradiction (see CPJ 153).[37] In response to a local disturbance, however, he restricted the rights of one community without hindering the rights of other communities throughout the empire.[38]

Nero, much like Claudius, responded negatively to *collegia* insofar as they were a perceived threat to civil order. In 59 CE, Tacitus recounts a scuffle at a theater in Pompeii between the residents of Nuceria and Pompeii during gladiatorial games. The fighting left many injured and dead. Tacitus recounts:

The Pompeiians as a community were debarred from holding any similar assembly for ten years, and the associations which they had formed *illegally* were dissolved. (*Ann.* 14.17 [Jackson, LCL])[39]

Much like the previous example of Flaccus's response to associations in Egypt and Claudius's response to associations in Rome, we have here a temporary police measure imposed by Nero. We may surmise from our evidence that whenever there was civil unrest in Rome or its provinces, the emperor and senate moved to remove associations which were considered illicit. These associations may have been formed without the direct approval of the senate and therefore were considered illegal. Nonetheless, as it has been shown, the policies enacted in Rome against associations were limited to Rome. And those policies enacted in provinces pertained only to the localized area of the disturbance, and for a temporary amount of time. For the greater part of the empire, especially in the Hellenized east, associations continued to flourish and grow in number.

The Ancient Association and Its Societal Roles

The Greco-Roman association refers to ancient groups that people opted to join.[40] These private groups were often small. Membership ranged from about ten people to around fifty, but some groups did have membership in the hundreds.[41] These groups would meet regularly to socialize, and to honor their earthly and divine benefactors.

Philip Harland proposes that these associations had external and internal activities that reflected their civic and religious relationships.[42] Externally, associations had relationships with wealthier members of their communities who became benefactors and, sometimes, leaders of the association. In the ancient world, social structure was maintained by the exchanging of benefits for honors.[43] Out of goodwill, those wealthier members of society would make donations to build temples, host festivals, support local associations, or become leaders of associations. Those who received these donations would then honor their benefactors in various ways, including making them special guests at meetings, proclaiming honors during a meeting, or erecting a statue or monument for the benefactor(s).[44] These social relations varied in their level of involvement from one group to another.[45]

Overall, all associations were in some sense religious, and each had a deity associated with the group. Internal relations included several activities such as worshiping the gods through cultic rituals of sacrifices and commensality.[46] These communal meals were intrinsic to the life of these associations, because it tied in directly to the socioreligious element of their lives.[47]

But these groups also had common funds for funerary activities, honorific decrees, and commensality.[48]

In the following section, I will present the primary functions and societal roles of these associations within their civic contexts. Because associations varied from location to location, there will be some differences regarding how associations related to their environments. But their commonalities outweigh their dissimilarities.

Identifying Ancient Associations and Their Heterogeneity

The main evidence for associations in the ancient Mediterranean comes from several types of epigraphical and papyrological documents, specifically four types that are most plentiful:

1. Honors or honorific decrees commending distinguished members of association or its benefactors and inscribed on steles. These were frequently set up in temples or sometimes affixed to the benefactor's home.
2. Membership lists.
3. Funerary monuments, and *koinon* tomb inscriptions.
4. Dedications to the deities or patrons of associations.[49]

These documents range in dates, from the fifth century BCE to the second or third centuries CE. Because our specific concern is Pauline assemblies, I will limit the discussion to evidence from Rome and Asia Minor. These documents illustrate several important features of ancient associations.

From the extant evidence, one is able to identify five common types of associations in the cities of Roman Asia. These guilds were drawn from "household connections, ethnic or geographic connections, neighborhood connections, occupational connections, and cult or temple connections."[50] As Kloppenborg and Ascough observe, "Associations likely served as vehicles by which various populations in the *polis* replicated and internalized the hierarchical structures of the ancient city and mimicked its honorific practices."[51] Furthermore, Pantelis Nigdelis observes that when people joined associations, they aimed at being "reintegrated into the life of the city as active citizens" by their shared identities as members of an association.[52] Members of associations aimed at internalizing the *polis* in their own meetings, and used their membership as a means of connecting themselves to the larger civic institution.

Familial associations made up a significant number of associations.[53] Ancient familial networks far surpassed what we would now consider relational. This network also included slaves and other dependents. An excellent example of a familial private association comes from Torre Nova in Italy, concerning the family of Agrippinilla.[54] In 160 CE, a large group of about four hundred initiates (μύσται) of Dionysus honored their priestess Agrippinilla with a statue (*IGUR* I 160). Harland draws from the study of Achille Vogliano who shows that "many of the main functionaries come from the families of Agrippinilla and her husband, M. Gavius Squilla Gallicanus, who was consul in 150 CE and proconsul of Asia in 165 CE."[55] The statue lists the names of 292 men and 110 women who were of free, manumitted, or servile status who were dependents of that household.[56] But once a familial association is established, it is common for membership to include friends of the family, and those with occupational and other indirect relationships to the family.

Those people who shared ethnicity or lived in the same geographic area also created associations based on their shared identity. Most ethnic associations were composed mainly of immigrants, and members could be of varying social and economic status. Membership in local associations was composed of those who lived in the same area: on the same street, district, or town. These local associations saw less variation in social status among its membership since those who lived in a close vicinity to each other reflected similar social brackets.[57]

Occupational associations were more homogenous because one's occupation is more often related to social status.[58] There was a wide range of occupational associations including clothing- or weaving-related groups; food-related groups; groups of potters, smiths, and artists; masonry groups; groups of bankers, merchants, and traders; physicians; and entertainment groups.[59] It should be noted that not all guilds were exclusive in their membership. For example, membership in occupational associations serves a group of people with similar professions, though their social status may differ. An inscription in Ephesus, dating to the mid-first century CE, details an association of fishermen and fish dealers who donated to the building of a fishery toll office (*IEph* 20 = *NewDocs* V5 = PH 247975).[60] The inscription lists donors in order of the size of their donations. Donations range from "four columns" or "30 denarii," to "five denarii" or less. The list represents not only social status but also the range of wealth among the membership of this association.

Social networks created through affiliation with specific cults or temples offered another avenue by which associations were formed. These associations were not connected to the official body of temple officials, but still used the temple for their group meetings. The membership of these cultic associations varied. For example, the association devoted to the Phrygian deity Sabazios was mainly composed of male membership, yet the association of Sabaziasts at Teos (a city on the coast of Ionia) honored a woman named Eubola.[61] The association of devotees to Demeter *Karpophores* is known at

Ephesus from the first and second centuries CE. Membership in this association, as well as others devoted to Demeter, could consist of both male and female leaders and initiates.[62]

Contrary to Wayne Meeks's observations, ancient Greco-Romans associations were not always socially homogenous.[63] Though the associations varied in their internal activities, they were interconnected socially and religiously. Ultimately, associations provided their members a sense of belonging and identity. [64]

Functions of the Ancient Association: Social and Religious

As Kloppenborg and Ascough observe, it is likely that most associations met for the purposes of sociability, often connected to the worship of a deity.[65] But was there any social advantage for a member of an association? Regarding occupational associations Kloppenborg says,

> The benefits sought by professional collegia were for the most part unconnected with their work. These included above all patronage in support of the common meals. And perhaps a wealthy patron might be persuaded to purchase buildings for the group's meetings or a common burial ground . . . collegia were more interested in the pursuit of honour than of economic advantage.[66]

Philip F. Venticinque has observed that associations, most especially those who had rules for moral behavior, sought to create and maintain bonds of trust between their members. In essence, an association not only reinforced familial relationship but also maintained strong social bonds between the members. These social bonds led to positive economic benefits for the entire group.[67]

Moreover, associations would foster feelings of pride for the *polis* or *patris*.[68] Some scholars, however, argue that associations were excluded from participation in civic life.[69] On the contrary, Van Nijf observes that several Lydian occupational associations referred to themselves as a tribe (φυλή), that possibly connotes that they had some form of political social status in the city.[70] Notice that the population of most Hellenistic Roman provinces were mainly craftsmen and traders.[71] If these groups considered themselves a φυλή in the traditional sense of the term, then this has major implications on the civic relationship between occupational associations and local governments. It seems to be the case that participation in the association did not mean that members no longer participated in the life of the *polis*. Rather, the relationship between the *polis* and ancient associations was non-conflicting.

An early third-century CE inscription from Philadelphia may shed some light on this issue (*IGLAM* 648 = *IGRR* IV 1632). This inscription records a number of significant details that alludes to the relationship between ancient associations and the *polis*: that the benefactor Aurelius Hermippos, who is "leader of the athletes" (ξυστάρχης), was honored by the *polis* as a "friend of the homeland" (φιλόπατρις); a mention of "the most revered association of elders" (τῷ σεμνοτάτῳ συνεδρίῳ τῆς γερουσίας); a mention of seven associations as "tribes" (φυλαί); a mention of the "sacred tribe of wool-workers" (ἡ ἱερὰ φυλὴ τῶν ἐριουργῶν). Another inscription, dated from the same period, also refers to "the sacred tribe of leather-workers" (ἡ ἱερὰ φυλὴ τῶν σκυτέων) (*IGLAM* 656). These terms may connote a network of relationships between the *polis* and the guilds. This evidence suggests that there are possible relationships between local governments and some ancient associations.[72]

As Ascough notes, these inscriptions are relatively late when considering how ancient associations functioned in the first century CE.[73] Yet, it is not uncommon for associations to imitate positions of leadership from their civic institutions. They used such titles as "secretary" (γραμματεύς), "treasurer" (τάμιας), "president" (ἐπιστάτης), and "superintendent" (ἐπιμελητής).[74] Furthermore, the activities of ancient associations would reflect those of their civic institutions: "passing decrees, granting honors, voting on decisions, electing leaders, and engaging in the conventions of diplomacy."[75] It is important to note that some foreigners in the Greek provinces, both freedmen and slaves, who could not join the civic assembly or council, would use the associations as a means to achieve an honorary position within the cities.[76] What we begin to notice is that the life of the *polis* and the communal life of the ancient association were not mutually exclusive. Moreover, associations in Asia Minor became recipients of benefaction and were often incorporated into the networks of the civic elite.[77]

Ancient associations were not just social guilds but also had religious dimensions. Though we may anachronistically understand *social* and *religious* as two separate categories, they were one and the same aspect in the ancient Greco-Roman world. For example, occupational associations in the north coast of the Black Sea worshipped the god Poseidon (*IBosp* 1134; 173-211 CE), and *The Most-High god* (θεός ὕψιστος) (*IBosp* 1283; 228 CE). Household associations in Phrygia worshipped Dionysus (*TAM* V1539; 100 BCE), and Dionysus *The Leader* (καθηγεμών) (*SEG* 41.1202; second century CE). Occupational guilds also honored the gods by erecting altars or other monuments throughout the Roman world.[78] Epigraphical evidence reveals that religion was an intrinsic part of virtually all ancient associations.

An aspect of the ancient associations were funerary activities. As previously mentioned, during Augustus's Principate restrictions were placed on *collegia*. They were to meet only once a month and could have a common fund only to assist members at funerals. Kloppenborg observes that classifying *collegia* by their principal activities is problematic since their activities could range from primarily cultic to primarily social.[79] Though Augustus limited Roman *collegia* to funerary activities, they were not solely established for funerals. It was not until the emperor Hadrian (117–138 CE) that funerary *collegia* were recognized within Roman law.[80]

Virtually all associations had funerary activities associated with membership, which included burial rituals, and feasts held in memory of the deceased member.[81] The importance for burial fluctuated between certain associations, which usually depended on the economic circumstances of the membership.

Harland compares two associations and how they dealt with funerary activities.[82] A *collegium* of the worshippers of Diana and Antinous, from Lanuvium, includes in its bylaws extensive details about funerary procedures in case a member should die (*CIL* XIV 2112 = *ILS* 7212; 136 CE).[83] Some of the funerary procedures include what to do if a non-paying member should die, and what to do if a member should die more than twenty miles away from the town (lines 20-40). Less concern is given to funerary activities, for example, with an association of worshippers of Bacchus in Athens. The rule of the *Iobakchoi* (*IG* II² 1368; 164/165 CE) is inscribed into a column and contains 163 lines of regulations for the community. Of the 163 lines, only the final five lines give instructions for the death of a member:

> If an Iobakchos dies, let there be a wreath up to the cost of five denarii and a single jar of wine shall be provided for those who attend the funeral. But no one who is absent from the funeral (itself) shall have any wine.[84]

Compared to the amount of space devoted to rules of conduct at the meeting, it might not come as a surprise that so little space is devoted to funerary activities. But taking into consideration that this group likely consisted of wealthier members (considering its fifty denarii initiation fee, monthly dues, and penalty fees), assistance for burial was not a major concern.[85]

Ancient Greco-Roman associations are, in essence, an ongoing social interaction between the community members and the *polis*. The association seems to be an extension of the immediate family and allows members to network with each other and with their civic institutions. This allowed the membership as well as the *polis* to benefit economically. Furthermore, associations provided their members a sense of belonging. As previously indicated, this sense of belonging was not in response to a declining civic institution. Rather, associations gave members the ability to contribute to the larger civic structures of the *polis*, while simultaneously participating in the life of their larger world.

Summary

This section sought to accomplish two goals: the first was to give a brief overview of ancient associations during the period of the late Republic to the early Principate; second, to emphasize how associations were not a monolithic phenomenon across the empire. Associations varied in several ways, including their external and internal activities, as well as their societal functions. Yet, these associations all provided their membership a means of socializing with one another and a means to worship their gods. It also gave them the means to create social networks which often granted social and economic advantages.

Paul and the Pauline assemblies emerged within this environment which was saturated with these guilds. This observation has led many to place Paul's communities and letters against the backdrop of ancient Greco-Roman associations. Is there enough evidence to suggest that Paul's assemblies were related in some way to associations? In the next section I will argue that there are analogies between the Pauline Christ assemblies and ancient associations but, nevertheless, there are differences. The following section will take a sociohistorical approach to understanding Paul's assemblies and their relationship to their wider Greco-Roman environment.

PAULINE CHRIST ASSEMBLIES

Important contributions to the sociohistorical study of early Christianity have been made by Edwin A. Judge, Gerd Theissen, John G. Gager, Abraham Malherbe, John H. Elliott, Wayne A. Meeks, and Richard Horsley.[86] It was Judge who emphasized that Christianity could not be understood within a metaphorical *bubble*, but that early Christianity was a social phenomenon that naturally reflected the social institutions of its civic contemporaries.[87] Judge goes on to suggest that associations help provide a contemporaneous analog to Christian assemblies, despite some of their differences.[88] Kloppenborg explains that sociohistorical scholars seek analogical comparisons in order to "identify similarity within difference in such a way that various aspects of the phenomena under consideration become intelligible."[89] The differences, however, can better inform us in our study of Pauline assemblies in four areas: (1) Paul's ability or inability to find a communal niche within his immediate civic context; (2) benefits of belonging to a Pauline assembly; (3) how these benefits were reflective of Greco-Roman polity; (4) and the ways internal relationships of Pauline assemblies were similar and distinguishable from Greco-Roman ancient associations.[90]

In this section, I shall elaborate on Pauline ecclesiology focusing on two questions: how does Paul understand the term ἐκκλησία, and how should we consider Paul's ecclesial social interactions with those outside the assemblies of Christ believers? While the task at hand seeks to understand Paul's ecclesiology and wider civic interactions, it must be noted, however, that each community Paul wrote to developed in different social situations. One cannot generalize about a universal "Pauline assembly."[91] Though there are significant differences between each community Paul wrote to, we will notice a shared "Pauline ecclesiology," and ethical links.

Paul's Ἐκκλησία and Ancient Associations

Scholars of the nineteenth century suggested that the earliest Christian groups imitated ancient Greco-Roman associations, especially in their inclusion of those of lesser means (e.g., *collegia tenuiorum*).[92] Wayne Meeks objects to such notions and argues that associations do not serve as useful models for understanding the earliest Christian communities.[93]

Meeks's contentions rely on differences between the Pauline Christ assemblies and associations, which, he suggests, outweigh their similarities.[94] First, he argues that Christian groups were much more inclusive "in terms of social stratification and other social categories than were the voluntary associations." He makes this argument based on the heterogeneity of the Pauline assemblies as opposed to the, supposed, "homogeneity" of associations. Second, Paul's groups did not use similar terminology in the description of his communities. Terms like *thiasos, factio, curia, corpus* are nowhere to be found in Paul's letters. Rather, argues Meeks, Paul's use of ἐκκλησία is more closely related to the Septuagint's use of this term as well as the biblical Hebrew phrase קְהַל לַיהוה (qāhāl YHWH).[95] Third, associations were a localized phenomenon as opposed to the translocal links of the Pauline assemblies. Fourth, like their Jewish counterparts, Pauline groups were sectarian as opposed to ancient associations.[96]

Meeks's study warrants close attention because he categorizes the Pauline assemblies as a uniform entity across the Mediterranean. His observations are, to a great extent, based on social data from ancient Corinth, which is contrasted over and against his conception of ancient associations. Kloppenborg observes, however, that it is incorrect to generalize about the makeup of associations.[97] As previously shown, associations were not uniform, and they varied in their membership. Membership in *collegia* could be a homogenous group (e.g., ethnic association like that of the Alexandrians; *IGLSkythia* II 153 = *IGRR* I 604 = PH 173253), or it could be a more heterogeneous group (e.g., the occupational association of fishermen from Ephesus; *IEph* 20 = *NewDocs* V5 = PH 247975).

Though Paul does not use similar titles and designations associated with associations, both Pauline assemblies and Jewish assemblies shared organizational characteristics with associations.[98] As Kloppenborg observes, there "is no a priori reason to assume that there was uniformity among the Pauline Churches, any more than one should assume a uniform organizational structure in associations. On the contrary, titles were highly voluble, local particularities abound, and in many instances, we have no indication of how officers were designated."[99] Notice how Paul, in the Corinthian correspondence, praises those who are in leadership positions. He only mentions Stephanas by name without attaching to him any official title (1 Cor 16:15; εἰς διακονίαν τοῖς ἁγίοις ἔταξαν ἑαυτούς). Furthermore, Paul in 1 Thess 5:12 describes the functions of those in leadership positions without listing their official titles (εἰδέναι τοὺς κοπιῶντας ἐν ὑμῖν καὶ προϊσταμένους ὑμῶν ἐν κυρίῳ καὶ νουθετοῦντας ὑμᾶς). As Kloppenborg suggests, Paul seems to be favorable to those who are in leadership positions among the assemblies and it seems likely that if these leaders had assumed special designations, Paul would have likely used them.[100]

Paul's use of the term ἐκκλησία and its historical background has long been a topic of interest.[101] Though this topic is beyond the scope of this study, it is important to note several important points. Meeks suggests that Paul's use of the term ἐκκλησία lies somewhere amid Greek polity and the larger Jewish tradition.[102] As Young-Ho Park observes, the term ἐκκλησία predominantly appears in the Deuteronomistic books of the Septuagint.[103] The many instances of ἐκκλησία in the Septuagint denotes the assembly of the whole nation, "or more accurately, the assembly *representing* the whole nation."[104] In contrast, the term συναγωγή was used for congregations not representing the whole nation.[105] In the Deuteronomistic books of the Septuagint, the main function of the ἐκκλησία was never to affirm a new covenant or religious agenda. Rather, its primary function was to reaffirm the covenant enacted from the ἐκκλησία at Sinai. Park observes:

> The ἐκκλησίαι at Mt. Sinai was the archetype of all subsequent ἐκκλησίαι for the Israelites, and Deuteronomy was nothing more or less than a record of an ἐκκλησία that reaffirmed what had been given "on the day of the ἐκκλησία" [Deut 4:10]. The occasions recorded as notable ἐκκλησίαι in the scrolls of the Hebrew scriptures were understood as "pivotal," points at which the national identity and the constitutional order were challenged and needed to be reestablished. In this way, the ἐκκλησία in Deuteronomy 31:30 became the first example of all pivotal gatherings thereafter.[106]

Thus, whenever the nation gathered, associated with the Jewish assembly at Jerusalem, they made that connection to that pivotal moment at Sinai.[107] Though Meeks's understanding of influences on Paul are important, it is unlikely that Paul simply took on the Septuagint's understanding or a political understanding of ἐκκλησία. Paul, rather, constructed a new reality unique to his assemblies. This reality is composed of a believer's relationship to God through Christ, which is expressed within the Pauline assemblies. Paul seeks to establish a new reality in which believers encounter a new way of life, primarily founded on the gospel he is preaching. This notion will be discussed later in this chapter.

Meeks also suggests that Paul's translocal activities differentiate his assemblies from the associations. He says that "each association, even those that served the internationally popular deities, was a self-contained local phenomenon."[108] Richard Ascough refutes Meeks's dichotomy by evidencing translocal relationships between associations while simultaneously minimizing the evidence of Paul's translocal relationship to his assemblies.[109] Ascough is correct when he argues against the claim that Paul is attempting some sort of organizational structure that he *imposed* on his assemblies.[110] Ascough presents evidence that he proposes to be translocal links between associations, but as Park suggests, the quoted evidence shows relationships between associations "mitigated by the civic authorities rather than direct relationships between remote communities."[111] Indeed, Paul did not impose a universal hierarchical structure upon the assemblies, but he did try to create a shared custom among his communities by encouraging certain behaviors, as well as encouraging his communities to elect representatives. I agree with Park who says that Paul's assemblies' translocal relationship was "not incidental but central" to the shared identity of the Pauline ἐκκλησίαι.[112] This shared identity is directly related to Paul's use of the term ἐκκλησία that is fashioned around a *new reality* which is constituted by the centrality of the gospel of Christ.

Ἐκκλησία and a New Reality in Christ

In the New Testament, 105 of the 133 instances of the term ἐκκλησία occur in the Pauline literature. The term appears a total of forty-four times in the undisputed letters of Paul.[113] Though the term appears to be conspicuously Pauline, it is probable that Paul did not introduce this term into early Christianity.[114] He even recounts how he persecuted the "church of God" (1 Cor 15:9; Gal 1:13), suggesting the term may have been previously used to acknowledge the assembly of Christ believers in Jerusalem.[115] Nonetheless, Paul's approach to the term is distinctive because he incorporates into his letters a *new reality* that is conveyed by its use.

Paul preaches a *new reality*. This new reality is one where Christ becomes intimately involved in the community, evoking a sense of solidarity among the various assemblies. Paul understands God working within the ἐκκλησία, but this notion is predicated on God working "in Christ" (ἐν χριστῷ) (e.g., 1

Thess 2:13). This section will proceed to distinguish Paul's use of the term ἐκκλησία. Then, I will argue that these assemblies are united as a distinct ἐκκλησία, by means of their faith in Christ. Finally, we will inquire into how Paul understood his relationship, and that of the ἐκκλησία, with their greater sociopolitical environment.

Young-Ho Park distinguishes five typical contexts for Paul's use of the term ἐκκλησία.[116] The instances of ἐκκλησία in Paul's letters can be classified according to five categories: (1) greetings; (2) translocal relationships between Paul's assemblies; (3) a plenary assembly as opposed to house groups; (4) the human abuse of the divine assembly; (5) and titles of *church* officials.[117] I will not reiterate the entirety of Park's important study. Rather, I will focus most on the first three categories since they are directly related to Paul's treatment of a *new reality* in Christ.

In the instances where Paul uses the term ἐκκλησία in the greetings of his letters (see 1 Cor 1:2; 2 Cor 1:1; Gal 1:2, 13, 22; 1 Thess 1:1; Philm 1:2), it is best to understand the term within its epistolary setting.[118] In one sense, the term ἐκκλησία was used during the Hellenistic age to describe the primary assembly of the *inhabitants* of a *district, village,* or *country* (δῆμος). During this period, the ἐκκλησία was the actual gathering of the people rather than an abstract idea of community or specific institution.[119] Oftentimes, directly writing to a δῆμος and addressing its inhabitants as one unified entity was quite meaningful because the sender acknowledged their importance within a civic context.[120] As previously suggested, the Septuagint's use of ἐκκλησία referred to the gathering of the whole people that was called to reaffirm the assembly at Sinai at the giving of the Decalogue. Park suggests that in Paul's greetings, where he uses ἐκκλησία, Paul "not only enhances the status of the recipients but also acquired for himself an honorary platform from which to speak to the ἐκκλησία, the gem of the civic glory of the Greek πόλεις."[121] This point is further evidenced in Paul's formula of greeting.

When Paul introduces himself in the greetings of his letters, he often included a title for himself such as δοῦλος (Rom 1:1; Phil 1:1), ἀπόστολος (Rom 1:1; 1 Cor 1:1; 2 Cor 1:1; Gal 1:1), or δέσμιος (Phlm 1).[122] Paul honors these communities by writing to them, giving these assemblies a sense of high-status. In many ways, those communities he addressed as ἐκκλησία are being honored. Though we will see how ἐκκλησίαι has a universal and translocal understanding, Paul's greeting to each ἐκκλησία should be understood as a greeting to that local community. David A. DeSilva, commenting on Paul's greeting to the Thessalonian believers, suggests that by addressing the group as an ἐκκλησία, he is granting them a "supra-local" honor.[123] The Thessalonians are being positively recognized because of their "eager reception of the gospel, their welcome of God's emissaries, and their endurance of affliction."[124] Moreover, Paul, in attaching titles to himself (likely a result of dispute about his authority or for the sake of empathy), grants himself an authority over the recipients of the letter. Samuel Byrskog observes that Paul's inclusion of titles for himself, paying particular attention to Romans, is Paul's attempt at laying out his credentials for writing a letter.[125] Furthermore, Paul suggests in 1-2 Corinthians (1 Cor 1:1; 2 Cor 1:1) and in Galatians (1:1, 11-12) that his authority was granted to him by God and is therefore qualified to preach the gospel of Christ to them.[126]

Addressing a group as an ἐκκλησία has translocal connotations. Though I will discuss in more detail the translocal system that Paul is promoting in the following chapter, I will make a few comments here. Paul does not use the term ἐκκλησία to refer to the multiple house groups which could be in one area. Rather, he uses the plural ἐκκλησίαι to address multiple assemblies in a certain province: 1 Cor 16:1 (Galatia), 19 (Asia); 2 Cor 8:1 (Macedonia); Gal 1:2; 1:22 (Judea); 1 Thess 2:14 (Judea). Or he uses the term with modifiers such as *all, every, no, other,* or by the adverb *everywhere* (1 Cor 7:17; 11:16; 14:33; 2 Cor 8:18). He can refer to all the ἐκκλησίαι as "gentile" (Rom 16:4) or generally as "all the churches of Christ" (Rom 16:6). As previously noted, Ascough disagrees that Paul sought to establish translocal links between his communities.[127] But I agree with Park who suggests that Paul was not trying to establish a uniform structure among the assemblies, but Paul was trying to establish a shared custom among the assemblies.[128] This shared custom is emphasized by God's work in the ἐκκλησία, and it is Paul's attempt at constructing a new reality which believers are now engaged in. Ultimately, God works within the ἐκκλησία but the ἐκκλησία also belongs to God.

One notices that in Paul's letters he never refers to the ἐκκλησία as belonging to one person or one group of people. In Paul's letters, there is a strong distinction between the plenary assembly and the numerous house groups.[129] On two occasions Paul uses the phrase "the whole church" (Rom 16:24; ὅλης τῆς ἐκκλησίας: 1 Cor 14:23; ἡ ἐκκλησία ὅλη). Moreover, notice that without the adjective "whole," ἐν ἐκκλησία can also refer to the plenary assembly (e.g., 1 Cor 11:18; 14:19, 28, 35). In this context, Paul was intentionally distinguishing the plenary meeting of believers in Corinth from the other smaller gatherings that could be expressed by the term οἶκος (1 Cor 11:34; 14:35; ἐν οἴκῳ: Rom 16:5; 1 Cor 16:19; Phlm 2; ἡ κατ'οἶκον . . . ἐκκλησία). When Paul refers to the "whole church" he is not referring to the "universal church" as proposed by Ernst Käsemann.[130] It is, nevertheless, a coming together of the entire Corinthian community "as one" (1 Cor 11:20; 14:23; ἐπί τό αὐτό). When they come together as one (1 Cor 11:20; συνερχομένων οὖν ὑμῶν ἐπὶ τὸ αὐτὸ), they not only celebrate the Lord's supper but also had a kind of symposium.[131] Whenever they come together, they come together as the ἐκκλησία τοῦ θεοῦ.

The "whole church" is also mentioned in Romans 16:23. Gaius, Paul says, not only hosted him but also the whole assembly. We learn that Paul had baptized Gaius and his household in 1 Cor 1:14. That Gaius was able to be a host and provide for the "whole church" at Corinth suggests that he was wealthy.[132] Also, notice how Gaius is a "host" (ξένος) to the whole church as opposed to the church, in some fashion, belonging to him. Nevertheless, the adjective "whole" would be unnecessary if the Corinthian believers met only as a single group.[133] The adverb "whole" in 1 Corinthians 14:23 further illustrates that all the believers from various house assemblies would meet in some way, at the expense and hospitality of Gaius.[134]

Regarding the relationship between οἶκος and ἐκκλησία, it is important to note that Paul rarely uses οἶκος to describe his understanding of the assemblies of Christ believers.[135] The phrase ἡ κατ᾽οἶκον . . . ἐκκλησία is used only three times in his letters (Rom 16:5; 1 Cor 16:19; Phlm 2).[136] It is never used to describe more than one group in a city and never used to describe any Corinthian group. Paul did not want the notion of ἐκκλησία to have solely a household connotation, or to be associated with one person or family. Rather, the assembly was gathered within the house but was never associated with the house itself. The assembly did not belong to any one person. The ἐκκλησία, however, did belong to God (e.g., 1 Cor 1:2; 2 Cor 1:1; ἐκκλησία τοῦ θεοῦ). The Pauline ἐκκλησία should not be understood as a household phenomenon, but rather having public dimensions. As Park observes, the "civic tone of the word ἐκκλησία substantially helped Paul in this struggle by reminding his audience of the public dimension of the church."[137] For this reason Paul rarely uses the term ἐκκλησία for household, even though the vast majority of Christ believers met within households.

In this section, I have explained the context in which Paul employs the term ἐκκλησία. In his greetings, Paul honored his communities by addressing them as an ἐκκλησία as well as granting them a new identity as the ἐκκλησία τοῦ θεοῦ. This ἐκκλησία remained distinct from the household, and therefore Paul refrains from identifying a smaller gathering of Christ believers as an ἐκκλησία belonging to one person. The ἐκκλησία did meet regularly at the house of patrons but the term is never associated with that person. Rather, as already mentioned, the ἐκκλησία belongs to God and to no one else. Paul understands his assemblies to be the ἐκκλησία τοῦ θεοῦ, and he sought to create a new reality which these Christ believers now lived in.

Negotiating between Realities

Thus far, it has been argued that Paul shared certain affinities with ancient Greco-Roman associations while, in various ways, remained distinct. Not only was Paul's terminology for his groups different (e.g., ἐκκλησία/ἐκκλησίαι), but he also tried to build relationships between the communities by means of his gospel.¹³⁸ This information raises a question; how does Paul ultimately understand his relationship, and that of his communities, to the wider Greco-Roman world? Though I will develop an answer to this question in chapter 5 of this study, I think it appropriate to make a few preliminary observations here.

Diaspora Jewish associations were complex in nature, especially when it came to their rights to congregate and worship.¹³⁹ A large-scale observation of Jewish assemblies suggests that they could "adopt, adapt, and develop ways of finding a place within civic society akin to the ways of other socioreligious groups in that setting."¹⁴⁰ Though Jewish assemblies could in fact assimilate in several ways with the greater Greco-Roman world, they rejected many other aspects of that society which were considered contrary to their own religious worldview. A similar act of assimilation can be seen with Christian groups in the second century.

It is not until the early second century CE that we have a better understanding of how some early Christian communities identified themselves, especially within their larger societal context. Pliny the Younger, appointed governor to Bithynia in 110 CE, in his correspondence with the emperor Trajan, describes the gatherings of Christians (*Christiani*). Of interest is how some Christians obeyed Trajan's edict restricting the meetings of associations. He writes:

> They also declared that the sum total of their guilt or error amounted to no more than this: they had met regularly before dawn on a fixed day to chant verses alternately among themselves in honour of Christ as if to a god, and also to bind themselves by oath, not for any criminal purpose, but to abstain from theft, robbery and adultery, to commit no breach of trust and not to deny a deposit when called upon to restore it. After this ceremony it had been their custom to disperse and reassemble later to take food of an ordinary, harmless kind; but they had in fact given up this practice since my edict, issued on your instructions, which banned all political societies. (*Ep.* 10.7-8 [Radice, LCL])

That Christians obeyed Trajan's edict likely meant that certain meetings, possibly those held at night, were avoided.¹⁴¹ Moreover, the Roman government also recognized these Christian groups as an association. Pliny's attestation here demonstrates that by 110 CE some Christian groups, at least some of those in Bithynia, regarded themselves as associations and were recognized as such by the Roman authorities.

Paul's self-understanding is unique, insofar as he does not understand his communities as Jewish assemblies or as associations, as we understand them, in the strict sense. Rather, Paul's self-understanding lies somewhere between Jewish assemblies and ancient associations. For Paul, I think, the issue is acculturation, that can be defined as contact of at least two autonomous cultural groups which eventually results in a "change in one or other of the two groups which results from contact."[142] In the context of Paul and the earliest movement of Christ followers, we should place acculturation in a framework of assimilation. Assimilation, in this regard, should be understood as acculturation without necessarily being integrated into the pervading culture.[143] Paul is on the cusp of forming a new religious identity, that is not completely Jewish and not completely Greco-Roman. Paul understands himself as a Jewish follower of Jesus Christ (Gal 1:13-14; 2:15 Phil 3:4-6). But faith in/of Jesus Christ means that he is no longer obligated to observe certain aspects of the Mosaic Law (Rom 2:16-29; 3:31; 8:3-4; 13:8-10; 1 Cor 7:19; Gal 5:13, 22-24). But preaching Christ to a largely non-Jewish population meant he had to find ways to assimilate without giving up his religious worldview.

One example of assimilation I would like to draw on comes from 1 Cor 6:1-11 and 1 Cor 8:1-11:1. In 1 Cor 6:1-11, Paul addresses an issue of taking a fellow Christ believer to court. What is interesting in this passage is how Paul wants the believers to avoid the civic magistrates. Though some have conjectured as to the possible historical situation of the Corinthian believers, I am more interested in Paul's reasoning.[144] In a series of rhetorical questions Paul declares that those outside the community of "saints" are "unrighteous" (ἄδικος) and are unworthy to judge the matters of the saints (1 Cor 6:1). Furthermore, he asserts the saints will judge the world and even the angels (1 Cor 6:2).[145] Moreover, if there are disputes among the Corinthian believers they should not appoint anyone to judge matters of the community who "amount to nothing in the church" (τοὺς ἐξουθενημένους ἐν τῇ ἐκκλησίᾳ) (1 Cor 6:4). Paul, it seems, is negotiating a new way life that begins in the ἐκκλησία τοῦ θεοῦ and extends to daily communal living. Because the Corinthian believers are sanctified "in Christ" (1 Cor 6:11) they must not associate with the unrighteous (1 Cor 6:9-10) in matters relating to the ἐκκλησία.

But this notion of separation seems to regard internal relationships as opposed to external relationships. Externally, the Corinthian believers still associate with non-believers and may even sit at table with them (1 Cor 10:27; cf. 1 Cor 14:24-25).[146] Paul admonished his assembly to avoid food offered to idols, possibly because he wanted to keep the integrity and solidarity of this community he is building.[147] Paul is urging a singularity of purpose.[148] Even though cultural and ethnic factors may intrude on the assembly's *new reality*, they must continue to live in a manner worthy of the gospel and of Christ (1 Cor 1:21; 7:32; 10:5,33; cf. 9:27; 15:58). As a reward, they will be "saved in the power of God" (1 Cor 1:18).

Here and elsewhere Paul is nuancing the relationship between his Christ assemblies and the larger civic world. He is attempting to preach his gospel in predominantly gentile territories and must use both the cultural and the social contexts to promote his gospel. As seen in 1 Cor 6:1-11, Paul does not have one method for understanding this relationship but must remain attentive to the particular needs of each community he writes to. Paul draws upon each community's immediate environment, revises it by means of his Hellenistic Jewishness, and uses it to preach his gospel.

Summary

Paul and his assemblies are negotiating their *new reality* in Christ to a dominant Greco-Roman culture. Though this new reality calls for adherence to a specific lifestyle, believers still have a relationship with their civic society. Paul, therefore, proposes that in Christ there is a *new creation*. The ἐκκλησία τοῦ θεοῦ, in which believers now live, is a *new creation*. It was inaugurated by the Christ-event. Though it is revealed within the ἐκκλησία, its fullness will not be fully manifested or fully revealed to the world until the parousia (e.g., Gal 6:15; 2 Cor 5:17). This *new creation* encompasses this new reality but also promises both cosmological and anthropological transformations. The topic of *new creation* will be the subject of chapter 5.

CONCLUSION

This chapter contextualized the Pauline assemblies. Our closest parallel to Pauline assemblies in the ancient world are Greco-Roman associations in certain respects. The general function of an association was to encourage sociability among the membership while, simultaneously, worshipping the association's patron deity. The deity would then protect the group and individual members in their daily lives. Associations helped create social networks among the various members and benefactors, and allowed both economic and social advantages. Ancient associations also offered members a sense of belonging that encouraged a positive feeling for their *polis*. In summary, the association allowed all peoples of varied social status to reap the benefits of membership. Ancient associations become a backdrop to the discussion of Pauline assemblies.

Pauline assemblies, ἐκκλησίαι, were Paul's attempt at assimilating to his Greco-Roman setting. Though Paul's definition of ἐκκλησία depended on Jewish (Septuagint) and Greco-Roman contexts (associations), Paul revised and made the term his own. The ἐκκλησία became an association, of sorts, that provided its members with internal benefits. Such benefits included the creation of new social networks. Paul's Christ assemblies offered a new way of life promising a postmortem transformation of the body and cosmic trans-formation of the world. To join a Pauline Christ assembly meant one believed and lived by the gospel of Christ. To live by the gospel meant being engaged in a new reality that included having faith, being transformed, and being pos-sessed and empowered by the Holy Spirit of God. To have this Spirit meant one has begun this transformative process, though one was still negotiating their lifestyle within the world.

Paul embraces a view of the cosmos that encompasses both a new reality and a *new creation*. His understanding of new creation embraces both a new cosmology and a new anthropology that are intrinsically linked to the Christ-event. In the following chapter, I attempt to show how the Christ-event is central to the concepts of "newness" and "creation." Paul's primary concern is not the Roman Empire. Paul preaches deliverance or vindication not over human enemies, but over the cosmic force of sin (Rom 8-11).

NOTES

1. Though it is common to refer to Paul's communities as "churches" or "church" in the general sense, I, however, have opted to use the word "assembly." The word "church" carries with it many modern connotations that can lead to an anachronistic interpretation of the earliest Pauline communities. Similarly, James D. G. Dunn, *Beginning from Jerusalem, Christianity in the Making* (Grand Rapids: William B. Eerdmans, 2009), 6 n.9.

2. Philip A. Harland, *Dynamics of Identity in the World of Early Christians: Associations, Judaeans, and Cultural Minorities* (New York: The Continuum International Publishing Group Inc, 2014), 25; John S. Kloppenborg, *Christ's Associations: Connecting and Belonging in the Ancient City* (New Haven/London: Yale University Press, 2020), 265–277.

3. Harland, *Associations, Synagogues, and Congregations*, 211. Harland also gives a history of scholarship regarding sociohistorical interpretations of early Christian and Jewish assemblies. See ibid., 177–212.

4. Συναγωγή in reference to Christ assemblies occurs in Jas 2:2 and in Ign. *Pol.* 4.2.

5. Kloppenborg, *Christ's Associations*, 19.

6. Ibid.

7. We should note that the early community of Christ believers at Rome was not founded by Paul. But this does not hinder Paul from preaching his gospel to them. It is important to consider how the beliefs of Roman believers in Christ may differ from that of communities which Paul founded.

8. Stephen G. Wilson, "Voluntary Associations: An Overview," in *Voluntary Associations in the Graeco-Roman World*, ed. John S. Kloppenborg and Stephen G. Wilson (London: Routledge, 1996), 1–15.

9. John S. Kloppenborg and Richard S. Ascough eds., *Greco Roman Associations: Texts, Translations, and Commentary. Vol I. Attica, Central Greece, Macedonia, Thrace*, BZNW 181 (Berlin: De Gruyter, 2011), 5.

10. Harland, *Dynamics of Identity in the World of Early Christians*, 27. Also Kloppenborg and Ascough, *Associations in the Greco-Roman World*, 5.

11. Harland, *Dynamics of Identity in the World of Early Christians*, 27. The role, function, and history of the Greco-Roman association will be discussed in the following sections on Pauline assemblies.

12. Cf. Nicholas R. E. Fisher, "Greek Associations, Symposia, and Clubs," in *Civilization of the Ancient Mediterranean: Greece and Rome*, ed. Michael Grant and Rachel Kitzinger (New York: Charles Scribner's Sons, 1988), 2:1167–1197. Also, Otto M. Van Nijf, *The Civic World of Professional Associations in the Roman East* (Amsterdam: J.C. Gieben, 1997), 5–11.

13. Kloppenborg and Ascough, *Associations in the Greco-Roman World*, 2.

14. See Cotter, "The Collegia and Roman Law, 74–89.

15. Luuk De Ligt, "Governmental Attitudes towards Markets and Collegia," in *Mercati permanenti e mercati periodici nel mondo romano*, Atti degli incontri capresi di storia dell'economia antica (Capri 13-15 ottobre 1997), ed. E. Lo Cascio (Bari: Edipuglia, 2000), 237–252, 243.

16. W. Jeffery Tatum, "Cicero's Opposition to the Lex Clodia de Collegiis," *CQ* 40 (1990): 187–194.

17. Cotter, "The Collegia and Roman Law," 76.

18. Adolf Berger, ed., *Encyclopedic Dictionary of Roman Law*, vol. 43.2 of *Transactions of the American Philosophical Society*, ed. Adolf Berger (Philadelphia: Independence Square, 1953), 555–556. Also, Ilias N. Arnaoutoglou, "Roman Law and Collegia in Asia Minor," *RIDA* 49 (2002): 27–44.

19. Arnaoutoglou, "Roman Law and Collegia in Asia Minor," 31. Also: Cotter, "The Collegia and Roman Law," 76; Kloppenborg and Ascough, *Greco-Roman Associations*, 219.

20. Ilias N. Arnaoutoglou, ""Collegia" in the Province of Egypt in the First Century AD," *AncSoc* 35 (2005): 197–216, 199.

21. *Dis manibus. Collegio symphoniacorum qui sacris publicis praestu sunt, quibus senatus c(oire) c(ogi) c(onvocari) permisit e lege Iulia ex auctoritate Aug(usti) ludorum causa* (*CIL* VI 2193 = *ILS* 4966).

22. Cotter, "The Collegia and Roman Law," 78.

23. I am indebted to the work of Ilias N. Arnaoutoglou whose history of the *senatus consultum de collogiis* I follow. See Arnaoutoglou, ""Collegia" in the Province of Egypt," 199–201.

24. *Kaput ex s(enatus) c(onsultum) p(opuli) R(omani): qui[bus res tenuior est, co]nvenire collegiumq(ue) habere liceat. Qui stipem menstruam conferre volen[t ad facienda sac]ra, in it collegium coeant, neq(ue) sub specie eius collegi nisi semel in mense c[oeant stipem co]nferendi causa, unde defuncti sepeliantur . . .* (*CIL* XIV 2112 = *ILS* 7212). Latin text as restored by De Light, "Governmental Attitudes towards Markets and Collegia," 246–47. Translation is by Arnaoutoglou, ""Collegia" in the Province of Egypt," 200.

25. Arnaoutoglou, ""*Collegia*" in the Province of Egypt," 200.

26. Kloppenborg and Ascough, *Associations in the Greco-Roman World*, 7.

27. De Ligt, "Governmental Attitudes towards Markets and Collegia, 247.

28. Arnaoutoglou, ""*Collegia*" in the Province of Egypt," 201. Also, Van Nijf, *The Civic World of Professional Associations*, 10, 31–69.

29. See *IG II2* 1339 (Attica; 57/56 BCE), which is dated to the year after the *Lex Clodia de collegiis.* Also: *SEG* 37:103 (Attica; 52/51 BCE); *AJA* 64 (1960) 269 = *SEG* 54:235 (Athens; ca. 50 BCE); *IG* V/2 266 (Mantineia; 46-44 BCE); *SEG* 43:59 (Rhamnous; 41/40 BCE); *IG II2* 1343 (Athens; 37/36 BCE); and *IG* V/1 210-212 (Sparta; 30-20 BCE); Kloppenborg and Ascough, *Greco Roman Associations*, 219. Arnaoutoglou, "Roman Law and Collegia in Asia Minor,"33. Cf. Richard S. Ascough, Philip A. Harland, and John S. Kloppenborg, eds., *Associations in the Greco-Roman World: A Sourcebook* (Waco: Baylor University Press, 2012). Contra Wendy Cotter who suggests that there is a lack of documentation on *collegia* in the western and eastern provinces. Cf. Cotter, "The Collegia and Roman Law," 74–89.

30. Cf. Harland, *Associations, Synagogues, and Congregations*, 49.

31. Wendy Cotter, for example, suggests that Tiberius had a general distrust of associations and this was relayed through his appointment of Flaccus as governor. See Cotter, "The Collegia and Roman Law," 79–80.

32. Arnaoutoglou, ""*Collegia*" in the Province of Egypt."

33. Slightly modified.

34. Arnaoutoglou, ""*Collegia*" in the Province of Egypt," 212.

35. Anthony A. Barrett, *Caligula: The Corruption of Power* (New Haven: Yale University Press, 1989), 230. Also, Cotter, "The Collegia and Roman Law," 80.

36. Smallwood, *The Jews Under Roman Rule*, 215. Also, De Ligt, "Governmental Attitudes towards Markets and Collegia," 248.

37. See my note on *The Letter of Claudius to the Alexandrians* on p. 50, n.123.

38. Smallwood, *The Jews Under Roman Rule*, 215. Also, Collins [*Between Athens and Jerusalem*, 120] says, "Claudius meant [in his reference to two embassies] that there should not be two delegations form Alexandria, as if the Jews inhabited a separate city. . . . He confirms the traditional Jewish right to live according to their ancestral laws, but he states unequivocally that they live in a city no their own. The Jews, in short, are not citizens, and are not Alexandrians."

39. Emphasis mine.

40. Wilson, "Voluntary Associations: An Overview," 2.

41. Harland, *Dynamics of Identity in the World of Early Christians*, 26.

42. Ibid., 26–28.

43. Ibid., 148.

44. Ibid. Cf. see J. E. Lendon, *Empire of Honour: The Art of Government in the Roman World* (Oxford: Oxford University Press, 1997).

45. Harland treats the external relations of voluntary associations more completely in, Harland, *Associations, Synagogues, and Congregations*, 115–76.

46. For a treatment of commensality in the ancient associations see Richard S. Ascough, "Forms of Commensality in Greco-Roman Associations," *CW* 102 (2008): 33–45.

47. Harland, *Dynamics of Identity in the World of Early Christians*, 27.

48. See Van Nijf, *The Civic World of Professional Associations, Passim.*

49. Kloppenborg and Ascough, *Associations in the Greco-Roman World*, 3. For less common, but equally important, epigraphical and papyrological evidence see ibid.

50. Harland, *Associations, Synagogues, and Congregations*, 29.

51. Kloppenborg and Ascough, *Associations in the Greco-Roman World*, 8. Similarly, Harland, *Associations, Synagogues, and Congregations*, 55–88, 103–106.

52. Pantelis M. Nigdelis, "Voluntary Associations in Roman Thessalonikē: In Search of Identity and Support in a Cosmopolitan Society," in *From Roman to Early Christian Thessalonikē: Studies in Religion and Archaeology*, HTS 64, ed., Laura Nasrallah, Charalambos Bakirtzis, and Steven J. Friesen (Cambridge: Harvard University Press, 2010), 13–48, esp. 36.

53. Harland, *Associations, Synagogues, and Congregations*, 30.

54. I am thankful for Philip Harland's observations on this familial association. See this and other examples in ibid., 30–33.

55. Ibid., 30. Cf. Achille Vogliano, "La grande iscrizione bacchica del Metropolitan Museum," *AJA* (1933): 215–231.

56. Harland, *Associations, Synagogues, and Congregations*, 30.

57. Ibid., 34–37.

58. Ibid., 38–44.

59. See Harland for related epigraphical evidence in Ibid., 39–40.

60. Cf. Kloppenborg and Ascough, *Associations in the Greco-Roman World*, 101–104. Also, Harland, *Associations, Synagogues, and Congregations*, 43.

61. Harland, *Associations, Synagogues, and Congregations*, 44–52.

62. Cf. Peter Herrmann, "Demeter Karpophoros in Sardeis," *REA* 100 (1998): 495–508.

63. Cf. Wayne Meeks, *The First Urban Christians: The Social World of the Apostle Paul,* 2nd ed. (New Haven: Yale University Press, 2003), 79.

64. Harland, *Associations, Synagogues, and Congregations*, 55.

65. Kloppenborg and Ascough, *Associations in the Greco-Roman World*, 5.

66. John S. Kloppenborg, "Collegia and Thiasoi: Issues in Function, Taxonomy, and membership," in *Voluntary Associations in the Graeco-Roman World*, ed. John S. Kloppenborg and Stephen G. Wilson (London: Routledge, 1996), 16–30, esp. 19.

67. Philip F. Venticinque, "Family Affairs: Guild Regulations and Family Relationships in Roman Egypt," *GRBS* 50 (2010): 273–294.

68. Harland, *Associations, Synagogues, and Congregations*, 101–112.

69. E.g. C. P. Jones, *The Roman World of Dio Chrysostom* (Cambridge: Harvard University Press, 1978), 80–81; M. I. Finley, *The Ancient Economy*, 2nd ed. (London: Hogarth, 1985), 136–138; Guy MacLean Rogers, *The Sacred Identity of Ephesos: Foundation Myths of a Roman City* (London: Routledge, 1991), 71–72. See Harland, *Associations, Synagogues, and Congregations*, 103.

70. Van Nijf, *The Civic World of Professional Associations*, 20–21.

71. Friedemann Quaß, *Die Honoratiorenschicht in den Städten des griechischen Ostens: Untersuchungen zur politischen und sozialen Entwicklung in hellenistischer und römischer Zeit* (Stuttgart: Steiner, 1993), 355–365.

72. Cf. Ascough, *Greco Roman Associations*, 185–186.

73. Ibid., 187. Cf. Van Nijf, *The Civic World of Professional Associations*, 184.

74. Cf. Franz Poland, *Geschichte des grichischen Vereinswesens* (Leipzig: Teubner, 1909), 376–387. Also, Harland, *Associations, Synagogues, and Congregations*, 106. For comparison, see the structure of Attic associations in Kloppenborg and Ascough, *Associations in the Greco-Roman World*, 11.

75. Harland, *Associations, Synagogues, and Congregations*, 106.

76. Kloppenborg and Ascough, *Associations in the Greco-Roman World*, 11

77. Cf. see *IGRR* I 787; *ISmyrna* 639; *ISardBR* 22; *IGR* I 800. Harland, *Associations, Synagogues, and Congregations*, 106–107. Also, Kloppenborg and Ascough, *Associations in the Greco-Roman World*, 11–12; Danker, *Benefactor*, 32–34.

78. Harland, *Associations, Synagogues, and Congregations*, 63 esp. n.5.

79. Kloppenborg, "Collegia and Thiasoi," 20–23.

80. Ibid., 21.

81. Van Nijf, *The Civic World of Professional Associations*, 38–55,

82. I am indebted to the work of Philip Harland for his observations on the funerary activities of ancient associations in *Associations, Synagogues, and Congregations*, 84–86. Also, Kloppenborg, *Christ's Associations*, 265–77.

83. Cf. Kloppenborg and Ascough, *Associations in the Greco-Roman World*, 194–98.

84. Translation from Kloppenborg and Ascough, *Greco-Roman Associations*, 248.

85. Two other notes on funerary activities of associations. Some associations would even construct communal cemeteries or tombs for their members. There is extensive evidence of communal burial plots in Rhodes (see *IkosPH* 155-159), and evidence of a communal tomb for an association of flax-workers in Smyrna (see *ISmyrna* 218; *IEph* 2213). Moreover, the burial plots of wealthier members, who bequeathed monetary gifts to their associations upon their deaths, were regularly taken care of. It would even be customary to congregate at the person's gravesite for a yearly commemoration of the benefactor's death (see *IEph* 1677, 2112, 2304; *SEG* 43.812). See Van Nijf, *The Civic World of Professional Associations*, 47. Also Harland, *Associations, Synagogues, and Congregations*, 85. On the Rhodian epitaphs see Peter M. Fraser, *Rhodian Funerary Monuments* (Oxford: Clarendon Press, 1977).

86. See Edwin A. Judge, *The Social Pattern of the Christian Groups in the First Century* (London: Tyndale Press, 1960); Edwin A. Judge, "The Social Identity of the First Christians: A Question of Method in Religious History," *JRH* 11 (1980): 201–217; Gerd Theissen, *Sociology of Early Palestinian Christianity*, trans. John Bowden (Philadelphia: Fortress Press, 1978); Gerd Theissen, *The Social Setting of Pauline Christianity: Essays on Corinth*, trans. John H. Schütz (Philadelphia: Fortress Press, 1982); John G. Gager, *Kingdom and Community: The Social World of Early Christianity* (Englewood Cliffs: Prentice Hall, 1975); Abraham J. Malherbe, *Social Aspects of Early Christianity*, 2nd ed. (Philadelphia: Fortress Press, 1983); John H. Elliott, *A Home for the Homeless: A Social-Scientific Criticism of 1 Peter: Its Situation and Strategy*, 2nd ed. (Minneapolis: Fortress Press, 1990); Meeks, *The First Urban Churches*; Richard Horsley, *Bandits, Prophets, and Messiahs: Popular*

Movements in the Time of Jesus (Harrisburg: Trinity Press International, 1985). Cf. Harland, *Dynamics of Identity in the World of Early Christians*, 4.

87. Judge, *The Social Pattern of the Christian Groups*, 14.

88. Ibid., 44.

89. John S. Kloppenborg, "Edwin Hatch, Churches and Collegia," in *Origins and Method: Towards a New Understanding of Judaism and Christianity. Essays in Honour of John C. Hurd*. JSNTSup 86, ed. Bradley H. McLean (Sheffield: Sheffield Academic, 1993), 212–238, 230.

90. Four observations based on Kloppenborg's insights. See Kloppenborg, "Edwin Hatch, Churches and Collegia," 230.

91. See John M. G. Barclay, "Thessalonica and Corinth: Social Contrasts in Pauline Christianity," *JSNT* 47 (1992): 49–74.

92. See Georg Heinrici, "Die Christengemeinde Kirinths und die religiösen Genossenschaften der Griechen," *ZWT* 19 (1876): 464–526; Georg Heinrici, *Der Zweite Brief an die Korinther*, 7 ed., Kritisch-exegetischer Kommentar über das Neue Testament, 6 (Göttingen: Vandenhoeck & Ruprecht, 1890); Edwin Hatch, *The Organization of the Early Christian Churches*, 4th ed. (London: Longmans, Green, 1892), 26–55.

93. Meeks, *The First Urban Christians*, 77–81. Similar arguments are made for the dissimilarity of Pauline assemblies and ancient Greco-Roman associations, see Robin Lane Fox, *Pagans and Christians* (New York: Knopf, 1986), 85–89, 324–325; Burkert, *Ancient Mystery Cults*, 2–4, 30–53. Cf. Harland, *Dynamics of Identity in the World of Early Christians*, 65

94. Meeks, *The First Urban Christians*, 77–81.

95. Wayne Meeks, "Corinthian Christians as Artificial Aliens," in *Paul Beyond the Judaism/Hellenism Divide*, ed. Troels Engberg-Pedersen (Louisville: Westminster John Knox Press, 2001), 129–138.

96. Cf. Harland, *Associations, Synagogues, and Congregations*, 178–182; Thomas Schmeller, *Eine sozialgeschichtliche Untersuchung paulinischer Gemeinden und griechisch-römischer Vereine*, SBS 162 (Stuttgart: Katholisches Bibelwork, 1995); Wayne O. McCready, "Ekklēsia and Voluntary Associations," in *Voluntary Associations in the Graeco-Roman World*, eds. John S. Kloppenborg and Stephen G. Wilson (London: Routledge, 1996), 59–73.

97. Kloppenborg, "Edwin Hatch, Churches and Collegia," 234–36.

98. Harland, *Associations, Synagogues, and Congregations*, 181.

99. Kloppenborg, "Edwin Hatch, Churches and Collegia," 232. Cf. Harland, *Associations, Synagogues, and Congregations*, 181.

100. Kloppenborg, "Edwin Hatch, Churches and Collegia," 233.

101. Young-Ho Park reviews the history of this topic and makes an important contribution to the function of the term ἐκκλησία in Paul's letters, as well as those factors that influenced Paul's usage of the term. I am indebted to his work on this topic. See Young-Ho Park, *Paul's Ekklesia as a Civic Assembly: Understanding the People of God in their Politico-Social World*, WUNT 2/393 (Tübingen: Mohr Siebeck, 2015).

102. Meeks, "Corinthian Christians as Artificial Aliens," 135.

103. Park, *Paul's Ekklesia as Civic Assembly*, 63–68.

104. See Park's summary statements on this topic in, Ibid., 96–97.

105. Ibid., 97.

106. Ibid., 89. Cf. Georg Braulik, "'Conservative Reform': Deuteronomy from the Perspective of the Sociology of Knowledge," *OTE* 12 (1999): 13–23.

107. The importance of Jerusalem, especially among diaspora Jews, is central to Jewish identity. See Barclay, *Jews in the Mediterranean Diaspora*, 417–424. On diasporic Jewish identity see John J. Collins, *Between Athens and Jerusalem, passim.*

108. Meeks, *The First Urban Christians*, 80.

109. Richard S. Ascough, "Translocal Relationships among Voluntary Associations and Early Christianity," *JECS* 5 (1997): 223–241; Richard S. Ascough, "Voluntary Associations and the Formation of Pauline Christian Communities," in *Vereine, Synagogen und Gemeinden im Kaiserzeitlichen Kleinasien*, ed. Andreas Gutsfeld and Dietrich-Alex Koch, STAC 25 (Tübingen: Mohr Siebeck, 2006), 149–184.

110. Meeks, *The First Urban Christians*, 79. Ascough also argues against "common teachings and practices" which some try to trace throughout Paul's letters. See Ascough, "Translocal Relationships," 239 n.82.

111. Park, *Paul's Ekklesia as Civic Assembly*, 116. E.g., *IG II2* 337, *IG II2* 1117, *CIG* 5853; Ascough, "Translocal Relationships," 228–234.

112. Park, *Paul's Ekklesia as Civic Assembly*, 116.

113. See Rom 16:1, 4, 5, 16, 23; 1 Cor 1:2; 4:17; 6:4; 7:17; 10:32; 11:16, 18, 22; 12:28; 14:4, 5, 12, 19, 23, 28, 33, 34, 35; 15:9; 16:1, 19 (twice); 2 Cor 1:1; 8:1, 18, 19, 23, 24; 11:8, 28; 12:13; Gal 1:2, 13, 22; Phil 3:6; 4:15; 1 Thess 1:1; 2:14; Phlm 2. Notice that the instances of the term ἐκκλησία found in 1 Cor 4:17 and Phil 4:15 are grammatically singular, but plural in meaning; cf. Karl L. Schmidt, "ἐκκλησία," *TDNT* 3:501–36.

114. Scholars tend to agree that early Christian usage of the term ἐκκλησία predates Paul. See Rudolf Bultmann, *Theology of the New Testament* (New York: Scribner, 1951), 1.94; Jürgen Becker, *Paul: Apostle to the Gentiles* (Louisville: Westminster/John Knox Press, 1993), 426–427; Ekkehard Stegemann and Wolfgang Stegemann, *The Jesus Movement: A Social History of its First Century* (Minneapolis: Fortress Press, 1999), 263. See Park, *Paul's Ekklesia as Civic Assembly*, 98–99; Schmidt, *TDNT* 3:507.

115. The origin of the phrase "church of God" is still debated. See Klaus Berger, "Volksversammlung und Gemeinde Gottes. Zu den Anfängen der christlichen Verwendung von 'ekklesia,'" *ZTK* 73 (1976): 167–207, especially 198–207. Also, Martin Hengell, *Between Jesus and Paul: Studies in the Earliest History of Christianity* (Philadelphia: Fortress Press, 1983), 83.

116. Here, I follow closely the work of Young-Ho Park whose contextualizing of Paul's use of ἐκκλησία I find most convincing. See Park, *Paul's Ekklesia as Civic Assembly*, 103–124.

117. Ibid., 103.

118. Cf. Sean A. Adams, "Paul's Letter Opening and Greek Epistolography: A Matter of Relationship," in *Paul and the Ancient Letter Form*, ed. Stanley E. Porter and Sean A. Adams (Leiden: Brill, 2010), 33–56.

119. Park, *Paul's Ekklesia as Civic Assembly*, 11.

120. Ibid., 105–106.

121. Ibid., 106.

122. It is only 1 Thessalonians that Paul does not add a title to his name. Charles A. Wanamaker suggests that in Romans, 1-2 Corinthians, and Galatians that Paul's status as apostle and his authority were matters of contention. In his greetings of the Philippians and Philemon Paul tries to empathize with his audience. 1 Thessalonians does not suggest that Paul's authority was in question. Furthermore, Paul's situation while writing to the Thessalonian believers was not as precarious as it was when writing to the Philippians or to Philemon. See Wanamaker, *The Epistles to the Thessalonians*, 68. Similar arguments are made by, Ben Witherington, *1 and 2 Thessalonians: A Socio-Rhetorical Commentary* (Grand Rapids: William B. Eerdmans, 2006), 48; Weima, *1-2 Thessalonians*, 65–66. Cf. Adams, "Paul's Letter Opening," 51.

123. David A. DeSilva, "'Worthy of His Kingdom': Honor Discourse and Social Engineering in 1 Thessalonians," *JSNT* 64 (1996): 49–79, 70.

124. Ibid., 70.

125. Samuel Byrskog, "Epistolography, Rhetoric and Letter Prescript: Romans 1.1-7 as a Test Case," *JSNT* 65 (1997): 27–46, 37.

126. Adams, "Paul's Letter Opening," 52.

127. Cf. Ascough, "Translocal Relationships."

128. Park, *Paul's Ekklesia as Civic Assembly*, 117–118.

129. Ibid., 116, 152–157.

130. Malherbe, *Social Aspects of Early*, 97. Cf. Käsemann, *Commentary on Romans*, 598.

131. Raymond F. Collins, *First Corinthians*, SP 7, ed. Daniel J. Harrington (Collegeville: Liturgical Press, 1999), 508.

132. Cf. Hultgren, *Paul's Letter to the Romans*, 598.

133. Jerome Murphy-O'Connor, *Paul: A Critical Life* (Clarendon Press: Oxford, 1996), 267.

134. Robert J. Banks, *Paul's Idea of Community* (Peabody: Hendrickson Publishers, 1994), 38. Cf. Gordon D. Fee, *The First Epistle to the Corinthians* (Grand Rapids: William B. Eerdmans, 1987), 683. Murphy-O'Connor [*Paul*, 267] tries to estimate the size of the Corinthian plenary assembly by analyzing archaeological evidence from Corinth. David Horrell ["Domestic Space and Christian Meetings at Corinth: Imagining New Contexts and the Buildings East of the Theatre," *NTS* 27 (2004): 349–369] suggests that there should be caution when employing archaeological evidence in such historical studies. Ultimately, Horrell, who further develops the argument of Murphy-O'Connor, says that their reconstructions of the Corinthian plenary assembly are "entirely imaginative" due to the present state of archaeological evidence. See Horrel, "Domestic Space and Christian Meetings at Corinth," 368.

135. Park, *Paul's Ekklesia as Civic Assembly*, 127.

136. See Hans-Josef Klause, *Hausgemeinde und Hauskirche im frühen Christentum* (Stuttgart: Verlag Katholisches Bibelwerk, 1981). Also, Roger W. Gehring, *House Church and Mission: The Importance of Household Structures in Early Christianity* (Peabody: Hendrickson Publishers, 2004).

137. Park, *Paul's Ekklesia as Civic Assembly*, 133.

138. Other likely differences include Paul's linear worldview; that time would ultimately end at the Parousia (e.g., 1 Cor 1:7–8; 4:5; 15:20–28; Phil 3:20–21; 1 Thess 1:9–19; 2:19; 3:13; 4:13–18; 5:1–11, 23). Also, one may conjecture that Paul's assemblies did not require mandatory fees for joining as did other ancient associations, nor did he require fees for group infractions (for initiation fees see, e.g., *AGRW* 310 = *CIL* XIV 2112 = *ILS* 7212 [Lanuvium, 136 CE]; *AGRW* 7 = *IG* II² 1368 [Athens, 164/165 CE]; *AGRW* 243 = *IG* XII,3 330 [Thera, 210-195 BCE]. For fines see, e.g., *AGRW* 7 = *IG* II² 1368 [Athens, 164/165 CE]; *AGRW* 301 = *PMich* V 244 [Tebtynis-Fayum, 43 CE]; *Philippi* II 133/G441 [Philippi, 2/3 century CE]).

139. For a fuller discussion on this topic see, e.g., Harland, *Associations, Synagogues and Congregations*, esp. 200–210; Harland, *Dynamics of Identity in the World of Early Christians* esp. 23–60.

140. Harland, *Associations, Synagogues and Congregations*, 199.

141. Harland, *Dynamics of Identity in the World of Early Christians*, 43.

142. John W. Berry, "Acculturation as Varies of Adaption," in *Acculturation: Theory, Models and Some New Findings*, ed. Amado M. Padilla (Boulder: Westview Press, 1980), 9–26, esp. 9.

143. See Milton M. Gordon, *Human Nature, Class, and Ethnicity* (New York: Oxford University Press, 1978). Also, Amado M. Padilla, "The Role of Cultural Awareness and Ethnic Loyalty in Acculturation," in *Acculturation: Theory, Models and Some New Findings*, ed. Amado M. Padilla (Boulder: Westview Press, 1980), 47–84.

144. For a history of interpretation of 1 Cor 8-11 see Rogers, *Gods and Idols*, 231–235, esp. 231–232 n.19; 233 n.21.

145. On the difficulty of interpretation regarding Paul's mention of "judging the angels" see Thiselton, *The First Epistle to the Corinthians*, 430–431.

146. Barclay, "Social Contrasts in Pauline Christianity," 57–60.

147. Horsley, *1 Corinthians*, ANTC, 146.

148. Collins, *First Corinthians*, 385.

Chapter 5

Between the ΚΟΣΜΟΣ and ΚΑΙΝΗ ΚΤΙΣΙΣ

In the previous chapters, I have shown that certain methods for detecting *hidden transcripts* are lacking in some studies. I have also argued that Paul is nuancing the relationship between his Christ assemblies and the larger civic world. Believers in Paul's Christ assemblies were called to live a harmonious life with all people, a life centered on the gospel of Christ. Paul called his communities to live in a new reality wherein a believer's primary allegiance is to their community. But, as I have argued, Paul suggested to his communities that even though they live in this new reality, believers still have a commitment to their larger civic community (e.g., Rom 13:1–7).[1]

Though Paul was not counter-imperial in a strict sense, he did not suggest that the civic authority was saved. Paul relativizes the place of the Roman Empire and includes it, although not in any explicit terms, in his critique of the physical κόσμος. For Paul, the death and resurrection of Christ was the pivotal moment in time that changed the course of history. The Christ-event in Paul's theology is the inaugural event for what he calls a "new creation" (Gal 6:15; 2 Cor 5:17). If you are "in Christ," you are a "new creation" (2 Cor 5:17).

The primary focus of this chapter is to understand the Pauline distinction between κόσμος and καινὴ κτίσις, and their cosmological and anthropological significance in Paul's eschatological soteriology. The scope of this question is broad, and scholars have devoted much time to this topic.[2] The intention of this chapter, however, is to understand how the dichotomy between κόσμος and καινὴ κτίσις characterizes Paul's nuanced relationship to the empire. The first section of this chapter will contextualize Paul's use of the term κόσμος, as the material creation. In 1 Corinthians and Romans, Paul describes the *world* as the arena of sin and death that comes under corruption due to Adam's sin.

Ultimately, sin and death reign over humanity and over creation. It is the Christ-event that has given hope to fallen humanity and, subsequently, to all creation.

The second section of this chapter will ask how humanity's relationship to the κόσμος is affected by the Christ-event. This section will be highlighted by three passages where the terms κτίσις/καινὴ κτίσις appear: Gal 6:11–18; 2 Cor 5:11–21; Rom 8:18–22. In each case, Paul emphasizes how the Christ-event reshaped the course of history. In the final section of this chapter, I will summarize practical translocal links among Paul's Christ assemblies. In establishing a translocal ethic across his communities, Paul suggests that to be "in Adam" is to be of the fading world, but to be "in Christ" is to be of the new creation. Though Paul does not directly mention Rome or the empire, Rome would likely fall under the category of being "in Adam."

Paul's eschatological soteriology functions on two different levels. The first level is cosmological, where Paul deals with the Christ-event and its implications on the cosmic forces of sin and death. The second level is anthropological, where Paul deals with the Christ-event and its implications on humanity's relationship to the κόσμος and to the καινὴ κτίσις. The cosmological level is highlighted by the Christ-event proper, while the anthropological level is highlighted by entering into the new creation. One enters the new creation by being "in Christ," which occurs by means of faith and baptism.

ΚΟΣΜΟΣ IN PAULINE THEOLOGY

Hans Dieter Betz summarizes Paul's eschatology and soteriology suggesting that salvation is based on: (1) the death and resurrection of Christ; (2) the "putting on" of, and dying and rising with Christ in baptism (e.g., Gal 3:26–28; Rom 6:3–4); (3) the gift of the Spirit of God (e.g., Gal 3:2–5; 5:16–25); (4) living in a "new creation" (Gal 6:15; 2 Cor 5:17).[3] From Betz's summary, one may draw the conclusion that salvation for Paul depends on whether or not one is "in Christ."

The phrase "in Christ" or "in the Lord" has several meanings.[4] Paul emphasizes that to be in Christ is not merely "to believe" in Jesus. To be "in Christ" is to share in a lived experience with the risen Lord (cf. 1 Cor 4:15; 2 Cor 2:17; Gal 2:19–24; 4:13; 5:10; Phil 2:29).[5] "New creation" (καινὴ κτίσις) is a Pauline phrase, explicitly used twice in his letters, that recapitulates Paul's eschatological soteriology (see Gal 6:15; 2 Cor 5:17). To participate in the new creation is to participate in a renewal of the individual believer, of the Pauline Christ assemblies, and of the "world" (κόσμος).[6] It is a concept which expresses the cessation of a *sinful* way of life in exchange for a more moral life in Christ.

Because Paul insists that there exists a new creation in Christ, it implies that there is an *old creation* not of Christ. Paul characterizes the *old creation* by primarily using the word κόσμος and/or the phrase "in Adam" (κόσμος; 1 Cor

1:20–21, 26–28; 2:12; 8:4–6; Adam motif; 1 Cor 15:21–22, 45–49; Rom 5:12–21).[7] The old way of life is one that encapsulates a *sinful* living prior to one's faith in Christ. Once you are "in Christ" you are a "new creation" and must conduct your life in a manner worthy of the gospel of Christ (cf. Phil 1:27).[8]

In this section I shall explain how Paul uses language of κόσμος ("world") to create an antithesis to the καινὴ κτίσις ("new creation"). As we shall see, κόσμος as described in 1 Corinthians is in direct opposition to God, on account of Adam's sin (1 Cor 5:14). Likewise in Romans, κόσμος is opposed to God insofar as it is directly corrupted by "sin" (ἁμαρτία) come into the world.[9] But whether Paul explains the "world" as sinful or as corrupted by sin, it has a direct effect on humanity.[10] Paul's purpose in using these terms to describe faith in Christ is to encourage believers to live out their faith in Christ, and this life in Christ will hopefully lead to resurrection and life everlasting.[11]

Sin and Death: Κόσμος in 1 Corinthians and Romans

How does Paul understand κόσμος in relationship to humanity? In Romans, Paul sees only two power structures at work in the world; sin and death (Rom 6:12–13; 7:4–6; 7:22–8:2; cf. 1 Cor 15:21–22). Considering the Christ-event, Paul understands that the physical creation is under the power of sin. The consequence of sin is death (Rom 5:12–14).[12] In 1 Corinthians, he suggests that the κόσμος is intrinsically linked with several negative aspects, including "flesh" (σάρξ) and "death" (θάνατος) (e.g., 1 Cor 10:18; 15:26).[13] Similarly, in Paul's letter to the Galatians both the "flesh" and the "Law" are cosmic powers warring with the Spirit of God (Gal 3:23–25; 4:5–6; cf. 1:4; 6:14).[14] Paul suggests that the κόσμος, exemplified by the sins of the σάρξ, has come under judgment because of the Christ-event (Gal 6:14).[15]

For Paul, the physical creation can be understood as sinful (opposed to God), corrupted on account of sin, and/or both.[16] A study contextualizing Paul's use of κόσμος in each of his letters, where the term appears, is beyond the scope of this study. I would like to draw on several examples from his letters, however, that best illustrate Paul's negative connotations relating to the κόσμος.[17] As I will argue, the κόσμος is controlled by the forces of sin and death. Rome does not seem to be a determinative factor in Paul's discussion of κόσμος. Ultimately, it will be shown how Paul's enemies are not of this world. Paul preaches deliverance and vindication not over human enemies but over the cosmic forces controlling/within the κόσμος, that are sin and death (cf. Rom 8–11).

The term κόσμος has been used in Greek literature from the time of Homer and conveys the sense of *building* and *establishing*. The connotation is that of *order* or *adornment*. It can also connote *humanity*.[18] Generally, the meaning of *order* and *adornment* applies in the New Testament.[19] Though an in-depth analysis of the non-biblical and biblical usage of the term κόσμος would be insightful for this discussion, it will suffice to mention briefly the Greco-Roman antecedents of the term that Paul develops in some of his letters.[20]

Paul's discussion of κόσμος in 1 Corinthians depends on the standard Greek linguistic usage of the term. The term would have been understood positively by the Corinthians suggesting order, unity, beauty, adornment, and so on.[21] When Paul uses this term, for example in 1 Cor 1:20, it can either have the positive connotation of the whole created order or it could be understood in a more neutral sense.[22] The same holds true in his letter to the Romans (e.g., Rom 1:18; 3:19).[23]

In 1 Cor 2:12–13 the "spirit of the world," in this context, should not be regarded as a demonic entity since it is not a rhetorical equivalent to "the Spirit from God."[24] The Spirit of God not only reveals divine wisdom but also communicates it. The spirit of the world, however, neither reveals divine wisdom nor communicates it.[25] Rather, as Gerd Theissen observes, the "spirit of the world" is a parallel to the "rulers of this age" (1 Cor 2:6).[26] Paul is making a distinction in the ways believers live with respect to the cross of Christ, as opposed to the way they lived prior to receiving the gospel. The cross meant a reorientation of life, embracing a new lifestyle which the Christ-event brings about (cf. 1 Cor 5:9–13; Gal 5:16–26).[27] The believers' reception of God's Spirit marks them off as distinct from the κόσμος. Moreover, Paul's use of the first-person plural in 1 Cor 2:12 (ἡμεῖς, ἐλάβομεν, εἰδῶμεν, ἡμῖν) draws a "social" distinction between Christ believers over against the κόσμος.[28] The reception and revelation of the Spirit calls believers to be distinct from the world that is categorized by "foolishness."[29]

Paul expands his ethical exhortations in 1 Cor 5–6. Though Paul is concerned with issues of purity and immorality, his primary concern is how the community of believers are to live a life that is pleasing to God (1 Cor 6:20).[30] In 5:9–10 Paul instructs the community not to "mingle with sexually immoral men" (συναναμίγνυσθαι πόρνοις).[31] Paul did not mean the sexually immoral, greedy, burglars, or idolaters of "this world" (οὐ πάντως . . . τοῦ κόσμου τούτου). These sexually immoral men, rather, are those who call themselves "brother" (ἀδελφός), likely someone from within their community of Christ believers. If a believer sought to disassociate with all immoral men, Paul admits, "You must therefore depart from the world" (ὠφείλετε ἄρα ἐκ τοῦ κόσμου ἐξελθεῖν) (1 Cor 5:10). Here, I would like to note two important points: the first point is that the κόσμος is where sinners/sin exist(s); the second point is that Paul's community must remain ethically distinct from the world.

The phrase ὁ κόσμος οὗτος carries with it negative connotations that may convey a "negative apocalyptic sense" in the Pauline letters. As Adams observes, "The κόσμος is a world which is populated by immoral and corrupt people, so numerous that believers cannot avoid contact with them."[32] In 1 Cor 5:5 Paul suggests that those who are caught in incestuous acts are to be delivered "to Satan for the destruction of the flesh" (1 Cor 5:5a). In this verse "flesh" (σάρξ) is associated with the work of Satan, as that which is under Satan's influence.[33] It is the sins of the flesh that corrupts the body (σῶμα) preventing the believer from union with God (cf. 1 Cor 6:17–20).[34] These deeds are understood within the realm of the unrighteous κόσμος (cf. Gal 1:4). Sin, ultimately, will lead to death (cf. 1 Cor 15:56).

Corinthian believers cannot escape sin and death and must find a way to balance both their life within the church, and their life within the κόσμος. Returning to 1 Cor 5:10b, Paul admits that the only way to avoid the ethically immoral of this world is to "go out" from it. But Paul is not suggesting a complete separation from the world itself. Paul acknowledges that there will always be contact with the outside world (1 Cor 6:1–11, 14–15; 7:40; 10:1–22), but warns about associating with such immoral peoples; "bad associations corrupts good morals" (1 Cor 15:33b). What is to be understood in 1 Cor 5–6 is that which exists outside the community of believers, the κόσμος, is a place of sin and death. For this reason, the community of Christ believers must remain committed to their call to follow Christ.

Following the discourse on the celebration of the Lord's Supper (1 Cor 11:17–26), Paul stresses that whoever partakes of the Lord's Supper unworthily will bring judgment upon themselves (1 Cor 11:27–34). The concern in this passage is judgment. Here, Paul incorporates judicial language to emphasize how improper moral behavior within the church will lead to suffering and death (11:29–30, 32). Paul uses the rhetorical device of *paronomasia*, which is the repetition of the same word stem in close proximity, to emphasize the judgment the community has incurred (κριν- κρίμα, διακρίνων, διεκ ρίνομεν, ἐκρινόμεθα, κρινόμενοι, κατακριθῶμεν, κρίμα).[35] As a community of Christ believers, they are bound to the Lord as one body (1 Cor 12:27) and any behavior that is unbecoming of their faith will only bring judgment and death. Of interest to this study is how Paul links their judgment to that of the κόσμος. The "world" here takes on the connotation of those who are not in Christ. He makes a distinction between the believers and the world. For Paul, Christ believers exist within the world but are not of this world (cf. John 17:15–16).[36] Ultimately, when the world is judged by God, it will be condemned (1 Cor 11:32). Believers are disciplined now, so that they may not be brought to the same fate that awaits the κόσμος.[37]

Though the Corinthian believers associated the noun κόσμος with *order* and *adornment*, Paul's description of it was not as flattering.[38] The world is where sin reigns. If the believer is of the world, he will be judged unto death along with the world. For this reason, the believer must remain distinct from the world. Moreover, in Romans, the κόσμος (physical creation) comes under the power of sin and awaits God's redemption at the eschaton.

The first instance of κόσμος appearing within the body of the letter (1:16–15:13) is in Rom 1:20. In Romans 1:18–3:20 Paul is developing an argument on the equal sinfulness of both Jew and gentile. The sub-proposition of the argument is that the wrath of God is revealed against all human ungodliness.[39] Ungodliness, at least in the context of this passage, is the notion that God's creation has forgotten its "creatureliness" and, as a result, sins against their Creator (cf. Rom 1:20, 25; 2:12). James Dunn highlights this notion in his definition of sin suggesting, "sin is that power which makes human beings forget their creatureliness and dependence on God, that power which prevents humankind from recognizing its true nature."[40] When Paul speaks of the κόσμος in 1:20, the term connotes positive aspects of *order* and *adornment*. Since its creation (κτίσις), God has endowed the κόσμος and all of God's creation (ποίημα) with God's deity so that even the gentiles could clearly perceive (νοούμενα καθορᾶται) God's eternal power in the things God has fashioned.[41]

Paul suggests that the revealed knowledge of God is perceivable in and through the κόσμος. What is revealed is God's eternal power, and divinity. Yet the gentiles ignored God's divinity in the κόσμος; they have forgotten to worship the Creator and instead worship the creature (Rom 1:25). The gentiles are the cause of their own sinfulness because they have ignored God's self-revelation in creation. Ultimately, the κόσμος carries positive connotations in this passage and throughout Romans.

In 1 Cor 1:20, Paul calls the wisdom of the world "foolish." By employing the aorist active of μωραίνω (*I make foolish, I show to be foolish*), Paul emphasizes how God has shown the physical κόσμος to be the place of foolishness.[42] Paul uses this same verb, μωραίνω, in Rom 1:22 but as an aorist passive (*to become* foolish). Here, "foolishness" is associated with those gentiles who have failed to recognize the Creator. The gentile becomes foolish on account of the κόσμος. In Romans the world and creation (κτίσις) are overtaken by the cosmic forces of sin and death.

Paul, in the passage in Rom 5:1–7:25, is making a rhetorical argument for his understanding of faith and righteousness, apart from observance of the Mosaic Law. In Rom 5:1–5, Paul offers the sub-proposition of his argument by means of an ethical exhortation. Paul emphasizes that the Law of Moses no longer brings righteousness, because the believers have been justified by faith in/of Christ. This faith is not devoid of ethical obligations but is ethically more rigorous than the Mosaic Law. The passage in Rom 5:12–21 draws on the significance of Christ's death by comparing and contrasting Adam, the biblical progenitor of humanity, and Christ.[43] Paul writes that Adam's sin has brought condemnation for all, and creation also suffers on account of this sin.

In Rom 5:12-14 Paul says that Adam's sin led to death, and death *infected* all of humanity.[44] The term κόσμος appears twice in these verses. In the first instance Paul writes, "Therefore, just as through one-man sin entered the world and death on account of sin, thus death came to all mankind, inasmuch as all have sinned (Rom 5:12)." In this passage, the κόσμος is corrupted by sin, "which entered the world" (εἰς τὸν κόσμον εἰσῆλθεν). Adam's transgression had cosmological implications; the world was good because sin and death were not a part of God's original creation.[45] But on account of Adam, all creation inherits the consequences of his sin.[46]

The second instance of the term κόσμος appears in Rom 5:13-14. Paul writes:

> For up to the time of the Law, sin was in the world, but sin is not reckoned when there is no Law. But death reigned (ἐβασίλευσεν) from Adam until Moses and even over those whose sins were not like the transgressions of Adam who is a type of the one who was to come.

Like Rom 5:12, the κόσμος is not equivalent to sin and death as it is in 1 Corinthians (cf. 1 Cor 1:20, 21; 3:19, 22). The powers of sin and death have invaded the world and, in some sense, have taken control (βασιλεύω) of the κόσμος. Death entered the world through sin and, as Paul emphasizes, "sin reigned through death" (ἐβασίλευσεν ἡ ἁμαρτία ἐν τῷ θανάτῳ, Rom 5:21). Death becomes the end result of sin, and death is the final and most climactic consequence of the power of sin (Rom 7:9–10, 13). Yet by Christ's death and resurrection believers, and subsequently all creation, will be freed from the reign of death (Rom 7:15–17).

Summary

In 1 Corinthians and in Romans, the κόσμος becomes the showground of sin and death. In 1 Corinthians Paul takes the common understanding of κόσμος, order and beauty, and adapts it. The κόσμος is not perceived as orderly but rather as unruly on account of Adam's sin. If a believer seeks to avoid sin and death, they must practice virtue in spite of what exists in the *world*. Romans more clearly presents the κόσμος as God's ordered creation that has been overtaken by the cosmic powers of sin and death. Though sin and death reign over the world, Christ will set all humanity free from bondage to sin's power. Yet in both of his letters, Paul stresses the role of sin and death as dominating forces. He even personifies them as a king who "rules" over creation (Rom 5:14, 17, 21). In 1 Corinthians, death becomes "the last enemy (ἐχθρός) to be destroyed" (1 Cor 15:26). It is interesting to note that even though Christ defeated death, death was only defeated by Christ's death. So too, death stands and awaits humanity (Rom 7:24), but it is Christ who frees humanity from death's tyranny. But like humankind, even the physical creation longs to be set free from the reign of sin.

THE HOPE OF ALL CREATION: ΚΑΙΝΉ ΚΤΙΣΙΣ

In several instances, Paul emphasizes his eschatological soteriology in language of *dying* and *rising* with Christ (e.g., Rom 6:1–11; 7:4–6; 8:3–4; 2 Cor 5:14–21; Gal 2:19–20; 5:24–25; 6:14–16; Phil 3:8–11). As noted earlier, the Pauline notion of dying and rising with Christ falls under the topic of *creation* (κτίσις) and *new creation* (καινὴ κτίσις) (e.g., Rom 8:8–25; 2 Cor 4:17–18; cf. Rom 8:9–11, 18–25; 1 Cor 6:13–14; 15:20–28, 35–58; 2 Cor 4:13–14; 5:1–5; Gal 6:7–8; Phil 3:10–11, 20–21; 1 Thess 4:13–18; 5:23). Κόσμος therefore stands in direct opposition to the new creation in Christ. The κόσμος is corrupted by Adam's sin. As a result, humanity inherits death (cf. Rom 7:9–10, 13).[47] Yet, what is promised by the Christ-event is a transformation of both fallen humanity and corrupted creation. A careful exegesis of Gal 6:11–18, 2 Cor 5:11–21, and Rom 8:18–22, where Paul explicitly writes about *creation* and *new creation*, reveals how the Christ-event involves not only the individual believer but all of God's creation. To make this argument, I propose that, for Paul, the Christ-event was the moment in which God inaugurated the new age. But if sin and death still reign within the κόσμος, this *new creation* will not be fully realized until the eschaton. All creation is led toward death on account of sin. But it is the death and resurrection of Christ, this gift of God, that has begun the final liberation of all creation from the bondage of sin and death.[48]

Galatians 6:11–18

Paul's letter to the Galatians contains one of the only two instances of the phrase καινὴ κτίσις (Gal 6:15; cf. 2 Cor 5:17). This phrase appears in the letter's conclusion. In Betz's commentary on Galatians, he suggests that the postscript in Galatians serves as the *conclusio*, or *peroratio*, of this apologetic letter. Betz writes, "The general purpose of the *peroratio* is twofold: it serves as a last chance to remind the judge or the audience of the case, and it tries to make a strong emotional impression upon them."[49] In this passage, Paul highlights three matters which have been at the heart of his letter: (1) The motivation of the Judaizers (6:12–13); (2) the centrality of the cross of Christ (6:14); (3) the ethical and moral obligations of the Galatian Christ believers (6:15).[50] Of interest to this study is Gal 6:14–15, which recapitulates Paul's argument throughout the letter. Paul writes,

But may I never boast except in the cross of our Lord Jesus Christ, through which the world (κόσμος) has been crucified to me and I to the world (κόσμος). For neither circumcision nor uncircumcision is anything, but a new creation (καινὴ κτίσις).

In Gal 6:14, Paul is contrasting a false "boasting" from a true "boasting." It is not a boasting of what happened to Paul, namely, circumcision, but what happened to him through Christ. As a consequence of this boasting, Paul, as well as all those who boast in the cross of Christ, is a *new creation* (καινὴ κτίσις) (Gal 6:15). Paul's notion of *new creation* is an eschatological concept that takes prominence in this letter.

It is important to note that the phrase *new creation* was an established technical term in Jewish apocalyptic literature. Ulrich Mell shows that the phrase "new creation" refers to an expected destruction of the world and its renewal.[51] The phrase is also equated with a few other phrases such as "new heavens and new earth" (Isa 65:17; 66:22; 1 En. 91:15; LAB 3:10; 2 Pet 3:13; Rev 21:1), "renewed creation" (4 Ezra 7:75; 2 Bar. 32:6; 57:2; LAB 32:17; 16:3), "renewal" (1QS IV, 25), and "new world" (2 Bar. 44:12).[52] Moyer Hubbard also focuses on *new creation* in both Jubilees and in *Joseph and Aseneth*. Hubbard suggests that *new creation* is depicted as a movement from death to life and is described using vocabulary of "Spirit," "newness," and "life." Furthermore, he shows how Aseneth, in Jos. Asen., breaks with her pantheistic religion and is described using language of "new creation" (e.g., Jos. Asen. 16).[53] Though Paul may not be drawing on all of these Jewish sources for his cosmological understanding of *new creation*, it is important to observe that Paul's use of καινὴ κτίσις suggests that he is at least aware of this larger tradition. Paul, therefore, challenges not only the Mosaic Law but also the κόσμος by means of his *new creation* theology.

Paul's anthropological and cosmological understanding of *new creation* addresses a change in the individual and in the cosmic order. The term κόσμος appears three times in this letter: 4:3; 6:14 (twice). Notice in the *peroratio*, 6:14, that κόσμος is not only the realm of "circumcision" but also of "uncircumcision." If Betz is correct, then the mention of the κόσμος here and its relationship to "circumcision" and "uncircumcision" leads the reader back to Paul's argument about the "elemental spirits of the world" in 4:3.[54] If one takes seriously his claim in 6:14, κόσμος is not simply just the "Jewish world of 'circumcision and uncircumcision'" but the κόσμος becomes the arena of Christ's victory over the forces of sin and death.[55] This notion is more fully appreciated in Paul's larger argument in Gal 3:26–4:11.

In Galatians, Paul is trying to dissuade the Galatian Christ believers from observing certain aspects of the Mosaic Law, primarily circumcision.[56] Paul establishes the basic proposition of the letter in 2:15–21 suggesting that one is made righteous by faith in/of Jesus Christ and not by observance of the Mosaic Law. Paul's fourth proof in 3:26–4:11 is his appeal to their shared experience in baptism.[57] Ultimately, it is their baptism "in Christ" (ἐν Χριστῷ) that separates them from the *world*. In baptism they become children of God and, both Jew and gentile, are delivered from bondage to the κόσμος. As Tobin observes, "Sonship and inheritance came through baptism and all that it implied and not through the law or its observance, which is slavery to the elemental principles of the universe."[58] Paul says that the Galatian believers are "in Christ Jesus." The reason that they are in Christ Jesus is that "as many as have been baptized into Christ have put on Christ" (3:26).[59]

The verb βαπτίζω first appears in Gal 3:27. Paul is emphasizing that the one who comes to Christ by faith can come into a relationship with Christ only by means of baptism. Paul says that they have received the Spirit by the "hearing of faith" (3:2). It is this faith that leads to a life in the Spirit.[60] Baptism then becomes an action of the faithful that not only signifies one's acceptance of Christ but allows Christ to be manifested within the believer. Baptism allows the believer to receive the divine "adoption of sons" and to receive the Spirit. To "put on Christ" (ἐνδύσασθαι Χριστόν) becomes a metaphor that expresses the spiritual transformation of the believer. As Dunn notes, the subject of the action implied by ἐβαπτίσθητε is God. He writes, "It is God who effects the incorporation into Christ, and he does it by baptizing ἐν πνεύματι, so that entry into the new relationship (καινὴ κτίσις -6:15) is birth κατὰ πνεῦμα (4:29)."[61]

Faith and baptism in Christ also destroy the identity markers of all those who come to Christ. Paul writes in Gal 3:28 that because of baptism in Christ, "There is neither Jew nor Greek, neither slave nor free, no male and female" (cf. Rom 10:12; 1 Cor 1:20–22; 12:13). This verse correlates directly to Paul's formulaic antithesis in Gal 6:15 and suggests that appearance is irrelevant to the reality they now live in Christ. Faith and baptism do not replace circumcision as a mere "sign" of the covenant (cf. Gen 17:10–14; Gal 5:6), but it is the manifestation of a new age wherein God deals with humanity according to the Christ-event. The use of the perfect tense of the verb σταυρόω, in Gal 6:14, suggests that Paul's crucifixion with Christ was a past event with ongoing significance. In Gal 6:15 Paul's use of the present tense of εἰμί suggests that the current reality of believers is the καινὴ κτίσις. Yet, Paul does not suggest that "this present evil age" (Gal 1:4) has completely dissipated. Rather, "this age" remains a force that one must continuously be liberated from.

Returning to Paul's fourth proof in Gal 3:26–4:11, Paul says that even though believers are now in Christ there is still a chance a believer could fall away. If the Galatians succumb to circumcision, then they will revert to their previous slavery to the κόσμος (Gal 4:1–11). In Gal 4:1–2, Paul wants to describe the historical condition of Israel under the Law. Often, Gal 4:1–2 may be oversimplified as a discussion of Greco-Roman guardianship.[62] Though Paul may be alluding to Greco-Roman law, it is also likely that he is considering Palestinian Jewish law of guardianship.[63] Rodrigo Morales observes that if one understands Gal 4:1–2 as referring to Greco-Roman law, then there are two "glaring discrepancies" between the application of these verses to Gal 4:3–7. The first discrepancy is the Father in Gal 4:3–7 is both alive and active, sending his son and adopting others as sons, whereas the father in Gal 4:1–2 is presumably dead since the minor is under guardians until the date set by his father in his will.[64] The second discrepancy is when the divine adoption of sons in 4:5 is compared with Greco-Roman guardianship in Gal 4:2. As Morales notes, Gal 4:3–7 "says nothing about leaving the status of minority, as Greco-Roman custom would dictate."[65] Taking the proposal of James M. Scott, Morales suggests that the "heir" of Gal 4:1 is not referring to the Greco-Roman legal system, but specifically to Israel as Abraham's original (collective) heir.[66]

As a whole, Gal 4:1–2 refers to Israel's historical situation as a νήπιος. In the Jewish prophetic literature (LXX) Israel can be referred to as a child whenever the text discusses Israel's lapse into idolatry (e.g., Hos 2; 11; Ezek 16). Though it may be difficult to suggest that Paul is directly alluding to these or similar texts in his discussion, it is plausible that these texts constitute a "stock motif describing Israel's history as a period of infancy and slavery to idols, something that the Law failed to remedy."[67] Therefore, Gal 4:1–2 describes Israel under the Law before the coming of Christ.

In Gal 4:3, Paul uses the first-person plural and is emphasized by καὶ ἡμεῖς. This usage can be understood as either exclusive (Jewish followers of Christ) or inclusive (Jewish and gentile followers of Christ). It seems that Paul's use of "you" in Gal 4:8 is referring to the gentile believers. Therefore, I consider that Paul's use of "we" in 4:3 is in an exclusive sense, namely, "we Jewish followers of Christ." So, when Paul speaks of the "elemental spirits of the *world*" (τὰ στοιχεῖα τοῦ κόσμου) in 4:3, he is referring to Israel's idolatrous history as a νήπιος. The Law of Moses is ineffective in bringing about salvation. Christ has redeemed Jewish followers of Christ from the curse of the Law (cf. Gal 3:13; 4:5), and God has granted them the gift of the Spirit. Yet the gift of the Spirit of God is not exclusive only to Jewish followers of Christ, but to all people who come to the faith. Because Israel has been redeemed from the curse of the Law, gentile followers of Christ also receive the blessing of Abraham through the Spirit. All who are of Christ are Abraham's offspring (Gal 3:29; εἰ δὲ ὑμεῖς Χριστοῦ, ἄρα τοῦ Ἀβραὰμ σπέρμα ἐστέ).

After addressing the Jewish followers of Christ in Gal 4:1–6, Paul turns his attention to the gentile followers of Christ in 4:7–11. In this passage, Paul wants to link the gentiles' former life to the former life of Jews under the Law. Paul states that the στοιχεῖα are "beings that by nature are not gods." Like the Law, the elemental spirits are weak and impotent. These spirits are ineffectual for salvation, just like the Law is impotent to grant life (cf. Gal 3:21).[68] Therefore to observe the Law of Moses is no different than reverting to the elemental spirits. As several commentators have noted, τὰ στοιχεῖα τοῦ κόσμου are the gods they have formerly worshipped.[69] Furthermore, the observance of the Law and worship of the elemental spirits both include calendrical observances. As De Boer observes, "Paul intentionally uses terms that cover both Jewish and pagan calendrical observances for he wants the Galatians to realize that by turning to the Law they are going back to where they came from. The observance of the Law is not a step forward, but a step backward!" (Gal 4:10).[70]

Ultimately, Paul emphasizes that the outpouring of the Spirit ends one's bondage to the Law and to the elemental spirits. Because of the Christ-event, all have been redeemed, Jew and gentile, circumcised and uncircumcised. The Spirit, which has been given to all believers by means of faith and baptism, signs the beginning of the eschatological age—the *new creation*. To glory in the Law or to glory in idolatry is to boast in one's slavery to those things that are neither gods nor grant life. The life, death, and resurrection of Christ, however, grants believers the ability to be free from their enslavement to those cosmic forces and to live life according to the new "rule" (κανών— Gal 6:16) of God the Father. Though believers live in the *new creation*, they are not immune to the world.

2 Corinthians 5:11–21

Second Corinthians 5:17 is the only other Pauline text where the phrase καινὴ κτίσις appears. This passage is part of Paul's larger argument in favor of his apostolic authority. It is a treatment of the theological, ethical, and spiritual superiority of a life in Christ.[71] Second Cor 5:11–21 is an exhortation; Paul and the faithful are known by God, and Christ's death and resurrection have brought about death to sin and a new life in Christ. Furthermore, by means of Christ's death and resurrection, God has begun to reconcile the *world* to himself and, therefore, believers should be reconciled to God.

Unlike 1 Corinthians, 2 Corinthians does not comprehensively link the term κόσμος with notions of sin or death. The term, for the most part, takes on the meaning of the "inhabited world" and has no obvious pejorative connotation.[72] In 2 Cor 7:10, the term κόσμος seems to be associated with "sorrow." Here κόσμος relates to θάνατος and is placed in opposition to God. Paul says, "For the sorrow that is according to God produces an irrevocable salvation; but the sorrow of the *world* produces death" (2 Cor 7:10). It is difficult within this context to ascertain whether Paul understands κόσμος as sinful humanity or in the apocalyptic sense of the sorrow of "this world."[73] I think this question should not overshadow Paul's main point in this verse. Paul suggests that what makes affliction beneficial is how one reacts to it.[74] "Worldly sorry" is a metaphor for alienation from God. If there is no repentance, no transformation of the human heart, then this sorrow leads to death.

In 5:17, Paul says that whoever is "in Christ" (ἐν Χριστῷ) is a "new creation" (καινὴ κτίσις). Taking into consideration our discussion of Gal 6:15, *new creation* here should be understood as the renewed created order. There is strong evidence that Paul is taking Isa 43:18 and Isa 65:17 as influential background to 2 Cor 5:17.[75] Although the phrase καινὴ κτίσις does not occur in Isaiah, "new heaven and new earth" (ὁ οὐρανὸς καινὸς καὶ ἡ γῆ καινή) in Isa 65:17 conveys the same idea.[76] Paul, by incorporating Isaianic creation theology, suggests that the cosmic destruction of the universe has occurred due to sin (2 Cor 5:19; cf. Isa 24–27, 34–35). But the Christ-event is the long-awaited final event of God's promised renewal of all creation. To say that ἐν Χριστῷ καινὴ κτίσις within this context of destruction and renewal is to suggest an inauguration of a new eschatological age.[77]

In 2 Cor 5:18–19 Paul emphasizes what he means by *new creation*. To be part of the *new creation* is for the *world* to be reconciled to God.[78] God, because of Christ's death and resurrection, is not counting their trespasses against humanity. God, rather, has positive saving actions for humanity. When comparing to Gal 6:14–15 Adams explains how the relationship between κόσμος and καινὴ κτίσις shifts: "In Gal 6:14–15, the cross of Christ announces the birth of the new creation and the *death* of the κόσμος. In 2 Cor 5:17–19, the death of Christ announces the birth of the new creation and the *reconciliation* of the κόσμος."[79]

Christ's death and resurrection significantly changes the course of all human history. Paul says that Christ's death and resurrection served "all" (πᾶς—occurs three times in 5:14–15).[80] Those who are "in Christ" no longer live for themselves but for Christ who died "on their behalf" (ὑπέρ αὐτῶν). To live in the *new creation* is not individualistic but communal. Christ, who died for all, has affected the course of human history and his death means "that all have died" (2 Cor 5:14c). Paul, here, is likely drawing on the Adam/Christ antithesis, which is most prominent in Rom 5 and 1 Cor 15. He suggests that Christ's death and resurrection has allowed believers to die to sin. No person is excluded from the scope of Christ's redemptive actions, but Christ's redemptive actions are applicable only to those who recognize the salvation offered by God through Christ. This notion will become more apparent in the discussion of *new creation* in Romans.

Romans 8:18–22

Although the phrase καινὴ κτίσις does not appear in Romans, the concept of *new creation* is a major eschatological point for Paul in Romans 1–8. Interestingly, κτίσις, among the undisputed letters of Paul, is only mentioned in Romans (cf. Col 1:15, 23). In Rom 1–8, the noun κτίσις is used twice in Rom 1 and five times in Rom 8. I agree with the argument of T. Ryan Jackson, who suggests that Paul employs creation imagery in Rom 1 and advances his argument toward creation's redemption and renewal in Rom 8.[81] In Romans, Paul argues that creation suffers because of sin, particularly the sin of Adam (Rom 5). Because creation has reaped the consequences of Adam's sin, it eagerly waits for the revelation of the children of God so it too may be transformed along with believers at the Parousia. In Romans 8, Paul is building upon an eschatological framework of the "already" and the "not yet." Though he speaks of the Christ-event as the "already," the final redemption of all creation is in the "not yet." He suggests the present suffering of all creation is incomparable to the future glory that is about to be revealed.[82] Creation awaits the parousia, for it too will be transformed with the "children of God."

The passage in Rom 8:18–22 focuses on the present enslavement and future liberation of all "creation" (κτίσις).[83] Several linguistic arguments have been offered as to how one should understand κτίσις in Rom 8.[84] I agree with the consensus view that κτίσις should be regarded as the "nonhuman creation."[85] In preparing to speak about *creation*, Paul deliberately evokes traditional Jewish apocalyptic images, while, at the same time, reinterpreting these images for his own purposes.[86] Tobin identifies four apocalyptic motifs that Paul employs.[87] The first is the contrast between present suffering and future glory (2 Cor 4:17; cf. 1 Pet 4:13; 5:10).[88] The second is the connection between the fate of humanity and *creation*, that is either associated with the fate of Adam (Gen 3:17–19; 5:29) or with the creation of a *new heaven and a new earth* (Isa 65:17; 66:22). The common theme in this apocalyptic framework is that the nonhuman κτίσις is intrinsically linked to the situation of humanity, and God will bring about their renewal in some future time.[89] The third motif is the notion that increased suffering and distress on a cosmic level will precede the final consummation of the world.[90] The final motif is the apocalyptic use of the birth pangs of a woman in labor.[91]

Paul revises these motifs to serve his own argument. One overarching way Paul reincorporates these themes in Romans is by placing them within an inclusive framework, that includes not only the children of Israel but also all of humanity. Jewish apocalyptic literature often pitted the Jewish people as a whole or the righteous among them, against the unrighteous who could be either gentiles or unrighteous Jews. Regarding Rom 8:19–22 Tobin observes:

> The "sons of God" (8:19) and the "children of God" (8:21) are not set over against any other group or groups of human beings from which they will be delivered or against which they will be vindicated. Rather, they will be freed from "slavery to decay"; (τῆς δουλείας τῆς φθορᾶς) into the freedom of the glory of the children of God. (8:21)[92]

For Paul, God's salvation is made available to all humanity. The salvation offered by God vindicates not only humanity but all creation from the cosmic forces of death and decay.

In Paul's eschatological point of view in Rom 8:18–22, Paul describes that the suffering of all creation, a suffering with Christ, will lead to being glorified with Christ. The Christ-event has cosmic implications. Paul states that the κτίσις has been made subject to "futility" (ματαιότης). The noun ματαιότης, as Dunn states, has the sense of uselessness "of an object which does not function as it was designed to do . . . or, more precisely, which has been given a role for which it was not designed and which is unreal or illusory" (cf. Rom 1:21).[93] Κτίσις has become subjected to sin and is held in "bondage to decay" (τῆς δουλείας τῆς φθορᾶς). Creation is not permanently corrupt, as seen in 1 Corinthians, but its enslavement to decay has been imposed upon it (Rom 8:20). Notice how the fate of humanity is linked to the fate of *creation*. On account of sin, both creation and humanity are in bondage to death and decay. Yet the freedom that is applied to the "children of God," the future resurrection of believers, will be applied to *creation*. Creation itself (αὐτὴ ἡ κτίσις) is the subject of the passive verb ἐλευθερωθήσεται; creation will be liberated (Rom 8:21).[94] It will be transformed along with humanity.

Summary

The passage in Rom 8:18–22, when taken into consideration with Gal 6:15 and 2 Cor 5:17, illustrates several points about Paul's understanding of καινὴ κτίσις. First *new creation* comes from an established motif in Jewish apocalyptic literature. Paul revises this motif to illustrate how the death and resurrection of Christ has brought an eschatological fulfillment to several prophecies from Jewish literature, including several Isaianic prophecies of a "new heaven and a new earth" (Isa 49:8; 65:17, 22). Second, *new creation* is crucial to the life of a follower of Christ. *New creation* promises an epistemological change of all Christ believers. Those "in Adam" remain within the old fading creation; a place of the "flesh" where sin, death, and decay rule. Those "in Christ" enter the *new creation*; a place where one walks by the Spirit in hope of a final resurrection from the dead. Third, Christ believers stand in contrast to sin. In 1 Corinthians and Galatians, believers stand in contrast to the κόσμος, which is described as the arena of sin and death. In Romans, however, all creation stands in opposition to their cosmic captor *who* is death and decay. Finally, Christ by his passion, death, and resurrection has inaugurated the *new creation*, which will be fully manifested at the eschaton. As seen in Rom 8:18–22, the redemption of creation is linked to that of humanity. It has already begun, but all creation eagerly awaits the final redemption of the "children of God." For the transformation and resurrection of believers is the sign that creation will be transformed. This sign is the "hope" for all who were saved by Christ, but they must wait "with patience" until the consummation of time.

A NEW REALITY IN CHRIST AND ROME

Paul's response to sin and death is his theology of καινὴ κτίσις ("new creation"). *New creation* becomes a motif that acknowledges, on account of Christ's death and resurrection, the "old way" of life has ended and this has resulted in a "new way" of life, a new reality. This "new way" of life can be explained using Paul's eschatological-soteriological understanding of *new creation*. Paul seeks to establish a common ethic among his communities to suggest that they now exist as a new reality. Sin has brought about corruption and, therefore, believers must remain distinct. They must live in a manner worthy of the gospel of Christ, so they may inherit the resurrection from the dead.

In his ethical exhortations, Paul conveys that this new reality, *new creation*, is a liberation from the old, pre-*Christian*, way of life. Furthermore, it is a liberation from nonhuman enemies, the cosmic forces of sin, death, and decay. Creation will be renewed (Rom 8:18–30) and those in Christ will receive the resurrection from the dead (Rom 6:5; 7:4–6; 8:11, 18–25; 1 Cor 6:13–14; 15:20–28, 35–58; 2 Cor 4:13–14; 5:1–5; Gal 6:7–8; 1 Thess 4:13–18; 5:23). In this section I will explore Paul's ethical exhortations relating to his appeals of living in a new reality, emphasized by his *new creation* theology. Then, I will describe the likely place of the Roman Empire in Paul's eschatological soteriology. Regarding the Roman Empire, I will attempt to show that it does not play a significant role in Paul's eschatological soteriology. The Roman Empire, like every other entity both political and otherwise that are not in Christ, will ultimately fade away (1 Cor 7:31). This message, however, is not one of political subversion. Paul is not specifically targeting the civic authority or any one group of people. Paul's message is rooted in the eschatological hope that all people may be saved in Christ, inheriting the resurrection from the dead. At the end, all that will remain is the new creation in Christ.

A New Reality in Christ

Paul seeks to establish a common "Christian" ethic among his communities. Though the Pauline assemblies varied in location and in their societal interactions with non-Christ believers, Paul, nonetheless, wanted to instill an ethic focused on the gospel which he preached. Paul suggested that a life in Christ meant a believer lived in a new reality. In this reality, they were not only filled with God's Spirit but also lived a life that was pleasing to God. Paul sought to create a translocal ethical link among his communities that is emphasized by his Spirit-filled language. He wanted to guide believers to live a life worthy of the gospel of Christ.

In his commentary on 1 Thessalonians, Charles Wanamaker suggests that Paul's primary goal was to preach the gospel in order to create followers of Christ, while simultaneously building a community of believers. Wanamaker says, "without a community to reinforce the new beliefs and values and to encourage proper Christian behavior and practice, it is unlikely that Paul's converts would have survived as Christians."[95] As previously noted, Wayne Meeks suggested that Paul's assemblies differed from their Greco-Roman counterparts because Paul's translocal activities particularly an imposition of a universal hierarchical structure.[96] Richard Ascough, contra Meeks, documented translocal links between ancient associations and dismissed claims of a Pauline hierarchy among the assemblies of Christ believers.[97] But, as Young-Ho Park observes, though Paul does not impose a unified structure on his assemblies he does seek to establish a shared ethic and practices among them.[98]

In 1 Corinthians 11:16, Paul seems to be encouraging a *translocal standard*, with regard to ethical practices, among his assemblies.[99] Though, in the larger passage of 1 Cor 11:2-16, when Paul is discussing head coverings, he says that there is no need for contention about such practices because "we have no such *custom* (συνήθεια), nor do the churches (ἐκκλησίαι) of God" (1 Cor 11:6b; cf. 1 Cor 8:7).[100] Park pays particular attention to the term συνήθεια within the larger context saying:

> It was not an *a priori* fixed regulation; nor was behavior in worship entrusted to a local congregation's disposal. This dynamic shows the dialectical nature of formulating communal ethos. Each community's reception of its organizational principle of "the whole church." The concept of the universal church, however, was still not yet apparent in Paul's writing. It was rather a network of the multiple ἐκκλησίαι. A Pattern of behavior became a custom not through imposition from the center but by unanimous acceptance by the majority of the local congregations.[101]

Park proposes that common ethical principles united Paul's assemblies, but Park does not describe what that ethic or uniting principle was. Paul encouraged the Christ assemblies to live in a particular manner that was reflective of their faith and their possession of the Holy Spirit.[102] As Gordon Fee suggests, the empowering of the Spirit is crucial to an understanding of Pauline ethics.[103] In this section, I will not attempt to describe Paul's *pneumatology*, across his letters.[104] Rather, I am seeking to illustrate how Paul's theology of faith, Spirit, transformation, and sanctification encourages a common lifestyle among the Christ assemblies. Though these elements are not equally empha-sized across his letters, Paul did encourage a new way of life by means of his ethical exhortations. This shared ethic becomes a translocal link among the assemblies of Christ believers.[105]

Scholars widely regard 1 Thessalonians as Paul's earliest extant letter, writ-ten sometime around 50 CE.[106] In Paul's first letter to the Thessalonians, one reads that the Holy Spirit, which is given to the believer, calls the believer to a life of holiness: "For God has not called us for the purpose of uncleanliness (ἀκαθαρσία), but in holiness (ἐν ἁγιασμῷ). Consequently, the one who rejects [these things] is not rejecting man, but God the one who indeed gives you his Holy Spirit (τὸν θεὸν τὸν [καὶ] διδόντα τὸ πνεῦμα αὐτοῦ τὸ ἅγιον εἰς ὑμᾶς)" (1 Thess 4:7-8). These verses end the larger pericope concerning instructions on sexual morality (1 Thess 4:3-8). Ultimately, Paul's logic in this passage is that his ethical instructions are not his but come from God. Paul is merely God's agent. Therefore, to reject this call to holiness is a rejection of God.

One notices here and elsewhere in the letter, that it is the indwelling of the Spirit which grants the believer the ability to become holy; "For you also became imitators of us and of the Lord, having received the word in much tribulation with joy of the Holy Spirit (πνεύματος ἁγίου)" (1 Thess 1:6; see also 1 Thess 1:5 [πνεῦμα ἁγίῳ]). For the Thessalonian believers, to possess the Spirit is a call to *sanctification* (cf. 1 Thess 4:3, 4, 7; ἁγιασμός). To avoid *uncleanliness* is a call to *sanctification*, both concerns of an ethical life.[107] The believers, possessed by the Holy Spirit, are now enabled to live sanctified lives. To be sanctified (ἁγιάζω) does not mean a separation from the world, but to live a distinct life within the world.[108] A similar way of life is encour-aged in the letter to the Galatians.

Paul's letter to the Galatians, written sometime between 50 and 55 CE,[109] describes a Spirit and flesh (σάρξ) dichotomy directly associated with both virtues and vices (Gal 5:1-6:10). Paul's moral exhortation in Gal 5:16-25 is quite straightforward. This passage, general in its ethical exhortation, sug-gests that he was not addressing a specific issue in the community. He was giving the Galatian believers a general rule to live their lives. This passage also helps us understand how Paul conceives of an ethical life apart from the Mosaic Law.[110]

In Gal 2:19-20, Paul suggests that he has "died to the Law," so that he may live in God. To live for God is how Paul conceptualizes the life of a believer.[111] Paul associates the flesh with a sinful reality that is opposed to God (e.g., Gal 2:17; 3:3, 22; 4:23, 29; 5:13, 16, 17, 24; 6:8). This life in the flesh is also associated with observance of the Law of Moses (e.g., Gal 3:3). The Spirit, however, is vigorously opposed to the flesh (e.g., 3:3; 4:29; 5:16;

17 [twice]; 6:8 [twice]). This dichotomy is exemplified in the moral exhortation in Gal 5:16-25. If the Galatian believers "walk" by the Spirit, are "led" by the Spirit, and "live" by the Spirit, the Spirit will produce virtues in them (Gal 5:22-23).[112] But if they "gratify the desires of the flesh (σάρξ)," vices which he lists in Gal 5:19-21, "they will not inherit the kingdom of God" (Gal 5:21). To live in the Spirit is to live a life in Christ. The more the believer adheres to a life in the Spirit, the more Christ is "formed" within them (Gal 4:19; μορφόω).[113]

Paul's first letter to the Corinthians, written in the spring between 53 and 55 CE,[114] again makes use of the Spirit/flesh dichotomy as seen in Galatians. In 1 Cor 2:10-16, Paul tells the Corinthian believers that they have all received the Spirit from God so that they may be able to understand the gifts of God that were given to them (1 Cor 2:12). The Spirit of God is contrary to the "spirit of the world" (πνεῦμα τοῦ κόσμου) because it is only the Spirit of God that reveals things that are beyond the limits of human knowledge.[115] The Spirit of God relates divine knowledge, only accessible by means of Christ's death and resurrection (1 Cor 2:8, 16). Anthony C. Thiselton observes,

> The logic of Paul's thought is that if, by analogy, one person cannot know the least accessible aspects of another human being unless that person is willing to place them in the public domain, even so we cannot expect that God's own thoughts, God's own purposes, God's own qualities, or God's own self could be open to scrutiny unless his spirit makes them accessible by an act of unveiling them.[116]

Paul teaches that revelation not only derives from the Spirit but also is granted to the believer on account of the Spirit (1 Cor 2:11).[117] The Spirit, therefore, reveals the mystery of God "since only the Spirit has connatural knowledge of God."[118] But if you should still be living a "fleshly" (1 Cor 3:3; σαρκικός) life, you either have not received the Spirit or you have the Spirit but continue to act contrarily to the Spirit.[119]

Regarding ethics and a way of life, what does the Spirit reveal? Paul says that the "unrighteous will not inherit the kingdom of God" (1 Cor 6:9a; ἄδικοι θεοῦ βασιλείαν οὐ κληρονομήσουσιν). He then lists vices that the Corinthian believers should avoid (1 Cor 9b-10), and reiterates that those who commit such deeds will not "inherit the kingdom of God" (1 Cor 6:10; βασιλείαν θεοῦ κληρονομήσουσιν).[120] In 1 Cor 6:11 Paul's use of the imperfect indicative form of εἰμί (ἦτε) indicates that the Corinthian believers were once involved in these acts of debauchery: "this is what you used to be" (1 Cor. 6:11a; καὶ ταῦτά τινες ἦτε). It is a reference to a "continuous habituation" by the Corinthians. "But (ἀλλά)," says Paul, "you were washed, you were sanctified (ἡγιάσθητε [cf. 1 Cor 1:2, 30]), you were justified in the name of the Lord Jesus Christ, and in the Spirit of our God" (1 Cor 6:11b). Paul indicates that the Corinthian believers should no longer engage in such actions because they have undergone a great spiritual transformation of conversion (cf. 1 Cor 12:13).[121] Now that the believers are sanctified by Christ and in the Spirit of God, they must live a life in accordance to their new identity. Similar to his lament against the Galatians (see Gal 3), Paul emphasizes that, by means of the Spirit, they are now one body in Christ sharing in this common experience of a new reality (1 Cor 12:12, 27; cf. Gal 4:19).[122] To live in this new reality is to live according to the gospel of Christ (1 Cor 15:1-2), in order to obtain salvation (1 Cor 15:2), the kingdom of God (1 Cor 6:9, 10; 15:24, 50), and the resurrection from the dead (1 Cor 15:12-23).

In Paul's letter to the Philippians, written sometime during his imprisonment in the mid-50s CE,[123] there is a strong call to unity by means of the "Spirit."[124] Paul says that the Philippian believers are to "only conduct themselves in a manner worthy of the gospel of Christ" (Μόνον ἀξίως τοῦ εὐαγγελίου τοῦ Χριστοῦ πολιτεύεσθε), and that they are to "stand firm in one Spirit" (στήκετε ἐν ἑνὶ πνεύματι) (Phil 1:27). In this verse, Paul is singling out several intimate relationships which highlight the Philippian believers' practice of an ethical life, practices which are *worthy* of the gospel of Christ.

In Phil 2:1, Paul mentions the κοινωνία πνεύματος ("fellowship in the Spirit") as one of the relational factors to live in a manner worthy of the gospel.[125] The mention of the Spirit in Phil 2:1, is a calling back to the "one Spirit" in Phil 1:27.[126] In and by the Spirit, the Philippian believers are united to Christ, and in Christ to one another, as well as to Paul. Being united in the one Spirit, they are then required to live in a manner worthy of the gospel of Christ (Phil 1:27). In his encouragement to the believers, Paul calls them to imitate him so that they may avoid false teachers (Phil 3:17) and they may exhibit behavior that will *physically* change their bodies (Phil 3:19-21: μετασχηματίζω). Their destiny is to live with Christ "in heaven," and they need to reflect this new reality while they "await" the savior (Phil 3:20). This new reality is also emphasized in Paul's letter to Philemon, but in an unpronounced way.

The letter to Philemon, possibly written in the mid-50s CE,[127] is unique among Paul's letters. The letter is personally written to Philemon, but also to the ἐκκλησία that gathers in his house. It regards Philemon's runaway slave, Onesimus.[128] Though the letter's intention is a personal matter for Philemon, Paul's specific mention of Apphia, Archippus, and the assembly makes it a public discourse as well. In this letter of only twenty-five verses, the Spirit of God is never mentioned or alluded to. Yet, Paul uses Philemon's faith in Christ as an example of ethical living. Paul says,

That the fellowship of your faith may become effectual in the acknowledgment of every good that is ours in Christ. For I have great joy and consolation from your love, because the hearts of the holy ones have been refreshed on account of you, brother. (Phlm 6-7)

Though Paul does not specifically detail Philemon's faithful actions, he does suggest that his "acknowledgment of every good" is on account of Christ, giving Paul "consolation" (παράκλησις). Furthermore, Philemon's faith and actions (Phlm 7; ἀναπέπαυται) lifted the moral of other believers. Paul uses the term σπλάγχνον, translated as "bowels," that identifies the seat of all emotions in ancient world, to recognize the great effect Philemon had on the believers.[129] In a sense, the public character of this letter not only praises Philemon for his faith and actions, but also encourages other believers to follow his example.

In Paul's second letter to the Corinthians, likely a composite of two or more letters dating from 55 to 56 CE,[130] he emphasizes that the Spirit enables the believer to live a new life by means of an intimate encounter with God in Christ (2 Cor 3:1-18). This encounter allows the believer to be transformed into the likeness of Christ (2 Cor 3:18).[131] Second Corinthians 3:7-18 can be divided into two parts: In 3:1-11, Paul appeals to the story of Moses whose face was veiled after descending from Sinai (Exod 34:29-30) to support his gospel, the new covenant, as superior to the old, fading, covenant;[132] in 3:12-18 Paul considers the "veil" covering Moses's face in Exod 34:29-35 in order to contrast the *veiled* ministry of Moses to the *unveiled* ministry of Christ (2 Cor 3:13, 14, 15, 18).[133] This larger passage is preceded by a verse that indicates that the Spirit of God gives life, while the written (Mosaic) Law "kills" (ἀποκτείνω) (2 Cor 3:6).

In 2 Cor 3:7-11, Paul infers that the new covenant, which is *written* by the Spirit of God, far exceeds the Mosaic Law, which is *carved in stone* (2 Cor 3:7; ἐντυπόω). It is the Spirit which reveals the greater glory of God, much greater than that revealed in the written Law (2 Cor 3:8). The written Law brings death, while the Spirit gives life (cf. 2 Cor 3:17). Moses, while on the mountain, only saw a portion of God's glory because no one could see God and live (cf. Exod 33:20). The new covenant, however, reveals the fullness of God's glory without killing, because it leads to an internalized revelation. The new covenant brings about an internal transformation (e.g., 2 Cor 3:3; 4:6, 16-18), as opposed to Moses's external revelation.[134]

Then, in 2 Cor 3:12-18, Paul shifts to the function of the Spirit in the lives of believers. Craig S. Keener notes:

The glory of the first covenant was limited, transient, and deadly, those who "turn to the Lord" receive the Spirit, hence the glory of the internalized, new

covenant law (3:3, 6-11, 16-17). For them the veil is removed, as it was for
Moses when he was before the Lord (3:16). All those on whose hearts the Spirit
inscribes the new covenant message are *transformed* to keep God's covenant,
as they continue to behold God's glory and know God. (cf. 3:3; Jer 31:32-34)[135]

The emphasis for Paul is an internalized transformation of the believer,
that, consequently, has ethical ramifications. Paul says, "But all of us, with
unveiled faces, gazing at the glory of the Lord as in a mirror, are transformed
into the same image from [one degree of] glory into [another degree of] glory
(τὴν αὐτὴν εἰκόνα μεταμορφούμεθα ἀπὸ δόξης εἰς δόξαν), just as from the
Lord who is the Spirit" (2 Cor 3:18).[136] This transformation likely refers to
the life, death, and resurrection of Christ now made manifest in them (2 Cor
4:7-15). This manifestation of Christ is a notion that focuses heavily on the
believers' Christ-like behavior, and this Christ-like behavior then becomes
visible to the world (cf. 2 Cor 4:6-7).[137] Just as Paul was empowered by this
transformation to preach the gospel and live according to the new covenant of
God in Christ (2 Cor 4:1), so too are the Corinthian believers called to live in
this new reality: "but we have renounced the hidden things of shame; neither
walking in craftiness nor adulterating the word of God, but by manifestation
of the truth, commending ourselves to every man's conscience in the sight of
God" (2 Cor 4:2; cf. 2 Cor 3:3, 18; 4:1).[138]

Paul's letter to the Romans, likely written in 57–58 CE,[139] contains the sec-
ond-largest amount of Spirit material among the undisputed Pauline letters.[140]
The noun "spirit" (πνεῦμα) appears thirty-one times and the adjective "spiritual" (πνευματικός) appears an additional three times.[141] But it is interesting to
note that in Rom 5-7, where Paul is most concerned with the ethical behavior of
the Roman believers, the Holy Spirit plays a minor role.[142] Before commenting
on Rom 5-7, I think it necessary to make a few remarks regarding the *Spirit of
God* in this letter. Though this section is not concerned with Pauline pneumatology, it is beneficial to make a few comments contextualizing this letter.

I think Tobin is correct when he observes that Paul's ethical exhortation
relies neither on the Mosaic Law nor to one's conforming to the world. It is
due, however, "to the transformation of their minds that is rooted in the newness of life through the baptism they all share."[143] Paul contrasts the Holy
Spirit as that which gives life, against the flesh (σάρξ), which is the source
of sin and death (Rom 8:1-17). There is a striking difference between Paul's
understanding of Spirit in Galatians when compared to Romans. In Galatians,
on the one hand, the Spirit frees the believer from bondage to the Law of
Moses and guides the believers in their ethical behavior (Gal 5:1-21). On the
other hand, the Spirit in Romans is no longer opposed to the Law of Moses,
and the Spirit itself becomes its own type of "law" (Rom 8:2). The Spirit
frees from sin and death, instead of freedom from bondage to the Mosaic

Law (Rom 6-7; cf. Gal 4:1-7, 8-11). One of Paul's intentions in writing to the Roman Christ assembly is to dispel any misgivings about him or the gospel he preaches, and, it seems, there was some backlash against Paul's theology as expressed in 1 Corinthians and Galatians.[144]

Nonetheless, when Paul begins his ethical exhortation in Rom 5, he emphasizes that both he and the Roman believers were justified by faith in God through Christ (Rom 5:1).[145] Because of this righteousness, they now stand "in grace," which has ethical consequences (Rom 5:2a). Paul emphasizes that the Mosaic Law does not bring about righteousness. They are justified by faith in/of Christ (Rom 4:24-25). Therefore, a virtuous life is one where righteousness is connected to both "faith" and to "this grace in which we stand." Paul, on account of both faith and grace, boasts in the practice of three virtues: character, patience, and hope (Rom 5:4).[146] It is important to note that Paul places the practice of these three virtues in the context of "affliction" (θλῖψις) (Rom 5:3). He highlights the relationship between affliction and the virtues, using the rhetorical figure of κλῖμαξ or *gradatio*.[147] In this way, Paul is emphasizing the relationship between the virtues, namely, that affliction produces character, character produces patience, and patience produces hope. Though the present situation of the Roman followers of Christ may be burdensome, Paul reassures them that their lives in Christ are only strengthened, "because the love of God has been poured out into our hearts through the Holy Spirit that is given to us" (Rom 5:5b). To live in faith and grace is to know the reality, faithfulness, and presence of God's love.[148]

This section has set out to show how Paul sought to create a translocal ethic among the assemblies he wrote to. He wanted to establish a shared ethic centered on the gospel of Christ, namely, that life in Christ meant they lived in a new reality. They are not only devoted to Christ, but also have formed social and ethical obligations to one another. They enter this new reality by means of baptism, and, being filled with the Holy Spirit, are empowered to live a life that pleasing to God by means of their new faith. In his letters, Paul employs language of sanctification, and "transformation" over and against "conforming" to the world (e.g., 1 Thess 4:3-8; 1 Cor 6:11; 12:13; Phil 3:19-21). Paul also uses Spirit-filled language to suggest that it is the Holy Spirit that guides believers to live a moral and ethical life (e.g., 1 Thess 4:3-8; Gal 5:1-6). Or he may use language of faith and grace as ethical principles which should guide the believer in the practice of virtue instead of vice (Phlm 6-7: Rom 5-7).

The Place of the Empire in God's New Creation

As emphasized throughout this chapter, Paul's enemies are not human. Though Paul is often arguing against agitators in his community, he is arguing not against them but against the forces that they are enslaved to. In

Galatians, Paul argued against observing certain aspects of the Mosaic Law. It once enslaved Jews as did the elemental spirits, which are not gods, that once enslaved the gentiles (Gal 4:1–11). Likewise, in Romans 8, Paul suggests that all creation is in bondage not to any human force but to sin. The place of Rome in Paul's eschatological soteriology is more nuanced than what some may claim. Looking at the passage in 1 Cor 15, one will be more able to assess not only the place of Rome in Paul's theology but also the place of all entities that are not in Christ.

The passage in 1 Cor 15 develops a theme that Paul has been incorporating into the entire letter, namely, the contrast between this *world*/age and the new age. For example, in 1 Cor 1:18–25 Paul divides humanity into two categories: the "saved" (σῳζόμενοι) and the "perishing" (ἀπολλύμενοι). This passage emphasizes that those who are being saved are being rescued from this κόσμος, which will eventually fade away (cf. 1 Cor 15:24). Those who are being saved are those "in Christ" (cf. 1 Cor 15:18). Those who are perishing are those who are not in Christ (cf. 1 Cor 15:22).

The final hope of all those who are in Christ, all those who live in a *new creation*, is the resurrection from the dead. The passage in 1 Cor 15:20–28 emphasizes Paul's insider/outsider language by explaining how the Christ-event has implications for those who have died in Christ (cf. Rom 6:1–11; 7:4–6; 2 Cor 5:14–21; Gal 2:19–20; 5:24–25; 6:14–16; Phil 3:8–11; 1 Thess 4:13-18). In 1 Cor 15:23–24, Paul gives a scenario of events that have begun with the Christ-event and explains the eschatological (future) implications of this event. Paul writes,

> But each one in his own order; Christ the first-fruits (ἀπαρχή), then those who belong to Christ at his *Parousia*, then the end (τέλος), when he shall handover the kingdom to the God and Father, when he shall destroy every principality (ἀρχή), and every authority (ἐξουσία), and every power (δύναμις). (1 Cor 15:24–25)

The *end* is defined as the moment when Christ will hand over the kingdom to the Father. The *end* is understood as the culmination of Christ's destruction of every principality, authority, and power. Paul emphasizes this point by citation of Ps 110:1b (= LXX Ps 109:1b) in 1 Cor 15:25.[149] The principalities and powers are enemies, and their destruction is identified by the subjugation as placement (τίθημι) under the feet of Christ (ὑπο τοὺς πόδας). Death (θάνατος) is the final enemy (1 Cor 15:26). Death is destroyed but has not been completely destroyed, hence the difficulty in translating the present passive καταργεῖται. It is both an enemy (ἐχθρός) and the "last sequentially" to be overcome."[150]

There are a number of passages in the Pauline and non-Pauline epistles where several "powers" are listed.[151] In every case where these "powers" are listed together, Paul has in mind those cosmic forces that are both subordinate to God and to God's Christ. But what makes these forces "powers" is their ability to intervene between God and God's creation, and their intervention is hostile toward creation. It would be difficult to identify these "powers" specifically in 1 Cor 15:24–25 as the Roman Empire. Note that Paul is calling to mind the intended cosmic order of God which is brought to perfection in Christ. Those forces which interfere with God's cosmic order are not human entities. Rather as seen in 1 Corinthians, and similarly in Romans, the entrance of sin into the κόσμος not only intervenes in God's intended plans but has subjected creation to "futility" (ματαιότης) (cf. Rom 8:18-22). The "powers" and "authorities" are cosmic forces which have "enslaved" humanity (cf. Gal 4:11). Christ becomes victorious over all cosmic powers, and death is the final enemy of humankind.

If we take Paul's language at face value, then Paul categorizes humanity as those who are being saved and those who are perishing. Rome as an entity, therefore, is part of the realm that is perishing, though it could be saved.[152] To make this point is not to insist that Paul is encouraging the active political subversion of the civic authority. Everything not in Christ will fade away. This does not negate the notion that Paul could see Roman power as opposed to God. Many aspects of Roman power could be seen in the category of the κόσμος, that which is under the control of sin and death. Paul could recognize aspects of Roman power as incompatible with the reign of God. But Paul was not opposed to Rome in such explicit language. Romans 13:1–7 understands the positive role of the civic authority in the political and economic stability of society. He did not directly call for a radical subversion of the empire. It therefore becomes difficult to make a claim that Paul fostered a counter-imperial rhetoric. One can conclude this discussion with the insights of John M.G. Barclay. He observes, "[Paul's] stance towards the Roman empire is neither simple opposition nor obedience: it is a field of human reality criss-crossed and contested (like all others) by the opposing forces of Flesh and Spirit and is subject to powers far greater than itself in the battle created by the gospel."[153]

Summary

Interpreters who take Paul's theology to oppose the Roman Empire or "imperial ideology" are often trapped within political categories created by Rome itself or by modern political commentators. When Paul makes distinctions, it is not a distinction between Jews and Greeks, slaves and free, but rather between those who are in Christ and those who are not in Christ. As Barclay observes, "Paul sees no significant differences between Romans and Greeks, only a categorical distinction between κόσμος and καινὴ κτίσις which was created by the cross (Gal 6:14–15): in shattering other classifications of culture and power, the world is divided anew around the event of Christ."[154] Paul seeks to center his communities on a unified ethic in Christ, that by being "in Christ" they not only live in a *new creation* but live in a manner which is worthy of the gospel.

The kingdom of God is never directly opposed to the emperor's kingdom. The kingdom of God is, however, seeking to overthrow the rule of sin by the reign of grace (Rom 5:12–21).[155] The kingdom of God reigns in order to destroy "every principality (ἀρχή), and every authority (ἐξουσία), and every power (δύναμις)" and to ultimately destroy "death" (θάνατος) (1 Cor 15:25, 26). "Powers" in Paul's letters are "comprehensive features of reality which penetrate (what we call) the 'political' sphere, but only as it is enmeshed in larger and more comprehensive force-fields."[156]

CONCLUSION

This chapter has sought to establish Paul's understanding of κόσμος, καινὴ κτίσις, and their relationship to humanity. The term κόσμος is often associated with connotations of "orderliness" and "beauty." When Paul uses this term in 1 Corinthians, the κόσμος becomes the place where sin and death, personified, reign over humanity. On account of Adam's sin, the physical creation has become corrupted.

In Romans, on account of Adam's sin, the κόσμος, the physical creation, has been subjected to futility. The κόσμος, therefore, is connected with the fate of humanity. Yet, through Christ's death and resurrection humanity and creation are being liberated from the cosmic forces of death and decay. Though a *new creation* has begun with Christ's death and resurrection, its fullness will neither manifest nor be revealed to the world until the parousia. As seen in Rom 8:18–22, the redemption promised to all creation (human and nonhuman) has begun but the subhuman creation eagerly awaits the final redemption of the "children of God."

Humanity cannot escape this world and must live within a *new creation* inaugurated by the Christ-event. In this new reality, manifested in the life of the community, believers not only walk by the Spirit but live a life in a manner worthy of the gospel. In this way they may inherit resurrection since Christ defeated sin and death by his own death.

The Roman Empire, as well as every other political power and people, is not excluded from the scope of Christ's redemptive actions. Paul's preaching included the hope that all will be saved through Christ (cf. Rom 8:24). Though Paul's hope is the salvation of humanity, all of humanity does not recognize the salvation offered by God through Christ. If you are not "in Christ" then one is not being saved. If one remains outside of God's grace, they are perishing. At the eschaton all those entities "in Adam" will cease to be, leaving only the *new creation*. Yet hope remains that those "in Adam" (including the Roman Empire?) will be saved "in Christ."

NOTES

1. See also Paul's larger exhortation in Roman 12–15, commanding believers to live a moral and harmonious life. See chapter 4 of this study.

2. E.g. see Gerhard Schneider, "Die Idee der Neuschöpfung beim Apostel Paulus und ihr religionsgeschichtlicher Hintergrund," *TThZ* 68 (1959): 257–270; Peter Stuhlmacher, "Erwägungen zum ontologischen Charakter der ΚΑΙΝΗ ΚΤΙΣΙΣ bei Paulus," *EvTh* 27 (1967): 1–35; Ulrich Mell, *Neue Schöpfung: eine tradition-sgeschichtliche und exegetische Studie zu einem soteriologischen Grundsatz pau-linischer Theologie*, BZNW 56 (Berlin: Walter de Gruyter, 1989); Edward Adams, *Constructing the World: A Study in Paul's Cosmological Language* (Edinburgh: T&T Clark, 2000); Moyer V. Hubbard, *New Creation in Paul's Letters and Thought*, SNTSMS 119 (Cambridge: Cambridge University Press, 2002); T. Ryan Jackson, *New Creation in Paul's Letters: A Study of the Historical and Social Setting of a Pauline Concept*, WUNT 2/272 (Tübingen: Mohr Siebeck, 2010).

3. Hans Dieter Betz, "Paul," *ABD* 5:186–201, esp. 196.

4. For the different ways that Paul uses the interchangeable phrases of "in Christ" and "in the Lord" see Dunn, *The Theology of Paul*, 397–99.

5. Ibid., 400.

6. Hubbard, *New Creation in Paul's Letters*, 233.

7. On language of "cosmos" and "creation" in Paul see Adams, *Constructing the World, passim*. On the figure of Adam and Paul's use of the phrase "in Adam" see, e.g., N. T. Wright, "Adam in Paul Chronology," in *SBL Seminar Papers*, vol. 22 (Chico: Scholars Press, 1983), 359–389; Felipe De Jesús Legarreta-Castillo, *The Figure of Adam in Romans 5 and 1 Corinthians 15: The New Creation and Its Ethical and Social Reconfiguration* (Minneapolis: Fortress Press, 2014). Legarreta-Castillo's state of the question is the most up-to-date summary on scholarly work investigating the Adam motif in Paul; see ibid., 5–32.

8. The fulfilling of the "law of Christ" (Gal 6:2) is important to this discussion. See John M. Barclay, *Obeying the Truth: Paul's Ethics in Galatians* (Vancouver: Regent College Publishing, 2005), esp. 125–142.

9. I am indebted to the work of Adams [*Constructing the World, passim*. A similar argument is made by Jackson, *New Creation in Paul's Letters*, 152–155] who demonstrates this relationship in his work.

10. Neil Elliott, however, argues for a political reading of cosmos and creation in Paul, especially in Romans 8–9. See Neil Elliott, "Creation, Cosmos, and Conflict

in Romans 8–9," in *Apocalyptic Paul: Cosmos and Anthropos in Romans 5–8*, ed. Beverly Roberts Gaventa (Waco: Baylor University Press, 2013), 131–156.

11. See Jewett, *Romans*, 519; N. T. Wright, *The Resurrection of the Son of God*, vol. 3 of *Christian Origins and the Question of God* (London: SPCK, 2003), 365–366.

12. See the discussion in John M. G. Barclay, "Under Grace: The Christ-Gift and the Construction of a Christian Habitus," in *Apocalyptic Paul: Cosmos and Anthropos in Romans 5–8*, ed. Beverly Roberts Gaventa (Waco: Baylor University Press, 2013), 59–76, esp. 59.

13. When Paul places the "flesh" against the "Spirit," an apparent antithesis arises; "For the mindset of the flesh is death, but the mindset of the Spirit is life" (Rom 8:6). See Dunn, *Theology of Paul*, 64–68.

14. Rodrigo J. Morales, *The Spirit and the Restoration of Israel: New Exodus and New Creation Motifs in Galatians*, WUNT 2/282 (Tübingen: Mohr Siebeck, 2010), 143.

15. Jackson, *New Creation in Paul's Letters*, 91. Cf. Marinus C. De Boer, "The Meaning of the Phrase ΤΑ ΣΤΟΙΧΕΙΑ ΤΟΥ ΚΟΣΜΟΥ in Galatians," *NTS* 53 (2007): 204–24.

16. Notice how Paul's description of κόσμος in 1 Cor is disorderly, whereas in Romans the κόσμος is ordered but corrupted because of sin entering the world. However, the description depends on the context the term is employed in. See Adams, *Constructing the World, passim*.

17. The noun κόσμος appears in Paul's undisputed letters thirty-six times. See Rom 1:8, 20; 3:6, 19; 4:13; 5:12, 13; 11:12, 15; 1 Cor 1:21, 27 [twice], 28; 2:12; 3:19, 22; 4:9, 13; 5:10 [twice]; 6:2 [twice]; 7:31 [twice], 33, 34; 8:4; 11:32; 14:10; 2 Cor 1:12; 5:19; 7:10; Gal 4:3; 6:14 [twice]; Phil 2:15.

18. Herman Sasse, "κοσμέω, κόσμος, κτλ," TDNT3:867–98.

19. Ibid., 3:883.

20. In the discussion of κόσμος, I am dependent upon the work of Edward Adams and his analysis of the term both in the larger Greco-Roman (philosophical) understanding, and for his insights on the term's usage in the Septuagint and other Jewish literature. See Adams, *Constructing the World*, 41–84. Cf. Werner Jaegar, *Paideia: The Ideals of Greek Culture*, vol. 1 of *Archaic Greece, the Mind of Athens*, trans. G. Hight (Oxford: Basil Blackwell, 1965), 150–184; Sasse, *TDNT* 3:868–880; Horst R. Balz, "κόσμος," *EDNT* 2:309–312; J. Guhrt, "κόσμος," *NIDNTT* 1:517–26.

21. Adams, *Constructing the World*, 100.

22. Anthony C. Thiselton, *The First Epistle to the Corinthians: A Commentary on the Greek Text*, NIGTC (Grand Rapids: William B. Eerdmans Publishing Company, 2000), 165.

23. Adams, *Constructing the World*, 155–56; Sasse, *TDNT* 3:893.

24. Adams, *Constructing the World*, 116; Thiselton, *The First Epistle to the Corinthians*, 262. On the "spirit of the world" as a demonic antithesis to God's Spirit, see E. Earle Ellis, *Prophecy and Hermeneutic in Early Christianity: New Testament Essays*, WUNT 18 (Tübingen: Mohr Siebeck, 1978), 29–30.

25. Cf. Simo Frestadius, "The Spirit and Wisdom in 1 Corinthians 2:1–13," *JBPR* 1 (2011): 52–70.

26. Gerd Theissen, *Psychological Aspects of Pauline Theology* (Edinburgh: T&T Clark, 1978), 360–361. Cf. Thiselton, *The First Epistle to the Corinthians*, 262.

27. Theissen, *Psychological Aspects*, 378.

28. Adams, *Constructing the World*, 116.

29. This call to be *distinct* is reminiscent of the Holiness Code: "You will be holy for I the LORD your God am Holy" (Lev 19:2; Cf. Lev 17–27).

30. See Raymond F. Collins, *Frist Corinthians*, SP 7, ed. Daniel J. Harrington (Collegeville: The Liturgical Press, 1999), 203; Also, Horsley, *1 Corinthians*, ANTC, 78.

31. On the translation of συναναμίγνυμι as "mingle," see David E. Garland, *1 Corinthians*, BECNT (Grand Rapids: Baker Academic, 2003), 185. Cf. Thiselton, *The First Epistle to the Corinthians*, 409.

32. Adams, *Constructing the World*, 125.

33. See the observation of Trevor Oswald Ling, *The Significance of Satan* (London: SPCK, 1961), 40–42.

34. George E. Ladd [*A Theology of the New Testament* (Grand Rapids: William B. Eerdmans Publishing Company, 1974), 469 n.4] lists the use of σάρξ in 1 Cor 5:5 as an ethical use of the term. Cf. Barth Campbell, "Flesh and Spirit in 1 Cor 5:5: An Exercise in Rhetorical Criticism of the NT," *JETS* 36 (1993): 331–342.

35. Collins, *First Corinthians*, 436. Cf. Thiselton, *The First Epistle to the Corinthians*, 898.

36. Though the formulation "not of this world" is a Johannine notion, we see Paul's own understanding of this difference in his letters. This topic will be further explored later in this chapter, in the discussion on *new creation*.

37. Fee, *The First Epistle*, 566.

38. Adams calls this method a *defamiliarization* of the conventional use and understanding of κόσμος. See Adams, *Constructing the World*, 105–149.

39. On the structure, genre, and purposes of Romans see Tobin, *Paul's Rhetoric in Its Contexts*, 79–103. For a discussion of the argument of 1:18–3:20 see Tobin, 104–123. See also Dunn, *Romans 1–8*, WBC 38A, 51–162.

40. Dunn, *Theology of Paul*, 112.

41. On the possible Hellenistic Jewish influence on Rom 1:20 see Dunn, *Romans*, 57–58; Craig S. Keener, *The Mind of the Spirit: Paul's Approach to Transformed Thinking* (Grand Rapids: Baker Academic, 2016), 12.

42. Cf. Thiselton, *The First Epistle to the Corinthians*, 165; G. Bertram, "μωρός. μωραίνω, κτλ," *TDNT* 4: 832–847.

43. For studies on this topic see Charles K. Barrett, *First Adam to Last: A Study in Pauline Theology* (New York: Charles Scribner's Sons, 1962); Robin Scroggs, *The Last Adam: A Study in Pauline Anthropology* (Philadelphia: Fortress, 1966); Richard H. Bell, "The Myth of Adam and the Myth of Christ in Romans 5.12-21," in *Paul, Luke and the Graeco-Roman World: Essays in Honour of A.J.M Wedderburn*, JSNTSup 217, ed. Alf Christophersen et al., (Sheffield: Sheffield Academic Press, 2002), 21–36.

44. Paul's use of Gen 1–3 is evident in this passage. For a study in early Jewish interpretations of Gen 1–3, and the variety of early Jewish interpretations of Adam,

see John R. Levison, *Portraits of Adam in Early Judaism: From Sirach to 2 Baruch*, JSPSup 1 (Sheffield: JSOT Press, 1988). Gen 1–3 is also treated by Hellenistic Jewish authors, e.g., Tobin, *Paul's Rhetoric*, 167–177.

45. Adams, *Constructing the World*, 173.

46. See a similar interpretation in Hellenistic Jewish literature: 4 Ezra 3:21; 2 Bar. 3:21; 48:42; 54:15; Apoc. Mos. 14:2; LAB 13:8. Cf. Tobin, *Paul's Rhetoric in Its Contexts*, 180, esp. 180 n.58.

47. Recall that Paul does not have a unified cosmology that is stretched across his letters. What is universal, however, is the thought that sin and death reign in the world over against humanity.

48. Cf. Barclay, "Under Grace," 59–60.

49. Betz, *Galatians*, 313. Similarly, J. Louis Martyn, *Galatians: A New Translation with Introduction and Commentary*, AB 33A (New Haven: Yale University Press, 1997), 559.

50. See Richard N. Longenecker, *Galatians*, WBC 41 (Dallas: Word Books, 1990), 301.

51. E.g. Jub. 4; 1 En. 7:2; see Mell, *Neue Schöpfung, passim*.

52. Mell, *Neue Schöpfung, passim*. Cf. Adams, *Constructing the World*, 226.

53. Hubbard, *New Creation in Paul's Letters*, 60–70. Cf. Rees Conrad Douglas, "Liminality and Conversion in Joseph and Aseneth," *JSP* (1988): 31–42. For general works on Jos. Asen. see Randall D. Chesnutt, "The Social Setting and Purpose of Joseph and Aseneth," *JSP* (1988): 21–48; Joseph C. O'Neil, "What is Joseph and Aseneth all About?" *Hen* 16 (1994): 189–198; Edith M. Humphrey, *Joseph and Aseneth* (Sheffield: Sheffield Academic, 2000); John J. Collins, "Joseph and Aseneth, Jewish or Christian?" *JSP* 14 (2005): 97–112.

54. Betz suggests that Paul is incorporating the rhetorical technique or *enumeratio* or *recapitulatio* (ἀνακεφαλαίωσις), which sharpens and sums up the main points of Paul's argument. See Betz, *Galatians*, 313. Cf. Lausberg, *Handbook of Literary Rhetoric*, 206.

55. Contra Hubbard, *New Creation in Paul's Letters*, 213.

56. It is difficult to ascertain to what extent the Galatian believers were observing the Mosaic Law. It would be interesting to examine whether the Galatians were being persuaded to keep the entire Torah or only certain practices, like circumcision and *kashrut*. Cf. Barclay, *Obeying the Truth*, 60–72.

57. Six proofs (*probationes*, πίστεις) are offered in support of Paul's proposition in 2:15–21. See Tobin, *Paul's Rhetoric in Its Contexts*, 64–66. Cf. Lausberg, *Handbook of Literary Rhetoric*, 160–161.

58. Ibid., 66.

59. James D. G. Dunn, *Baptism in the Holy Spirit: A Re-Examination of the New Testament Teaching on the Gift of the Spirit in relation to Pentecostalism Today*, SBT 2/15 (Naperville: Alec R. Allenson Inc., 1970), 109–110.

60. Gordon Fee, *God's Empowering Presence: The Holy Spirit in the Letters of Paul* (Grand Rapids: Baker Academic, 1994), 383.

61. Dunn, *Baptism in the Holy Spirit*, 111–112.

62. E.g. Betz, *Galatians*, 202–204; Frank J. Matera, *Galatians*, SP 9 (Collegeville: The Liturgical Press, 1992), 154–155; James D. G. Dunn, *The Epistle to the Galatians*, BNTC (Grand Rapids: Baker Academic, 1993), 210–211.

63. I am grateful for the work of Morales [*The Spirit and the Restoration of Israel*, 114–131] for whose treatment of Gal 4:1–7 I closely follow. Cf. James M. Scott, *Adoption as Sons of God: An Exegetical Investigation into the Background of* ΥΙΟΘΕΣΙΑ *in the Pauline Corupus*, WUNT 2/48 (Tübingen: Mohr Siebeck, 1992), 128–131.

64. Morales, *The Spirit and the Restoration of Israel*, 115–116.

65. Ibid., 116.

66. See Scott, *Adoption as Sons*, 128–129.

67. Morales, *The Spirit and the Restoration of Israel*, 119–121, at 121.

68. Martyn, *Galatians*, 412. See also, De Boer, "The Meaning of the Phrase," 204–224.

69. See Betz, *Galatians*, 223–226; Dunn, *Galatians*, 149–150; Tobin, *Paul's Rhetoric in Its Contexts*, 66.

70. De Boer, "The Meaning of the Phrase," 216. Cf. Troy W. Martin, "Pagan and Judeo-Christian Time-Keeping Schemes in Galatians 4.10 and Col 2.16," *NTS* (1996): 105–119.

71. George G. Guthrie, *2 Corinthians*, BECNT (Grand Rapids: Baker Academic, 2015), 150.

72. Victor P. Furnish, *II Corinthians: Translated with Introduction, Notes, and Commentary,* AB 32A (Garden City: Doubleday & Company, 1984), 127.

73. Adams, *Constructing the World*, 236.

74. Cf. Murray J. Harris, *The Second Epistle to the Corinthians: A Commentary on the Greek Text*, NIGTC (Grand Rapids: Eerdmans, 2005), 541.

75. For a thorough study of Isaiah motifs in 2 Corinthians see Mark Gignilliat, *Paul and Isaiah's Servants: Paul's Theological Reading of Isaiah 40–66 in 2 Corinthians 5.14–6.10*, LNTS (London: T&T Clark, 2007). We should note that even though Paul may see Isaiah in the background of his writing, the Corinthian believers may not have understood the full message of Paul's literary technique.

76. See G. K. Beale, "The Old Testament Background of Reconciliation in 2 Corinthians 5–7 and its Bearing on the Literary Problem of 2 Corinthians 6:14–7:1," *NTS* 35 (1989): 550–581.

77. Ralph P. Martin, *2 Corinthians*, WBC (Waco: Word Books, 1986), 152. Cf. Gignilliat, *Paul and Isaiah's Servants*, 98.

78. Beale, "The Old Testament Background," 553.

79. Adams, *Constructing the World*, 236.

80. On the universal effect of Christ's death and resurrection see Harris, *The Second Epistle to the Corinthians*, 421–422.

81. Jackson, *New Creation in Paul's Letters*, 150. Cf. Peter Stuhlmacher, *Paul's Letter to the Romans*, trans. Scott J. Hafemann (Edinburgh: T&T Clark, 1994); John Bolt, "The Relation Between Creation and Redemption in Romans 8:8–27," *CTJ* 30 (1995): 34–51.

82. Notice how Paul often connects the suffering of all believers with the passion and death of Christ. See 2 Cor 4:7–14; 6:1–10; 7:3; 13:3–4; Gal 2:19–20; Phil 3:4–11, 20–21; 1 Thess 4:13–18; 5:10. Cf. Tobin, *Paul's Rhetoric in Its Contexts*, 289 n. 34.

83. I am grateful for the observations of Thomas H. Tobin, whose structuring of Paul's theological argument I follow. See Tobin, *Paul's Rhetoric in Its Contexts*, 289–298.

84. For a list of possibilities see Brendan Byrne, *Romans*, SP 6 (Collegeville: Liturgical Press, 1996), 255–256. For a history of research on ἡ κτίσις in Rom 8, see Olle Christofferson, *The Earnest Expectation of the Creation: The Flood-Tradition as Matrix of Romans 8:18–27*, ConBNT 23 (Stockholm: Almqvist and Wiksell, 1990). Three options for κτίσις have received considerable attention: (1) Κτίσις as the unbelieving human world; see J. G. Gager, "Functional Diversity in Paul's Use of End-Time Language," *JBL* 89 (1970): 327–330; Nikolaus Walter "Gottes Zorn und das 'Harren der Kreatur,' Zur Korrespondenz zwischen Römer 1, 18–32 und 8, 19–22," in *Christus Bezeugen: Festschrift für Wolfgang Trilling zum 65 Geburstag*, ed. T Holtz (Leipzig: St. Benno-Verlag, 1989), 219–228; (2) Κτίσις as unbelievers and the nonhuman creation see Horst R. Balz, *Heilsvertrauen und Welterfahrung: Strukturen der paulinischen Eschatologie nach Römer 8, 18-39*, BEvT 59 (Munich: Kaiser, 1971); Käsemann, *Commentary on Romans*, 223; (3) Κτίσις as nonhuman creation see Brendan Byrne, *"Sons of God – Seed of Abraham:" A Study of the Idea of Sonship of God of all Christians in Paul Against the Jewish Background*, AnBib 83 (Rome: Biblical Institute Press, 1979); Christofferson, *The Earnest Expectation*, 139; most modern commentaries. Cf. Adams, *Constructing the World*, 176.

85. For an analysis of the debate and for the meaning of κτίσις in Rom 8, see Harry Hahne, *The Corruption and Redemption of Creation: Nature in Romans 8.19-22 and Jewish Apocalyptic Literature*, LNTS 336 (London: Bloomsbury, 2006), 176–181; Also Jonathan Moo, "Romans 8.19-22 and Isaiah's Cosmic Covenant," *NTS* 54 (2008): 74–89, esp 75–77.

86. Dunn, *Romans*, 467; Tobin, *Paul's Rhetoric in its Context*, 289–290.

87. Tobin, *Paul's Rhetoric in its Context*, 289–290.

88. Dan 7:17–27; Wis 2–5; 2 Macc 7; 1 En. 102–104; 2 Bar. 15:8.

89. On the relationship between Adam and creation see Jub. 4:26; 2 Bar. 56:5–7; 4 Ezra 7:10–15.

90. Dan 7:21–22, 25–27; 12:1–3; 4 Ezra 5:1–13; 6:13–24; 9:1–3; 2 Bar. 25:2–3; 48:30–41; 70:2–10; Sib. Or. 1:62–65; 2:154–173; 3:632–656, 796–806.

91. Ps 48:6; Isa 13:8; 26:16–17; 66:7–8; Jer 4:31; 1 En. 62:4; 4 Ezra 10:6–16; 1QHa 3:7–18; Cf. 1 Thess 5:3. On Jewish apocalyptic literature see Edward Adams, *The Stars Will Fall from Heaven: Cosmic Catastrophe in the New Testament and Its World*, LNTS 347 (London: T&T Clark, 2007), 52–100.

92. Tobin, *Paul's Rhetoric in Its Contexts*, 291.

93. Dunn, *Romans*, 470.

94. Jackson, *New Creation in Paul's Letters*, 162.

95. Wanamaker, *The Epistles to the Thessalonians*, 15.

96. Meeks, *The First Urban Christians*, 79

97. Ascough, "Translocal Relationships," 223–241, at 228–234.

98. Park, *Paul's Ekklesia as a Civic Assembly*, 115–116.

99. Ibid., 115.

100. The larger pericope in 1 Cor 11:2-16 is one of the more debated Pauline passages. For a discussion on the topic, see Elizabeth Schüssler Fiorenza, *In Memory of Her: A Feminist Theological Reconstruction of Christian Origins* (New York: Crossroads, 1983), 227–228; Thiselton, *The First Epistle to the Corinthians*, 258–259; Victor Paul Furnish, *The Theology of the First Letter to the Corinthians* (Cambridge: Cambridge University Press, 1999), 77; Troy W. Martin, "Paul's Argument From Nature For the Veil in 1 Corinthians 11:13-15: A Testicle Instead of a Head Covering," *JBL 123* (2004): 75–84.

101. Park, *Paul's Ekklesia as Civic Assembly*, 115.

102. Paul does not use the Spirit to only speak about ethical teachings. On the complexity of Paul's use of πνεῦμα see, e.g., Gary T. Cage, *The Holy Spirit: A Sourcebook with Commentary* (Reno: Charlotte House Publishers, 1995), especially 494. Also, John Levinson, *Filled with the Spirit* (Grand Rapids: William B. Eerdmans, 2009).

103. Fee, *God's Empowering Presence*, 878. Similarly, Volker Rabens, *The Holy Spirit and Ethics in Paul: Transformation and Empowering for Religious-Ethical Life*, 2nd ed. (Minneapolis: Fortress Press, 2013), 20.

104. The most extensive study on Pauline pneumatology was undertaken by Fee, *God's Empowering Presence*. Also see Friedrich Wilhelm Horn, "Wandel im Geist: zur pneumatologischen Begründung der Ethik bei Paulus," *KD* 38 (1992): 149–70; James D. G. Dunn, "Towards the Spirit of Christ: The Emergence of Distinctive Features of Christian Pneumatology," in *The Work of the Spirit: Pneumatology and Pentecostalism*, ed. M. Welker (Grand Rapids: William B. Eerdmans, 2006), 3–26. On Pauline ethics and the Spirit, e.g. see Eckhard J. Schnabel, "How Paul Developed His Ethics," in *Understanding Paul's Ethics: Twentieth-Century Approaches*, ed. Brian S. Rosner (Exeter; Paternoster Press, 1995), 167–197; André Munzinger, *Discerning the Spirits: Theological and Ethical Hermeneutics in Paul*, SNTSMS 140 (Cambridge: Cambridge University Press, 2007).

105. The section will discuss each of Paul's letters in chronological order, following consensus dating: 1 Thess; Gal; 1 Cor; Phil; Phlm; 2 Cor; Rom. For a discussion regarding Pauline chronology, and authorship of the New Testament letters see Porter, *The Apostle Paul*.

106. Abraham J. Malherbe, *The Letters to the Thessalonian*, AB 32B (New York: Yale Doubleday, 2000), 13. M. Eugene Boring notes that we should not understand Paul's theology in his letters as progressing. Rather, Paul's theology "changed over the years, but this is a matter of adapting and rethinking his core convictions under the pressure of new situations, not an evolutionary development from primitive to sophisticated." See Boring, *I & II Thessalonians*, 9.

107. Ibid., 141.

108. Ibid., 142. Cf. 1 Cor 1:2; 6:11.

109. Hans Dieter Betz argues that chronologically dating Galatians among the other undisputed letters is difficult, since there is little evidence to go on. Theological

positions do shift between Romans and Galatians, suggesting that Galatians was written sometime before Romans. An earlier date for the letter is often proposed and accepted by most scholars. See Betz, *Galatians*, 11–12. Cf. Longenecker, *Galatians*, WBC 41, lxxii–lxxvii.

110. Cf. Tobin, *Paul's Rhetoric in Its Contexts*, 67.

111. "To live in God" as a concept is also found in Romans 6:10, 11 (with the addition of ". . . in Christ Jesus"). This concept is opposed to "live for oneself" (ζῆν ἑαυτῷ), cf. Romans 14:7; 2 Cor 5:15. See Betz, *Galatians*, 122, 122 n.82.

112. Matera, *Galatians*, 205.

113. Raben, *The Holy Spirit and Ethics in Paul*, 173.

114. On the dating of this letter see, e.g., Fee, *The First Epistle to the Corinthians*, 15. The unity of the letter has been questioned as well, arguing that 1-2 Corinthians are composites of multiple letters Paul had written to the community. See, e.g., Jerome Murphy-O'Conner, *Paul: A Critical Life* (Oxford: Oxford University Press), 255; Furnish, *II Corinthians*, 54–55; Hans Dieter Betz, *2 Corinthians 8 and 9: A Commentary on Two Administrative Letters of the Apostle Paul* (Philadelphia: Fortress Press, 1985), 3–36.

115. Garland, *1 Corinthians*, BECNT, 99.

116. Thiselton, *The First Epistle to the Corinthians*, 258–259.

117. Collins, *First Corinthians*, 132. Cf. Thiselton, *The First Epistle to the Corinthians*, 259–264.

118. Collins, *First Corinthians*, 133.

119. Cf. Fee, *God's Empowering Presence*, 110.

120. Notice the language about the "kingdom of God" and vice lists is strikingly similar to the language of Galatians 5:19-21.

121. Dunn, *Baptism in the Holy Spirit*, 121. Similarly, Fee, *The First Epistle to the Corinthians*, 604 n.24.

122. Cf. Dunn, *Baptism in the Holy Spirit*, 103.

123. On the debates surrounding the provenance of Paul's letter to the Philippians, see Bonnie B. Thurston and Judith M. Ryan, *Philippians and Philemon*, SP 10, ed. Daniel J. Harrington (Collegeville: Liturgical Press, 2005), 28–30; Fee, *Paul's Letter/*

124. Cf. Frederick F. Bruce, *Philippians* (San Francisco: Harper & Row, 1983), 19.

125. Rabens, *The Holy Spirit and Ethics in* Paul, 240.

126. Gordon Fee, *Philippians* (Downers Grove: IVP Academic, 1999), 84–85; Fee, *Paul's*, 181.

127. The date of this letter often depends on where one places Paul with regard to his imprisonment. Those who argue Paul wrote the letter during his imprisonment in Ephesus will date the letter to 55 CE. Those who accept the tradition of Acts 23:33–27:2 date the letter to 58 CE during his imprisonment in Caesarea. The traditional dating from Rome places the letter around 61 CE. See Joseph A. Fitzmyer, *The Letter to Philemon: A New Translation with Introduction and Commentary*, AB 34C (New York: Doubleday, 1964), 9–10; Melick, *Philippians, Colossians, Philemon*, NAC 32, 139–140; Daniel L. Migliore, *Philippians and Romans* (Louisville: Westminster John Knox Press, 2014), 190–192.

128. The identity of Onesimus is debated. Allen Dwight Callaghan, *Embassy of Onesimus: The Letter of Paul to Philemon* (Valley Forge: Trinity Press International,

1997), 44–54, identifies Onesimus as the estranged brother of Philemon; his theory is unpersuasive; James L. Houlden, *Paul's Letters From Prison* (London: SCM, 1970), 226, contests that Philemon sent Onesimus to Paul on an errand, and while with Paul converted proving himself helpful to Paul. Cf. Wendy Cotter, ""Welcome Him as you would Welcome Me" (Philemon 17): Does Paul Call for Virtue or the Actualization of a Vision?" in *From Judaism to Christianity – Tradition and Transition: A Festschrift for Thomas H. Tobin S.J., on the Occasion of His Sixty-Fifth Birthday* (Leiden: Brill, 2010), 185–206. See also Murphey O'Conner, *Paul*, 176–179.

129. Helmut Koester, "σπλάγχνον," *TDNT* 7: 555. Notice that σπλάγχνα is parallel to καρδία. As Koester notes, "The word . . . is used for the whole person which in the depths of its emotional life has experienced refreshment through the consolation of love." Also, Melick, *Philippians, Colossian, Philemon*, 356.

130. Furnish, *II Corinthians*, 54–55. For a more detailed discussion see Harris, *The Second Epistle to the Corinthians*, 30–48.

131. I am indebted to the work of Volker Rabens for his exegesis on 2 Cor 3:18. See Rabens, *The Holy Spirit and Ethics in Paul*, 174–203.

132. Furnish, *II Corinthian*, 225.

133. Guthrie, *2 Corinthians*, BECNT, 217.

134. Craig S. Keener, *1-2 Corinthians* (Cambridge: Cambridge University Press, 2005), 168.

135. Ibid., 169. Emphasis mine.

136. Cf. Harris, *The Second Epistle to the Corinthians*, 313–19.

137. Rabens, *The Holy Spirit and Ethics in Paul, 193.* Also, Harris, *The Second Epistle to the Corinthians*, 316.

138. Rabens, *The Holy Spirit and Ethics in Paul*, 199.

139. Fitzmyer, *Romans*, 87. Similarly, Joseph B. Lightfoot, *The Epistle of St. Paul to the Galatians* (Grand Rapids: Zondervan, 1967), 40,43. Hultgren, *Paul's Letter to the Romans*, 2–5, suggests that Paul could have written Romans any time between 55 and 58 CE.

140. First Corinthians contains the most Spirit material. See Fee, *God's Empowering Presence*, 472.

141. See ibid., 472 n.2. For instances of "Spirit" (πνεῦμα) see Rom 1:4, 9; 2:29; 5:5; 7:6; 8:2, 4, 5 [twice], 6, 9 [thrice], 10, 11 [twice], 143, 14, 15 [twice], 16 [twice], 23, 26 [twice], 27; 9:1; 12:11; 14:17; 15:13, 16, 19, 30. In Rom 8:1, variant manuscripts also contain the term "Spirit." For instances of "spiritual" (πνευματικός) see 1:11; 7:14; 15:27.

142. Notice that the Holy Spirit is described as either the Spirit of God or the Spirit of Christ, e.g., Rom 8:2, 9 (Spirit of Christ); Rom 8:14 (Spirit of God).

143. Tobin, *Paul's Rhetoric in its Context*, 389. Cf. Fee, *God's Empowering Presence*, 634, who suggests that the Holy Spirit is central to Paul's ethical exhortations in Roman.

144. For a more detailed discussion on these misgivings, as well as differences between Paul's pneumatology in Galatians when compared to Romans, see Tobin, *Paul's Rhetoric in its Context*, 155–158, 273–288.

145. Fitzmyer, *Romans: A New Translation*, 393.

146. Tobin notes that Paul is drawing on his ethical material from his earlier letters. See Tobin, *Paul's Rhetoric in its Context*, 159. Also, Dunn, *Romans*, WBC 38A-B , 251–252.

147. This rhetorical figure is a progressive elaboration of a reduplication, *anadiplosis*: /...x/x...y/y...z. See Quintilian, *Inst.* 9.3.54; 9.4.34; Demetrius, *Eloc.* 270. Lausberg, *Handbook of Literary Rhetoric*, 159.

148. Hultgren, *Paul's Letter to the Romans*, 208.

149. Martinus C. de Boer, *The Defeat of Death: Apocalyptic Eschatology in 1 Corinthians 15 and Romans 5*, JSNTSup 22 (Sheffield: JSOT Press, 1988), 115.

150. Thiselton, *The First Epistle to the Corinthians*, 1235.

151. For a complete list of references see Dunn, *Theology of Paul*, 105. I am also indebted for Dunn's work on the identity of the "powers" in Pauline literature. I closely follow his argument here. See ibid., 105–110.

152. Consider the role of Christianity in the empire post Constantine I.

153. John M. G. Barclay, *Pauline Churches and Diaspora Jews*, WUNT 275 (Tübingen: Mohr Siebeck, 2011), 383–387, at 386.

154. Ibid., 384.

155. Ibid.

156. Ibid.

Conclusion

Reconsidering Paul and Empire

This study has sought to explore counter-imperial interpretations of the undisputed letters of Paul. Some political interpreters of Paul suggest that Paul, either openly or covertly, criticized the Roman Empire. Some commentators even suggest that Paul sought a political subversion of sorts. A collection of counter-imperial interpretations of Paul, three volumes of essays edited by Richard Horsley, has brought great attention to this subject.[1] These volumes, and more recent publications, grew as a result of the Society of Biblical Literature's section on Paul and Politics which has been an ongoing consultation between several scholars for several decades.[2]

This study is a rhetorical, sociopolitical, and theological reading of Paul's letters. It has argued that, while Paul wrote in a predominantly Greco-Roman and Jewish environment, he was not steeped in *politics* as such. Paul's thought should not be confined under the category of *political* or *apolitical*. Paul's thought, however, should primarily be understood in the context of his preaching. Namely, Paul preached the gospel of Christ in contexts of κόσμος and καινὴ κτίσις. I have attempted to show that Paul's dealings with the civic authority were more nuanced than previously thought. Consequently, for Paul, you were either among those "being saved" or those "perishing"; you are either "in Christ" or "in Adam." All things not "in Christ" will eventually fade away leaving only the *new creation* in Christ. The redemptive actions of God in Christ, however, are not limited to certain peoples. Paul's hope is that all may be saved, rather than subverted. Though Paul wrote in a society heavily influenced by the Roman Empire, I have argued that the empire has remarkably little role in Paul's eschatological soteriology.

SUMMARY

The five chapters of this study have sought to understand Paul's undisputed letters rhetorically, sociopolitically, and theologically.

Chapter 1 focuses on the state of the question. Several scholars have located in Paul's undisputed letters a direct challenge to the authority of the emperor and/or the Roman Empire. Two larger issues appear in this discussion: first is the notion that Paul used terms that were first used for the emperor, for Christ. The use of parallel terminology, thereby, undermined the emperor's authority. In a world that was heavily influenced by the imperial cult, Paul's use of parallel terms seems divisive; the second issue is Paul incorporated *coded speech* in his letters. This allowed his readers to understand his subversive claims about Rome, but if the letter were intercepted by the Roman authority, his *hidden transcript* would go unnoticed.

In my analysis of these arguments, I contended that these claims were misplaced on several accounts. First, the notion that the imperial cult was a ubiquitous monolithic phenomenon across the empire is much exaggerated. Extant archaeological evidence suggests that even after an emperor, or member of the imperial family, was divinized they were not on par with the Olympian gods. Rather, the early imperial cult was established as a means of securing benefaction from the emperor. Second, parallel terminology, found in Roman propaganda, which Paul "incorporates" into his letters, does not take into account Paul's own background. Paul, a Hellenized Jew, preached Christ as the fulfillment of Jewish scriptures. Paul not only adopted language from the context of his communities but also adapted it in order to persuade others to his gospel. If Rome took seriously Paul's Jewishness, as we should, then it will not strike us as odd that Paul addresses the emperor as neither "god" nor "lord." But in the tradition of Jewish scripture, Paul can understand the imperial authority as divinely ordained (Rom 13:1–7). Finally, the argument for hidden transcripts takes special pleading after previous arguments fall short of their goal. Paul very openly proclaims the gospel of Christ and does not seem to hide this information. Paul's letters were not public discourses, but private documents written to small Christ assemblies. Each letter contained specific information pertaining only to that community, hence Paul's openness toward them. If Paul spoke in code, then why would he insist on the lordship of Christ? If he spoke in code, why would he openly admit that some in the household of Caesar accepted the gospel (Phil 4:22)?

Chapter 2 specifically focuses on the notion of *figured speech* in Paul's rhetoric. If Paul incorporated hidden transcripts into his letters, Paul would likely be using *figured speech*. Figured speech is the rhetorical device where a person says one thing but means another. Of the three main categories of figured speech, ἔμφασις, πλάγιον, and ἐναντίον, ἔμφασις (implied meaning) is the only category used in cases of propriety and in circumstances when it was unsafe to openly speak. Of the several methods for detecting ἔμφασις in speech, the two most prominent methods that are argued for Paul's use of hidden transcripts are audience-dependent irony and *aposiopesis*. Audience-dependent irony is when the historical content of the text supplies the reader with the irony at play. Normally, this would be hinted at within the text by short phrases, leaving the audience to turn the intentionally ambiguous into the politically allusive. Ἔμφασις can also be detected by *aposiopesis*; when an expression is omitted, which is usually made known by an abrupt stop in the sentence. Of the three passages that some scholars suggest contain subversive *hidden transcripts*—1 Thess 2:13–16, Phil 3, Rom 13:1–7—there is no indication that Paul incorporated figured speech into those passages. It is important to understand that my argument does not deny that Paul *could have* incorporated subtext in his letters, though I would deny any subversive agenda. Rather, my argument suggests that the methods that have been employed thus far are not sound. *Figured speech* gives the inquisitor another helpful tool in the study of the Pauline letters.

Moreover, because of Paul's Jewishness, it should seem awkward to suggest Paul would want to subvert the empire in his letters. Though Jews and Romans did not have a perfect relationship, they did have a mutual understanding where, more often than not, Rome respected the rights of the Jews to worship. For Paul, a Jew, to say that that the emperor is not "divine" would not be shocking. Conversely, for Paul, and any other Jew, to honor a pagan king or emperor was not out of the ordinary. The civil authority has their power because God has ordained it as such. Therefore, by revering their civil authorities, believers are ultimately honoring God (Rom 13:1–7). In fact, it would seem odd to deny that Rome secured the political, economic, and social well-being of the empire. If Paul sought to subvert the empire, he never offers a substitute beyond the metaphysical.

Chapter 3 contextualized the civic situation of Paul, by understanding how Rome functioned as a political power in from the late Republic to early Principate. This chapter also considered Rome's relationship to foreign cults. Rome considered itself as the preeminent political world power in the first century CE, and this was only accentuated by Augustus's rise to power.

Because Rome understood its place in the world as unique it sought to preserve itself as that unique power, as culturally superior. Foreigners and their cults were expected to assimilate to Roman culture. In this way, non-Roman cults became more tolerable by the authorities. Rome allowed outsiders to worship freely if Rome was not undermined. The only situations when Rome intervened against foreign cults were when those cults were perceived to threaten, politically or otherwise, the republic/empire. The cult of Bacchus, of Isis, and of Yahweh were tolerated insofar as they were not perceived as threatening. But when they were considered to be of some risk, they were suppressed on a local level. Regarding the Pauline communities, how should one understand Paul's relationship to the greater Greco-Roman world? Paul was Jewish, but his communities did not associate with the synagogues, or prayer-houses, of the Jews. Paul did recognize his assemblies as ἐκκλησίαι. Moreover, he likely understood his relationship to the wider Greco-Roman world as a positive one, rather than as a negative one.

Chapter 4 of this study shows that Paul's identification of his Christ assemblies as the ἐκκλησία τοῦ θεοῦ derived partly from his understanding of Greco-Roman ancient associations. Paul's ἐκκλησίαι, Jewish assemblies, and Greco-Roman ancient associations have significant parallels since they all developed within similar civic contexts. The general function of an ancient association was sociability among membership while, simultaneously, worshipping the associations patron deity. It included peoples of varied social status and all members benefited from engaging in their associations. Pauline assemblies, though similar, established a new way of life. Christ assemblies, just like other Greco-Romans in ancient associations, had to follow their ethical bylaws when they gathered. But unlike ancient associations, Paul's associations offered a new lifestyle that promised physical and spiritual transformation. Moreover, it promised a future resurrection from the dead. To join a Pauline Christ assembly, the ἐκκλησία, meant that one accepted the gospel of Christ. By means of baptism one receives the Spirit, receives the divine adoption, and as a consequence one must now live in a manner worthy of the gospel. To be a part of the ἐκκλησία τοῦ θεοῦ meant that you were empowered by the Holy Spirit and you were to "walk by the Spirit" (Gal 5:16; cf. Rom 8:4). According to Paul, the Spirit sanctifies and transforms the life of the believer.

As a result of this research, chapter 5 concluded that Paul was not concerned with the place of the Roman Empire, and it does not take any prominent place in his eschatological soteriology. I attempted to show, however, that Paul understood the universe in terms of κόσμος or καινὴ κτίσις; "in Adam" or "in Christ." Paul categorizes humanity as those who are being saved or those who are perishing. Those who are saved exist in a *new creation*, that was inaugurated by the passion, death, and resurrection of Christ. In the *new creation*, believers live in a new reality. Empowered by the Spirit of God, believers not only practice a life of virtue within and outside their local ἐκκλησία but are promised eternal life and resurrection from the dead. Those who are perishing, however, are still enslaved to the cosmic powers of sin and death. Paul, therefore, unifies his community under a common ethic; to live a life worthy of the gospel of Christ. This *new reality* will preserve them from reverting to enslavement to sin.

Paul does not make a distinction between Jews and Greeks, or slaves and free, only between those being saved in Christ and those who are perishing.

God's kingdom wages war against the cosmic forces of sin, death, and decay. The enemies in Paul's letters are the cosmic forces of sin and death who seek to enslave humanity, and the subhuman creation, under their power. But Christ, at the eschaton, will not only permanently liberate all creation from these forces but will put *Death* to death.

This study examined Paul's relationship to his greater Greco-Roman environment. Considering his Hellenistic Jewish background as well as his training in ancient rhetoric, one may reach the conclusion that Paul was comfortable insofar as he felt freedom in his ability to preach the gospel of Christ. Though Paul depended on several areas of Greco-Roman culture, they were adopted and adapted in the service of his preaching. I am certainly not the first to make these arguments, but I think my argument further illuminates the issue of Paul and politics. This study has furthered the argument that Paul did not seek to subvert and/or undermine the Roman Empire.

This study takes seriously the rhetorical, sociopolitical, and theological background of Paul. This study aimed to answer, "What is Paul thinking?" and "How is Paul's theology a reflection of the *world* in which he lives?" I have sought to answer this question not only by trying to understand Paul's rhetoric, but also how the gospel of Christ shaped his mind. In many ways, to ask about the *authorial intent* of any writer, especially ancient writers, is a most difficult question. Yet, a critical examination will help illuminate important nuances that have not received enough attention. It is my hope that this study will advance the argument for Paul's understanding of *self* and *identity* in a world that is so distant from our present. I desire that it may be a helpful model for further positive interpretations of biblical literature.

NOTES

1. Horsley, *Paul and Empire*; Horsley, *Paul and Politics*; Horsley, *Paul and the Roman*.

2. See the collection of essays published by the SBL on empire studies in the New Testament; Adam Winn, ed., *An Introduction to Empire in the New Testament* (Atlanta: SBL Press, 2016).

Bibliography

PRIMARY SOURCES

Athenaeus. Edited and Translated by S. Douglas Olson. 8 vols. LCL. Cambridge, Harvard University Press, 2007–12.

Cicero. *In Catilinam 1–4. Pro Murena. Pro Sulla. Pro Flacco*. Translated by C. Macdonald. LCL 324. Cambridge: Harvard University Press, 1976.

———. *On Duties*. Translated by Walter Miller. LCL. Cambridge: Harvard University Press, 1913.

———. *On the Orator: Books 1–2*. Translated by E. W. Sutton and H. Rackham. LCL. Cambridge, MA: Harvard University Press, 1942.

———. *Letters to Quintus and Brutus. Letter Fragments. Letter to Octavian. Invectives. Handbook of Electioneering*. Edited and Translated by D. R. Shackleton Bailey. LCL. Cambridge: Harvard University Press, 2002.

Dio Cassius. *Roman History*. Translated by Earnest Cary and Herbert B. Foster. 9 vols. LCL. Cambridge, MA: Harvard University Press, 1914–27.

Dionysius of Halicarnassus. *Roman Antiquities*. Translated by Earnest Cary. 7 vols. LCL. Cambridge: Harvard University Press, 1937–50.

Euripides. *Bacchae. Iphigenia at Aulis. Rhesus*. Edited and Translated by David Kovacs. LCL. Cambridge: Harvard University Press, 2003.

Homer. *Odyssey*. Translated by A. T. Murray. Revised by George E. Dimock. 2 vols. LCL. Cambridge: Harvard University Press, 1919.

Horace. Translated by H. Rushton Fairclough. LCL. Cambridge: Harvard University Press, 1926.

Isidorus. *The Four Greek Hymns of Isidorus and the Cult of Isis*. Edited and Translated by Vera Frederika Vanderlip. ASP 12. Toronto: A.M. Hakkert LTD, 1972.

Josephus. *Against Apion: Translation and Commentary*. Edited and Translated by John M.G. Barclay. Leiden: Brill, 2013.

Josephus. Translated by H. St. J. Thackeray et al. 10 vols. LCL. Cambridge: Harvard University Press, 1926–65.

Livy. Translated by B. O. Foster. 14 vols. LCL. Cambridge: Harvard University Press, 1919–59.

Ovid. Translated by Frank Justus Miller. Revised by G. P. Goold. 6 vols. LCL. Cambridge: Harvard University Press, 1916–31.

Pausanias. Edited by R. E. Wycherley. 5 vols. LCL. Cambridge: Harvard University Press, 1918–35.

Philo. Translated by F. H. Colson, G. H. Whitaker, and R. Marcus. 12 vols. LCL. Cambridge: Harvard University Presss, 1929–62.

Pliny the Younger. Translated by Betty Radice. 2 vols. LCL. Cambridge: Harvard University Press, 1969.

Plutarch. Translated by Frank Cole Babbitt. 15 vols. LCL. Cambridge: Harvard University Press, 1936–69.

Polybius. Edited and Translated by S. Douglas Olson. Translated by W. R. Paton. Revised by F. W. Walbank and Christian Habicht. 6 vols. LCL. Cambridge: Harvard University Press, 2010–12.

Pseudo Demetrius. *Demetrius on Style.* Translated by W. Rhys Roberts. Cambridge: University Press, 1902.

Pseudo Dionysus of Halicarnassus. *I Discorsi Figurati I e II (Ars Rhet. VIII e IX us. Rad.): Pseudo-Dionigi di Alicarnasso.* Translated by Stefano Dentice Di Accadia. Pisa: Fabrizio Serra Editore, 2010.

Pseudo Hermogenes. *Invention and Method: Two Rhetorical Treatises from the Hermogenic Corpus.* Translated by George A. Kennedy. Atlanta: Society of Biblical Literature, 2005.

Quintilian. Edited and Translated by Donald A. Russell. 5 vols. LCL. Cambridge: Harvard University Press, 2002.

Rhetorica ad Herennium. Translated by Harry Caplan. LCL. Cambridge: Harvard University Press, 1954.

Suetonius. *Lives of the Caesars.* Translated by J. C. Rolfe. 2 vols. LCL. Cambridge: Harvard University Press, 1914.

Tacitus. *Histories.* Translated by Clifford H. Moore. 5 vols. LCL. Cambridge: Harvard University Press, 1925–37.

Virgil. Translated by H. Rushton Fairclough. Revised by G. P. Goold. 2 vols. LCL. Cambridge: Harvard University Press, 1918.

SECONDARY SOURCES

Abraham Malherbe, *Social Aspects of Early Christianity.* Philadelphia: Fortress Press, 1983.

Abraham Smith, ""Unmasking the Powers:" Toward a Postcolonial Analysis of 1 Thessalonians." Pages 47–66 in *Paul and the Roman Imperial Order.* Edited by Richard A. Horsley. Harrisburg: Trinity Press International, 2004.

Adams, Edward. *Constructing the World: A Study in Paul's Cosmological Language.* Edinburgh: T&T Clark, 2000.

———. *The Stars Will Fall from Heaven: Cosmic Catastrophe in the New Testament and Its World*. LNTS 347. London: T&T Clark, 2007.

Adams, Sean A. "Paul's Letter Opening and Greek Epistolography: A Matter of Relationship." Pages 33–56 in *Paul and the Ancient Letter Form*. Edited by Stanley E. Porter and Sean A. Adams. Leiden: Brill, 2010.

Agosoto, Efrain. "Patronage and Commendation, Imperial and Anti-Imperial." Pages 103–24 in *Paul and Empire: Religion and Power in the Roman Imperial Society*. Edited by Richard A. Horsley. Harrisburg: Trinity Press International, 1997.

Ahl, Frederick. "The Art of Safe Criticism in Greece and Rome," *AJP* 105 (1984): 174–208.

Albert, Sigrid. *Bellum iustum: die Theorie des "gerechten Krieges" und ihre praktische Bedeutung für die auswärtigen Auseinandersetzungen Roms in republikanischer Zeit*. Frankfurter althistorische Studien 10. Kallmünz: Lassleben, 1980.

Alvar, James. *Romanising Oriental Gods: Myth, Salvation and Ethics in the Cults of Cybele, Isis, and Mithras*. Edited and Translated by Richard Gordon. Leiden: Brill, 2008.

Amphoux, C. B. "1 Th 2,14–16: Quel Juifs sont-ils mis en cause par Paul?" *FNT* 16 (2003): 85–101.

Ando, Clifford. *Imperial Ideology and Provincial Loyalty in the Roman Empire*. Berkeley: University of California Press, 2000.

Antaya, Roger. "The Etymology of Pomerium." *AJP* (1980): 184–89.

Applebaum, Shimon. *Jews and Christians in Ancient Cyrene*. SJLA 28. Leiden: Brill, 1979.

Arnaoutoglou, Ilias N. "Roman Law and Collegia in Asia Minor." *RIDA* 49 (2002): 27–44.

———. ""Collegia" in the Province of Egypt in the First Century AD." *AncSoc* 35 (2005): 197–216.

———. "Forms of Commensality in Greco-Roman Associations." *CW* 102 (2008): 33–45.

Ascough, Richard S. "Translocal Relationships among Voluntary Associations and Early Christianity." *JECS* 5 (1997): 223–41.

———. "Voluntary Associations and the Formation of Pauline Christian Communities." Pages 149–84 in *Vereine, Synagogen und Gemeinden im Kaiserzeitlichen Kleinasien*. Edited by Andreas Gutsfeld and Dietrich-Alex Koch. STAC 25. Tübingen: Mohr Siebeck, 2006.

Ascough, Richard S., Philip A. Harland, and John S. Kloppenborg, eds. *Associations in the Greco-Roman World: A Sourcebook*. Waco: Baylor University Press, 2012.

Bailey, Cyril. *Phases in the Religion of Ancient Rome*. Westport: Greenwood Press, 1972.

Balz, Horst R. *Heilsvertrauen und Welterfahrung: Strukturen der paulinischen Eschatologie nach Römer 8, 18–39*. BEvT 59. Munich: Kaiser, 1971.

Banks, Robert J. *Paul's Idea of Community*. Peabody: Hendrickson Publishers, 1994.

Barclay, John M. G. "Thessalonica and Corinth: Social Contrasts in Pauline Christianity." *JSNT* 47 (1992): 49–74.

————. *Jews in the Mediterranean Diaspora: From Alexander to Trajan (323 BCE – 117 CE)*. Berkley: University of California Press, 1996.

————. *Obeying the Truth: Paul's Ethics in Galatians*. Vancouver: Regent College Publishing, 2005.

————. *Pauline Churches and Diaspora Jews*. WUNT 275. Tübingen: Mohr Siebeck, 2011.

————. "Under Grace: The Christ-Gift and the Construction of a Christian Habitus." Pages 59–76 in *Apocalyptic Paul: Cosmos and Anthropos in Romans 5–8*. Edited by Beverly Roberts Gaventa. Waco: Baylor University Press, 2013.

Barrett, Anthony A. *Caligula: The Corruption of Power*. New Haven: Yale University Press, 1989.

————. *Livia: First Lady of Imperial Rome*. New Haven: Yale University Press, 2002.

Barrett, C. K. *A Commentary on the Epistle to the Romans*. HNTC. New York: Harper & Brothers, 1932.

Barrett, Charles K. *First Adam to Last: A Study in Pauline Theology*. New York: Charles Scribner's Sons, 1962.

Bartsch, Shadi. *Actors in the Audience: Theatricality and Doublespeak from Nero to Hadrian*. Cambridge: Harvard University Press, 1994.

Beale, G. K. "The Old Testament Background of Reconciliation in 2 Corinthians 5–7 and its Bearing on the Literary Problem of 2 Corinthians 6:14–7:1." *NTS* 35 (1989): 550–81.

Beard, Mary, John North, and Simon Price, *Religions of Rome: A History*, 2 vols. Cambridge: Cambridge University Press, 1998.

Becker, Jürgen. *Paul: Apostle to the Gentiles*. Louisville: Westminster/John Knox Press, 1993.

Bell, Richard H. "The Myth of Adam and the Myth of Christ in Romans 5.12–21." Pages 21–36 in *Paul, Luke and the Graeco-Roman World: Essays in Honour of A.J.M Wedderburn*. JSNTSup 217. Edited by Alf Christophersen, Carsten Claussen, Jörg Frey, and Bruce Longenecker. Sheffield: Sheffield Academic Press, 2002.

Berger, Adolf, ed. *Encyclopedic Dictionary of Roman Law*. Vol. 43.2 of *Transactions of the American Philosophical Society*. Edited by Adolf Berger. Philadelphia: Independence Square, 1953.

Berger, Klaus. "Volksversammlung und Gemeinde Gottes. Zu den Anfängen der christlichen Verwendung von 'ekklesia.'" *ZTK* 73 (1976): 167–207.

Berry, John W. "Acculturation as Varies of Adaption." Pages 9–26 in *Acculturation: Theory, Models and Some New Findings*. Edited by Amado M. Padilla. Boulder: Westview Press, 1980.

Bertschmann, Dorothea H. *Bowing Before Christ—Nodding to the State? Reading Paul Politically with Oliver O'Donovan and John Howard Yoder*, LNTS 502. London: Bloomsbury, 2014.

————. "The Good, the Bad and the State—Romans 13.1–7 and the Dynamics of Love." *NTS* 60 (2014): 232–49.

Betz, Hans Dieter. *Galatians: A Commentary on Paul's Letter to the Churches in Galatia*. Hermeneia. Philadelphia: Fortress Press, 1979.

———. *2 Corinthians 8 and 9: A Commentary on Two Administrative Letters of the Apostle Paul*. Philadelphia: Fortress Press, 1985.

Betz, Hans Dieter and E. W. Smith. "De Iside et Osiride (Moralia 351c–384c)." Pages 36–84 in *Plutarch's Theological Writings and Early Christian Literature*. Leiden: Brill, 1975.

Bickerman, Elias J. *The Jews in the Greek Age*. Cambridge: Harvard University, 1988.

Bitner, Bradley J. "Coinage and Colonial Identity: Corinthian Numismatics and the Corinthian Correspondence." Pages 151–88 in *The First Urban Churches*, vol. 1, ed. James R. Harrison and L. L. Welborn (Atlanda: SBL Press, 2015).

Boatwright, M. T. "The Pomerial Extension of Augustus." *Hist* (1986): 13–27.

Bockmuehl, Markus. *The Epistle to the Philippians*. BNTC. Peabody, MA: Hendrickson, 1998.

Borg, Marcus. "A New Context for Romans 13." *NTS* 19 (1972): 205–18.

Boring, M. Eugene. *I & II Thessaloians: A Commentary*. Louisville: Westminster John Knox Press, 2015.

Bowden, Hugh. *Mystery Cults of the Ancient World*. Princeton: Princeton University Press, 2010.

Brady, Thomas A. *The Reception of the Egyptian Cults by the Greeks (330–30 B.C)*. University of Missouri Studies. Vol. 10. Columbia: University of Missouri, 1935.

Braulik, Georg. "'Conservative Reform:' Deuteronomy from the Perspective of the Sociology of Knowledge." *OTE* 12 (1999): 13–23.

Bruce, Frederick F. *Philippians*. San Francisco: Harper & Row, 1983.

Brunt, P. A. *Roman Imperial Themes*. Oxford: Clarendon Press, 1990.

Brunt, P. A. and J. M. Moore. *Introduction to Res Gestae Divi Augusti, By Augustus*. Translated by P.A. Brunt and J. M. Moore. Oxford: Oxford University Press, 1967.

Bryan, Christopher. *Render to Caesar: Jesus, the Early Church, and the Roman Superpower*. Oxford: Oxford University Press, 2005.

Bultmann, Rudolf. *Theology of the New Testament*. New York: Scribner, 1951.

Burkert, Walter. *Ancient Mystery Cults*. Cambridge: Harvard University Press, 1987.

Byrne, Brendan. *"Sons of God—Seed of Abraham:" A Study of the Idea of Sonship of God of all Christians in Paul Against the Jewish Background*. AnBib 83. Rome: Biblical Institute Press, 1979.

———. *Romans*. SP 6. Collegeville: Liturgical Press, 1996.

Byrskog, Samuel. "Epistolography, Rhetoric and Letter Prescript: Romans 1.1–7 as a Test Case." *JSNT* 65 (1997): 27.

Cadwallader, Alan. "Assessing the Potential of Archaeological Discoveries for the Interpretation of New Testament Texts: The Case of a Gladiator Fragment from Colossae and the Letter to the Colossians." Pages 41–66 in *The First Urban Churches 1: Methodological Foundations*. Edited by James R. Harrison and L. L. Welborn. Atlanta: SBL Press, 2015.

Cage, Gary T., ed. *The Holy Spirit: A Sourcebook with Commentary*. Reno: Charlotte House Publishers, 1995.

Callaghan, Allen Dwight. *Embassy of Onesimus: The Letter of Paul to Philemon*. Valley Forge: Trinity Press International, 1997.

Camery-Hogatt, Jerry. *Irony in Mark's Gospel: Text and Subtext*. SNTSMS. Cambridge: Cambridge University Press, 1992.

Campbell, Barth. "Flesh and Spirit in 1 Cor 5:5: An Exercise in Rhetorical Criticism of the NT." *JETS* 36 (1993): 331–42.

Carney, Tom. *The Shape of the Past*. Lawrence: Coronado Press, 1975.

Carter, John M. *The Battle of Actium: The Rise & Triumph of Augustus Caesar*. London: Hamilton, 1970.

Cassidy, R. "The Politization of Paul: Romans 13:1–7 in Recent Discussion." *ExpTim* 121 (2010): 383–89.

Charlesworth, James H. ed. *The Dead Sea Scrolls: Hebrew, Aramaic, and Greek Texts with English Translations: Volume 1: Rule of the Community and Related Documents*. Tübingen: J. C. V. Mohr Paul Siebeck, 1994.

Chesnutt, Randall D. "The Social Setting and Purpose of Joseph and Aseneth." *JSP* (1988): 21–48.

Cheung, Alex T. *Idol Food in Corinth: Jewish Background and Pauline Legacy*. JSNT 176. Sheffield: Sheffield Academic Press, 1999.

Christofferson, Olle. *The Earnest Expectation of the Creation: The Flood-Tradition as Matrix of Romans 8:18–27*. ConBNT 23. Stockholm: Almqvist and Wiksell, 1990.

Churchill, J. Bradford. "Ex Qua Vellent Facerent: Roman Magistrates' Authority Over Praeda and Manubiae." *TAPA* 129 (1999): 85–116.

Cohick, Lynn H. "Philippians and Empire: Paul's Engagement with Imperialism and the Imperial Cult." Pages 166–82 in *Jesus is Lord, Caesar is Not: Evaluating Empire in New Testament Studies*. Edited by Scot McKnight and J. B. Modica. Downers Grove: InterVarsity Press, 2013.

Coleman, Thomas H. "Binding Obligations in Romans 13:7: A Semantic Field and Social Context." *TynBul* 48 (1997): 307–27.

Collins, John J. *Jewish Wisdom in the Hellenistic Age*. Louisville: Westminster John Knox, 1997.

———. *Between Athens and Jerusalem: Jewish Identity in the Hellenistic Diaspora*. 2nd ed. Grand Rapids: Eerdmans, 2000.

———. "Joseph and Aseneth, Jewish or Christian?" *JSP* 14 (2005): 97–112.

Collins, Raymond F. *First Corinthians*. SP 7. Edited by Daniel J. Harrington. Collegeville: Liturgical Press, 1999.

Cornell, Tim. "The End of Roman Imperial Expansion." Pages 139–70 in *War and Society in the Roman World*. Edited by John Rich and Graham Shipley. London: Routledge, 1993.

Cotter, Wendy. "The Collegia and Roman Law: State Restrictions on Voluntary Associations 60 BCE—200 CE." Pages 74–89 in *Voluntary Associations in the Graeco-Roman World*. Edited by John S. Kloppenborg and S. G. Wilson. London: Routledge, 1996.

———. ed., *Miracles in Greco-Roman Antiquity: A Sourcebook for the Study of New Testament Miracle Stories*. New York: Routledge, 1999.

———. ""Welcome Him as you would Welcome Me" (Philemon 17): Does Paul Call for Virtue or the Actualization of a Vision?" Pages 185–206 in *From Judaism to Christianity—Tradition and Transition: A Festschrift for Thomas H. Tobin S. J., on the Occasion of His Sixty-Fifth Birthday*. Leiden: Brill, 2010.

Cumont, Franz. *Oriental Religions in Roman Paganism*. New York: Dover, 1956.

Damon, Cynthia, ed. *Res Gestae Divi Augusti*. Bryn Mawr: Bryn Mawr Commentaries, 1995.

Danker, Frederick W. *Benefactor: Epigraphic Study of a Graeco-Roman and New Testament Semantic Field*. St. Louis: Clayton Publishing House, 1982.

De Boer, Martinus C. *The Defeat of Death: Apocalyptic Eschatology in 1 Corinthians 15 and Romans 5*. JSNTSup 22. Sheffield: JSOT Press, 1988.

———. "The Meaning of the Phrase TA ΣΤΟΙΧΕΙΑ ΤΟΥ ΚΟΣΜΟΥ in Galatians." *NTS* 53 (2007): 204–24.

De Ligt, Luuk. "Governmental Attitudes Towards Markets and Collegia." Pages 237–52 in *Mercati permanenti e mercati periodici nel mondo romano*, Atti degli incontri capresi di storia dell'economia antica (Capri 13–15 ottobre 1997). Edited by E. Lo Cascio. Bari: Edipuglia, 2000.

De Vos, Craig Steven. *Church and Community Conflicts: The Relationships of the Thessalonian, Corinthian, and Philippian Churches with Their Wider Civic Communities.*, SBLDS 168. Atlanta: Scholars Press, 1999.

Deissmann, Adolf. *Light from the Ancient East: The New Testament Illustrated by Recently Discovered Texts of the Graeco-Roman World*. New and Completely Rev. Ed. with Eighty-five Illustrations from the Latest German. Edited and Translated by Lionel R. M. Strachan. London; New York: Harper, 1927.

DeSilva, David A. "'Worthy of His Kingdom': Honor Discourse and Social Engineering in 1 Thessalonians." *JSNT* 64 (1996): 49–79.

Dmitriev, Sviatoslav. *City Government in Hellenistic and Roman Asia Minor*. Oxford: Oxford University Press, 2005.

Donfried, Karl P. "The Imperial Cults of Thessalonica and Political Conflict in 1 Thessalonians." Pages 215–23 in *Paul and Empire: Religion and Power in the Roman Imperial Society*. Edited by Richard A. Horsley. Harrisburg: Trinity Press International, 1997.

Douglas, Rees Conrad. "Liminality and Conversion in Joseph and Aseneth," *JSP* (1988): 31–42.

Dunand, François. "Le syncrétisme isiaque à la fin de l'époque hellénistique." Pages 79–93 in *Les syncrétismes dans les religions grecque et romaine: Colloque de Strasbourg (9–11 join 1971)*. Edited by Françoise Dunand and Pierre Levêque. Paris: Presses Universitaires, 1973.

Dunn, James D. G. *Baptism in the Holy Spirit: A Re-Examination of the New Testament Teaching on the Gift of the Spirit in relation to Pentecostalism Today*. SBT 2/15. Naperville: Alec R. Allenson Inc., 1970.

———. *Romans*. WBC 38A–B. Dallas: Word Books, 1988.

———. *The Epistle to the Galatians*. BNTC. Grand Rapids: Baker Academic, 1993.

———. *The Theology of Paul the Apostle*. Grand Rapids: William B. Eerdmans Publishing Company, 1998.

———. "Towards the Spirit of Christ: The Emergence of Distinctive Features of Christian Pneumatology." Pages 3–26 in *The Work of the Spirit: Pneumatology and Pentecostalism*. Edited by M. Welker. Grand Rapids: William B. Eerdmans, 2006.

———. *Beginning from Jerusalem, Christianity in the Making*. Grand Rapids: William B. Eerdmans, 2009.

Dyson, Stephen L. "Native Revolt Patterns in the Roman Empire." *ANRW* (1975): 138–75.

Easton, B. S. "New Testament Ethical Lists." *JBL* 51 (1932): 1–12.

Edwards, Catherine. *The Politics of Immorality in Ancient Rome.* Cambridge: Cambridge University Press, 1993.

Elliott, John H. *A Home for the Homeless: A Social-Scientific Criticism of 1 Peter: Its Situation and Strategy.* 2nd ed. Minneapolis: Fortress Press, 1990.

Elliott, Neil. *The Rhetoric of Romans: Argumentative Constraint: and Strategy and Paul's Dialogue with Judaism.* JSNT 49. Sheffield: Sheffield Press, 1990.

———. *Liberating Paul: The Justice of God and the Politics of the Apostle.* Maryknoll: Orbis, 1994.

———. "The Anti-Imperial Message of the Cross." Pages 167–83 in *Paul and Empire: Religion and Power in the Roman Imperial Society.* Edited by Richard A. Horsley. Harrisburg: Trinity Press International, 1997.

———. "Paul and the Politics of Empire." Pages 17–39 in *Paul and Empire: Religion and Power in the Roman Imperial Society.* Edited by Richard A. Horsley. Harrisburg: Trinity Press International, 1997.

———. "Romans 13:1–7 in the Context of Imperial Propaganda," Pages 184–205 in *Paul and Empire: Religion and Power in the Roman Imperial Society.* Edited by Richard A. Horsley. Harrisburg: Trinity Press International, 1997.

———. "The Apostle Paul's Self-Presentation as Anti-Imperial Performance." Pages 67–88 in *Paul and the Roman Imperial Order.* Edited by Richard Horsley. Harrisburg: Trinity Press International, 2004.

———. "Disciplining the Hope of the Poor in Ancient Rome," Pages 177–97 in *Christian Origins.* Vol. 1 of *A People's History of Christianity.* Edited by Richard Horsley. Minneapolis: Fortress Press, 2005.

———. "The Letter to the Romans." Pages 194–219 in *A Postcolonial Commentary on the New Testaments Writings.* Edited by F.F. Segovia and R. S. Sugirtharajah. New York: T & T Clark, 2007.

———. "Blasphemed Among the Nations': Pursuing an Anti-Imperial 'Intertextuality' in Roman.," Pages 213–33 in *As It Is Written: Studying Paul's Use of Scripture.* Edited by Stanley E. Porter and C. D. Stanley. Leiden: Brill, 2008.

———. *The Arrogance of Nations: Reading Romans in the Shadow of Empire.* Minneapolis: Fortress Press, 2008.

———. "Paul's Political Christology: Samples from Romans." Pages 39–51 in *Reading Paul in Context: Explorations in Identity Formation.* Edited by K. Ehrensperger and J. B. Tucker. London: T & T Clark, 2010.

———. "Creation, Cosmos, and Conflict in Romans 8–9." Pages 131–56 in *Apocalyptic Paul: Cosmos and Anthropos in Romans 5–8.* Edited by Beverly Roberts Gaventa. Waco: Baylor University Press, 2013.

Ellis, E. Earle. *Prophecy and Hermeneutic in Early Christianity: New Testament Essays.* WUNT 18. Tübingen: Mohr Siebeck, 1978.

Erskine, Andrew. *Roman Imperialism.* Edinburgh: Edinburgh University Press, 2010.

Fee, Gordon D. *The First Epistle to the Corinthians*. Grand Rapids: William B. Eerdmans, 1987.

———. *God's Empowering Presence: The Holy Spirit in the Letters of Paul*. Grand Rapids: Baker Academic, 1994.

———. *Paul's Letter to the Philippians*. NICNT. Grand Rapids: William B. Eerdmans, 1995.

———. *Philippians*. Downers Grove: IVP Academic, 1999.

Feldman, Louis H. *Jew and Gentile in the Ancient World: Attitudes and Interactions from Alexander to Justinian*. Princeton: Princeton University, 1993.

Finley, Moses I. *The Ancient Economy*. 2nd ed. London: Hogarth, 1985.

———. "Empire in the Greco-Roman World." *GR* 25 (1978): 1–15.

Fiorenza, Elizabeth Schüssler. *In Memory of Her: A Feminist Theological Reconstruction of Christian Origins*. New York: Crossroads, 1983.

Fisher, Nicholas R. E. "Greek Associations, Symposia, and Clubs," Pages 1167–97 in vol. 2 of *Civilization of the Ancient Mediterranean: Greece and Rome*. Edited by Michael Grant and Rachel Kitzinger. New York: Charles Scribner's Sons, 1988.

Fishwick, Duncan. *The Imperial Cult in the Latin West: Studies in the Ruler Cult of the Western Provinces of the Roman Empire*. 3 vols. Leiden: Brill, 1987.

———. "Votive Offerings to the Emperor?" *ZPE* 80 (1990): 121–30.

Fitzgerald, John T. *Cracks in an Earthen Vessel: An Examination of the Catalogues of Hardships in the Corinthian Correspondence*. Atlanta: Scholars Press, 1988.

Fitzmyer, Joseph A. *The Letter to Philemon: A New Translation with Introduction and Commentary*. AB 34C. New York: Doubleday, 1964.

———. *Romans: A New Translation with Introduction and Commentary*. AB 33. New Haven: Yale University Press, 1993.

Forman, M. *The Politics of Inheritance in Rome*. Cambridge: Cambridge University Press, 2011.

Fowl, Stephen E. *Philippians*, The Two Horizons New Testament Commentary. Grand Rapids: Eerdmans, 2005.

Fox, Robin Lane. *Pagans and Christians*. New York: Knopf, 1986.

France, R. T. *The Gospel of Mark*. NIGTC. Grand Rapids: William B. Eerdmans Publishing Company, 2002.

Frank, Tenney. "Mercantilism and Rome's Foreign Policy." *AHR* 18 (1912–13): 233–52.

———. *Roman Imperialism*. New York: Macmillan, 1914.

Fraser, Peter M. *Ptolemaic Alexandria*. 3 vols. Oxford: Clarendon Press, 1972.

———. *Rhodian Funerary Monuments*. Oxford: Clarendon Press, 1977.

Freedman, David Noel, ed. *The Anchor Bible Dictionary*. 6 vols. New York: Doubleday, 1992.

Freidrich, J., W. Puhlmann, and P. Stuhlmacher. "Zur historischen Situation und Intention von Rom. 13.1–7." *ZTK* 73 (1976): 131–66.

Frestadius, Simo. "The Spirit and Wisdom in 1 Corinthians 2:1–13." *JBPR* 1 (2011): 52–70.

Furnish, Victor Paul. *II Corinthians*. AB 32A. Garden City: Doubleday, 1984.

———. *The Theology of the First Letter to the Corinthians*. Cambridge: Cambridge University Press, 1999.

Gager, J. G. "Functional Diversity in Paul's Use of End-Time Language." *JBL* 89 (1970): 327–30.

———. *Kingdom and Community: The Social World of Early Christianity*. Englewood Cliffs: Prentice Hall, 1975.

Gambetti, Sandra. *The Alexandrian Riots of 38CE and the Persecution of the Jews: A Historical Reconstruction*. Leiden: Brill, 2009.

Garland, David E. *1 Corinthians*. BECNT. Grand Rapids: Baker Academic, 2003.

Gehring, Roger W. *House Church and Mission: The Importance of Household Structures in Early Christianity*. Peabody: Hendrickson Publishers, 2004.

Georgi, Dieter. "Who is the True Prophet." *HTR* 79 (1986): 100–26.

———. *Theocracy in Paul's Praxis and Theology*. Minneapolis: Fortress, 1991.

———. "God Turned Upside Down." Page 148–57 in *Paul and Empire: Religion and Power in the Roman Imperial Society*. Edited by Richard A. Horsley. Harrisburg: Trinity Press International, 1997.

Gignilliat, Mark. *Paul and Isaiah's Servants: Paul's Theological Reading of Isaiah 40–66 in 2 Corinthians 5.14–6.10*. LNTS. London: T&T Clark, 2007.

Gilliard, Frank D. "The Problem of the Antisemitic Comma Between 1 Thessalonians 2.14 and 15." *NTS* 35 (1989): 481–502.

Giovanni, Adalberto "The Parthenon, the Treasury of Athena, and the Tribute of the Allies." Pages 164–84 in *The Athenian Empire*. Edited by Polly Low. Edinburgh: Edinburgh University Press, 2008.

Goodenough, Erwin Ramsdell. *The Politics of Philo Judaeus*. New Haven: Yale University Press, 1938.

———. *An Introduction to Philo Judaeus*. 2nd ed. Oxford: Basil Blackwell, 1962.

Goodman, Martin. *Rome and Jerusalem: The Clash of Ancient Civilizations*. London: Allen Lane, 2007.

Gordon, Milton M. *Human Nature, Class, and Ethnicity*. New York: Oxford University Press, 1978.

Gradel, Ittai. *Emperor Worship and Roman Religion*. Oxford: Oxford University Press, 2002.

Grether, Gertrude. "Livia and the Roman Imperial Cult." *AJP* 67 (1946): 222–52.

Griffiths, J. Gwyn. *Plutarch's de Iside et Osiride*. Cardiff: University of Wales Press, 1970.

Gruen, Erich S. *The Hellenistic World and the Coming of Rome*. 2 vols. Berkley: University of California Press, 1984.

———. *Heritage and Hellenism: The Reinvention of Jewish Tradition*. HCS 30. Berkeley: University of California Press, 1998.

———. *Studies in Greek Culture and Roman Policy*. Leiden: Brill, 1990.

———. *Diaspora: Jews amidst Greeks and Romans*. Cambridge: Harvard University Press, 2002.

Guthrie, George H. *2 Corinthians*. BECNT. Grand Rapids: Baker Academic, 2015.

Harland, Philip A. *Associations, Synagogues, and Congregations: Claiming a Place in Ancient Mediterranean Society*. Minneapolis: Fortress Press, 2003.

————. *Dynamics of Identity in the World of Early Christians: Associations, Judaeans, and Cultural Minorities.* New York: The Continuum International Publishing Group Inc, 2014.

Harrington, R. M. *The Dawn of Empire: Rome's Rise to World Power.* Ithaca: Cornell University Press, 1971.

Harris, Murray J. *The Second Epistle to the Corinthians: A Commentary on the Greek Text.* NIGTC. Grand Rapids: Eerdmans, 2005.

Harris, William V. *War and Imperialism in Republican Rome: 327–70 B.C.* Oxford: Clarendon Press, 1985.

Harrison, James R. *Paul and the Imperial Authorities at Thessalonica and Rome: A Study in the Conflict of Ideology.* WUNT 273. Tübingen: Mohr Siebeck, 2011.

Hatch, Edwin. *The Organization of the Early Christian Churches.* 4th ed. London: Longmans, Green, 1892.

Hays, Richard. *Echoes of Scripture in the Letters of Paul.* New Haven: Yale University Press, 1989.

Heath, Malcolm. "Pseudo-Dionysius 'Art of Rhetoric' 8–11: Figured Speech, Declamation, and criticism," *AJP* 124 (2003): 81–105, 82.

Heilig, Christoph. *Hidden Criticism? The Methodology and Plausibility of the Search for a Counter-Imperial Subtext in Paul.* Minneapolis: Fortress Press, 2015

Heinrici, Georg. "Die Christengemeinde Kirinths und die religiösen Genossenschaften der Griechen." *ZWT* 19 (1876): 464–526.

————. *Der Zweite Brief an die Korinther.* 7th ed. Kritisch-exegetischer Kommentar über das Neue Testament, 6. Göttingen: Vandenhoeck & Ruprecht, 1890.

Hendrix, Holland Lee. "Thessalonicans Honor Romans." ThD diss., Harvard University, 1984.

Hengel, Martin. *Judaism and Hellenism: Studies in their Encounter in Palestine During the Early Hellenistic Period.* 2 vols. Translated by John Bowden. London: SCM Press LTD, 1974.

————. *Between Jesus and Paul: Studies in the Earliest History of Christianity.* Philadelphia: Fortress Press, 1983.

Hebert, Andrew C. "God and Caesar: Examining the Differences between Counter-Imperial and Post-Colonial Hermeneutics." *CTR* 11 (2014): 91–100.

Herbert, Musurillo ed. *The Acts of the Pagan Martyrs*: *Acta Alexandrinorum.* New York: Arno Press, 1979.

Herrmann, Peter. "Demeter Karpophoros in Sardeis." *REA* 100 (1998): 495–508.

Herzog, William R. II. "Dissembling, a Weapon of the Weak: The Case of Christ and Caesar in Mark 12:13–17 and Romans 13:1–7," *PRSt* (1994): 339–59.

Heyob, Sharon Kelly. *The Cult of Isis among Women in the Graeco-Roman World.* Leiden: Brill, 1975.

Hobson, John A. *Imperialism: A Study.* Ann Arbor: University of Michigan Press, 1965.

Holleaux, Maurice. *Rome, la Grèce et les monarchies hellénistiques au IIIe siècle avant J. C. (273–205).* BEHEH. Paris: Éditions E. de Boccard, 1921.

Holtz, Traugott. "On the Background of 1 Thessalonians 2:1–12." Pages 69–80 in *The Thessalonians Debate: Methodological Discord or Methodological Synthesis?*

Edited by. Karl P. Donfried and Johannes Beutler. Grand Rapids: Eerdmans, 2000).

Hopfner, Theodore. *Plutarch über Isis und Osiris*. Darmstadt: Wissenchaftliche Buchgesellschaft, 1967.

Hopkins, Keith. *Conquerors and Slaves,* Sociological Studies in Roman History 1. Cambridge: Cambridge University Press, 1978.

———. *Death and Renewal*. Cambridge: Cambridge University Press, 1983.

Horn, Friedrich Wilhelm. "Wandel im Geist: zur pneumatologischen Begründung der Ethik bei Paulus." *KD* 38 (1992): 149–70.

Horrell, David. "Domestic Space and Christian Meetings at Corinth: Imagining New Contexts and the Buildings East of the Theatre." *NTS* 27 (2004): 349–69.

Horsley, Richard. *Bandits, Prophets, and Messiahs: Popular Movements in the Time of Jesus*. Harrisburg: Trinity Press International, 1985.

Horsley, Richard A. "1 Corinthians: A Case Study of Paul's Assembly as an Alternative Society." Pages 242–52 in *Paul and Empire: Religion and Power in the Roman Imperial Society*. Edited by Richard A. Horsley. Harrisburg: Trinity Press International, 1997.

———. *1 Corinthians*, ANTC. Nashville: Abingdon Press, 1998.

———. *Paul and Politics*, 72–102. See also Richard A. Horsley, *1 Corinthians*, ANTC (Nashville: Abingdon Press, 1998).

———. "Rhetoric and Empire—and 1 Corinthians," Pages 72–102 in *Paul and Politics: Ekklesia, Israel, Imperium, Interpretations: Essays in Honor of Krister Stendahl*. Edited by Richard A. Horsley. Harrisburg: Trinity Press International, 2000.

———. *Paul and Politics: Ekklesia, Israel, Imperium, Interpretations: Essays in Honor of Krister Stendahl*. Harrisburg: Trinity Press International, 2000.

———. "Rhetoric and Empire." Pages 72–102 in *Paul and Politics: Ekklesia, Israel, Imperium, Interpretations: Essays in Honor of Krister Stendahl*. Edited by Richard A. Horsley. Harrisburg: Trinity Press International, 2000.

———. *Jesus and Empire: The Kingdom of God and the New World Disorder*. Minneapolis: Fortress, 2002.

———. ed. *Hidden Transcripts and the Arts of Resistance: Applying the Work of James C. Scott to Jesus and Paul*. Atlanta: Society of Biblical Literature, 2004.

———. ed. *Paul and the Roman Imperial Order*. Harrisburg: Trinity Press International, 2004.

Houlden, James L. *Paul's Letters from Prison*. London: SCM, 1970.

Hubbard, Moyer V. *New Creation in Paul's Letters and Thought*. SNTSMS 119. Cambridge: Cambridge University Press, 2002.

Hultgren, Arland J. *Paul's Letter to the Romans: A Commentary*. Grand Rapids, MI: William B. Eerdmans, 2011.

Humphrey, Edith M. *Joseph and Aseneth*. Sheffield: Sheffield Academic, 2000.

Hurtado, Larry W. *Lord Jesus Christ: Devotion to Jesus in Earliest Christianity*. Grand Rapids: William B. Eerdmans, 2003.

Itgenshorst, Tanja. "Roman Commanders and Hellenistic Kings: On the 'Hellenization' of the Republican Triumph." *AncSoc* 36 (2006): 51–68.

Jackson, T. Ryan. *New Creation in Paul's Letters: A Study of the Historical and Social Setting of a Pauline Concept.* WUNT 2/272. Tübingen: Mohr Siebeck, 2010.

Jaegar, Werner. *Paideia: The Ideals of Greek Culture.* Vol. 1 of *Archaic Greece, the Mind of Athens.* Translated by G. Hight. Oxford: Basil Blackwell, 1965.

Jedan, Christoph. *Stoic Virtues: Chrysippus and the Religious Foundations of Stoic Ethics.* New York: Continuum, 2009.

Jewett, Robert. *Romans: A Commentary.* Hermeneia. Edited by Helmut Koester. Minneapolis: Fortress Press, 2007.

Johanson, Bruce C. *To all the Brethren: A Text-Linguistic and Rhetorical Approach to 1 Thessalonians.* ConBNT. Stockholm: Almqvist & Wiksell Internation, 1991.

John Bolt. "The Relation between Creation and Redemption in Romans 8:8–27." *CTJ* 30 (1995): 34–51.

Jones, C. P. *The Roman World of Dio Chrysostom.* Cambridge: Harvard University Press, 1978.

Judge, Edwin A. *The Social Pattern of the Christian Groups in the First Century.* London: Tyndale Press, 1960.

———. "The Decrees of Caesar at Thessalonica." *RTR* 1 (1971): 1–7.

———. "The Social Identity of the First Christians: A Question of Method in Religious History." *JRH* 11 (1980): 201–17.

Kallas, James. "Rom xiii:1–7: An Interpolation." *NTS* 11 (1964–1965): 365–74.

Käsemann, Ernst. *Commentary on Romans.* Translated and Edited by G. W. Bromiley. Grand Rapids: Eerdmans, 1980.

Kasher, Aryeh. *The Jews in Hellenistic and Roman Egypt: The Struggle for Equal Rights.* Tübingen: Mohr Siebeck, 1985.

Kaylor, R. David. *Paul's Covenant Community: Jew and Gentile in Romans.* Atlanta: John Knox, 1988.

Kee, Howard Clark. *Miracle in the Early Christian World: A Study in Sociohistorical Method.* New Haven: Yale University Press, 1983.

Keener, Craig S. *1–2 Corinthians.* Cambridge: Cambridge University Press, 2005.

———. *The Mind of the Spirit: Paul's Approach to Transformed Thinking.* Grand Rapids: Baker Academic, 2016.

Kerényi, Carl. *Dionysos: Archetypal Image of Indestructible Life.* Vol. 2 of *Archetypal Images in Greek Religion.* Translated by Ralph Manheim. Routledge: London, 1976.

Kim, Seyoon. *Christ and Caesar: The Gospel and the Roman Empire in the Writings of Paul and Luke.* Grand Rapids: William B. Eerdmans, 2008.

Kittel, Gerhard, and Gerhard Friedrich, eds. *Theological Dictionary of the New Testament.* Translated by Geoffrey W. Bromiley. 10 vols. Grand Rapids: William B. Eerdmans, 1964–76.

Klause, Hans-Josef. *Hausgemeinde und Hauskirche im frühen Christentum.* Stuttgart: Verlag Katholisches Bibelwerk, 1981.

Kloppenborg, John S. "Edwin Hatch, Churches and Collegia." Pages 212–38 in *Origins and Method: Towards a New Understanding of Judaism and Christianity. Essays in Honour of John C. Hurd.* JSNTSup 86. Edited by Bradley H. McLean. Sheffield: Sheffield Academic, 1993.

————. "Collegia and Thiasoi: Issues in Function, Taxonomy, and membership." Pages 16–30 in *Voluntary Associations in the Graeco-Roman World*. Edited John S. Kloppenborg and Stephen G. Wilson. London: Routledge, 1996.

————. *Christ's Associations: Connecting and Belonging in the Ancient City*. New Haven/London: Yale University Press, 2020.

Kloppenborg, John S., and Richard S. Ascough eds. *Greco Roman Associations: Texts, Translations, and Commentary. Vol I. Attica, Central Greece, Macedonia, Thrace*. BZNW 181. Berlin: De Gruyter, 2011.

Knibb, Michael A. "Rule of the Community." Pages 793–97 in *Encyclopedia of the Dead Sea Scrolls*. Edited by Lawrence H. Shiffman and James C. VanderKam. Vol. 2. Oxford: Oxford University Press, 2000.

Knust, Jennifer Wright. "Paul and the Politics of Virtue and Vice." Pages 155–73 in *Paul and the Roman Imperial Order*. Edited by Richard A. Horsley (Harrisburg: Trinity Press International, 2004).

Koester, Helmut. "Imperial Ideology and Paul's Eschatology in 1 Thessalonians." Pages 158–66 in *Paul and Empire: Religion and Power in the Roman Imperial Society*. Edited by Richard A. Horsley. Harrisburg: Trinity Press International, 1997.

Ladd, George E. *A Theology of the New Testament*. Grand Rapids: William B. Eerdmans Publishing Company, 1974.

Larsen, J. A. O. "Roman Greece." Pages 259–498 in vol. 4 of *An Economic Survey of Ancient Rome*. Edited by Tenney Frank. Baltimore: The John Hopkins Press, 1938.

Lategan, Bernard C. "The Quality of Young Democracies from a Constitutional Perspective." Pages 95–114 in *Democracy Under Scrutiny: Elites, Citizens, Cultures*. Edited by U. J. Van Beck. Opladen: Barbara Budrich, 2010.

————. "Romans 13:1–7: A Review of Post-1989 Readings." *Scriptura (S)* 110 (2012): 259–72.

Lausberg, Heinrich. *Handbook of Literary Rhetoric: A Foundation for Literary Study*. Edited by David E. Orton and R. Dean Anderson. Translated by Matthew T. Bliss et al. Brill: Leiden, 1998.

Legarreta-Castillo, Felipe De Jesús. *The Figure of Adam in Romans 5 and 1 Corinthians 15: The New Creation and Its Ethical and Social Reconfiguration*. Minneapolis: Fortress Press, 2014.

Lendon, J. E. *Empire of Honour: The Art of Government in the Roman World*. Oxford: Clarendon Press, 1997.

Lenin, Vladimir I. *Imperialism, the Highest Stage of Capitalism: A Popular Outline*. New York: International Publishers, 1939.

Levinson, John. *Filled with the Spirit*. Grand Rapids: William B. Eerdmans, 2009.**

Lightfoot, Joseph B. *The Epistle of St. Paul to the Galatians*. Grand Rapids: Zondervan, 1967.

Lincoln, Andrew T. *Paradise Now and Not Yet: Studies in the Role of the Heavenly Dimension in Paul's Thought with Special Reference to his Eschatology*, SNTSMS 43. Cambridge: Cambridge University Press, 1981.

Ling, Trevor Oswald. *The Significance of Satan*. London: SPCK, 1961.

Long, A. A. and D. N. Sedley. *The Hellenistic Philosophers*, 2 vols. (Cambridge: Cambridge University Press, 1987.

Longenecker, Richard N. *Galatians*. WBC 41. Dallas: Word Books, 1990.

Lopez, Davina C. *Apostle to the Conquered: Reimagining Paul's Mission*. Minneapolis: Fortress Press, 2008.

Lyons, George. *Pauline Autobiography: Toward a New Understanding*. SBLDS 73. Atlanta: Scholars Press, 1985.

Maier, Harry O. *Picturing Paul in Empire: Imperial Image, Text and Persuasion in Colossians, Ephesians and the Pastoral Epistles*. London: Bloomsbury, 2013.

Malaise, Michel. *Les conditions de pénétration et de diffusion des cultes égyptiens en Italie*. Leiden: Brill, 1972.

Malherbe, Abraham J. "'Gentle as a Nurse:' The Cynic Background to 1 Thess ii." *NovT* 12 (1970): 203–17.

———. *Social Aspects of Early Christianity*. 2nd ed. Philadelphia: Fortress Press, 1983.

———. *The Letters to the Thessalonian*. AB 32B. New York: Doubleday, 2000.

Marchal, Joseph A. *The Politics of Heaven: Women, Gender and Empire in the Study of Paul*. Minneapolis; Fortress, 2008.

———. "Imperial Intersections and Initial Inquiries: Toward a Feminist, Postcolonial Analysis of Philippians." Pages 146–60 in *The Colonized Apostle: Paul Through Postcolonial Eyes*. Edited by Christopher D. Stanly. Minneapolis; Fortress Press, 2011.

Marshall, I. Howard. *1 and 2 Thessalonians: Based on the Revised Standard Version*. NCB. Grand Rapids: Eerdmans, 9.

Martin, Ralph P. *2 Corinthians*. WBC. Waco: Word Books, 1986.

Martin, Troy W. "Pagan and Judeo-Christian Time-Keeping Schemes in Galatians 4.10 and Col 2.16." *NTS* (1996): 105–19.

———. "Paul's Argument From Nature for the Veil in 1 Corinthians 11:13–15: A Testicle Instead of a Head Covering." *JBL 123* (2004): 75–84.

———. *Apostolic Confirmation and Legitimation in an Early Christian Faith Document: A Commentary on the First Epistle of the Apostle Peter*, NIGTC. Grand Rapids: Eerdmans, forthcoming.

Martyn, J. Louis. *Galatians: A New Translation with Introduction and Commentary*. AB 33A. New Haven: Yale University Press, 1997.

Metcalf, William E., ed. *The Oxford Handbook of Greek and Roman Coinage*. Oxford: Oxford University Press, 2012.

McCabe, Elizabeth A. *An Examination of the Isis Cult with Preliminary Exploration into New Testament Studies*. Lanham: University Press of America, 2008.

McCready, Wayne O. "Ekklēsia and Voluntary Associations." Pages 59–73 in *Voluntary Associations in the Graeco-Roman World*. Edited by John S. Kloppenborg and Stephen G. Wilson. London: Routledge, 1996.

McDonald, James H. "Romans 13:1–7: A Test Case for New Testament Interpretation." *NTS* 35 (1989): 540–43.

McEleney, Neil J. "Vice Lists of the Pastoral Epistles." *CBQ* (1974): 203–29.

Meeks, Wayne. "Corinthian Christians as Artificial Aliens." Pages 129–38 in *Paul Beyond the Judaism/Hellenism Divide*. Edited by Troels Engberg-Pedersen. Louisville: Westminster John Knox Press, 2001.

———. *The First Urban Christians: The Social World of the Apostle Paul*. 2nd ed. New Haven: Yale University Press, 2003.

Melick Jr., Richard R., *Philippians, Colossians, Philemon*. NAC 32. Nashville: Broadman Press, 1991.

Mell, Ulrich. *Neue Schöpfung: eine traditionsgeschichtliche und exegetische Studie zu einem soteriologischen Grundsatz paulinischer Theologie*. BZNW 56. Berlin: Walter de Gruyter, 1989.

Migliore, Daniel L. *Philippians and Romans*. Louisville: Westminster John Knox Press, 2014.

Mitchell, Stephen. *Anatolia: Land, Men, and Gods in Asia Minor*. 2 vols. Oxford: Clarendon Press, 1993.

Mitford, T. B. "A Cypriot Oath of Allegiance to Tiberius." *JRS* 1 (1930): 75–79.

Moehring, Horst R. "The Persecution of the Jews and the Adherents of the Isis Cult at Rome A.D. 19." *NovT* 3 (1959): 293–304.

Momigliano, Arnaldo. Review of *An Introduction to Philo Judaeus*. Edited by E. R. Goodenough, *JRS* 34 (1944): 163–65.

———. *Alien Wisdom: The Limits of Hellenization*. London: Cambridge University Press, 1975.

Mommsen, Theodor. *The Provinces of the Roman Empire from Caesar to Diocletian*. 2 vols. Translated by William P. Dickson. New York: C. Scribner's Sons, 1887.

Morales, Rodrigo J. *The Spirit and the Restoration of Israel: New Exodus and New Creation Motifs in Galatians*. WUNT 2/282. Tübingen: Mohr Siebeck, 2010.

Moskalew, Walter. "Fetial Rituals and the Rhetoric of the Just War." *Classical Outlook* 67 (1990): 105–10.

Munro, Winsome. *Authority in Paul and Peter: The Identification of a Pastoral Stratum in the Pauline Corpus and 1 Peter*, SNTSMS 45. Cambridge: Cambridge University Press, 1983.

Munzinger, André. *Discerning the Spirits: Theological and Ethical Hermeneutics in Paul*. SNTSMS 140. Cambridge: Cambridge University Press, 2007.

Murphy-O'Connor, Jerome. *Paul: A Critical Life*. Clarendon Press: Oxford, 1996.

Nanos, Mark D. "The Inter- and Intra- Jewish Political context of Paul's Letter to the Galatians," Pages 146–59 in *Paul and Politics: Ekklesia, Israel, Imperium, Interpretations: Essays in Honor of Krister Stendahl*. Edited by Richard A. Horsley. Harrisburg: Trinity Press International, 2000.

Nicolet, Claude "'Consul Togatus:' Remarques sur le Vocabulaire Politique de Cicéron et de Tite-Live." *REL* 38: 236–54.

Niehoff, Maren. *Philo on Jewish Identity and Culture*. Tübingen: Mohr Siebeck, 2001.

Nigdelis, Pantelis M. "Voluntary Associations in Roman Thessalonikē: In Search of Identity and Support in a Cosmopolitan Society." Pages 13–48 in *From Roman to Early Christian Thessalonikē: Studies in Religion and Archaeology*. HTS

64. Edited by Laura Nasrallah, Charalambos Bakirtzis, and Steven J. Friesen. Cambridge: Harvard University Press, 2010.

Nock, Arthur Darby. "Religious Developments from the Close of the Republic to the Death of Nero," Pages 465–522 in volume 10 of *The Cambridge Ancient History*. 14 vols. Edited by S.A. Cook, F. E Adcock, and M.P. Charlesworth. Cambridge: Cambridge University Press, 1934.

―――. "Deification and Julian," Pages 833–84 in vol. 2 of *Arthur Darby Nock: Essays on Religion and the Ancient World*. Edited by Zeph Stewart. 2 vols. New York: Oxford University Press, 1986.

O'Neil, Joseph C. *Paul's Letter to the Romans*. Middlesex: Penguin Books, 1975.

―――. "What is Joseph and Aseneth all About?" *Hen* 16 (1994): 189–98.

Oakes, Peter. *Philippians: From People to Letter*. Cambridge: Cambridge University Press, 2001.

―――. "Re-mapping the Universe: Paul and the Emperor in 1 Thessalonians and Philippians." *JSNT* 21 (2005): 301–22.

Oakley, Stephen. "The Roman Conquest of Italy." Pages 9–37 in *War and Society in the Roman World*. Edited by John Rich and Graham Shipley. London: Routledge, 1993.

Ochsenmeier, Erwin. "Romans 12,17–13,7 and the Justice of God: Two Neglected Features of Paul's Argument." *ETL* 89 (2013): 361–82.

Oropeza, Bj. "Situational Immorality—Paul's 'Vice Lists' at Corinth." *ExpTim* 110 (1998): 9–10.

Oster, Richard. "Numismatic Windows into the Social World of Early Christianity: A Methodological Inquiry." *JBL* 101 (1982): 195–23.

Otto, Walter F. *Dionysus: Myth and Cult*. Translated by Robert B. Palmer. Bloomington: Indiana University Press, 1965.

Oudshoorn, Daniel. *Pauline Politics: An Examination of Various Perspectives*, vol. 1 of *Paul and the Uprising of the Dead*. Eugene: Cascade Books, 2020.

Padilla, Amado M. "The Role of Cultural Awareness and Ethnic Loyalty in Acculturation." Pages 47–84 in *Acculturation: Theory, Models and Some New Findings*. Edited by Amado M. Padilla. Boulder: Westview Press, 1980.

Park, Young-Ho. *Paul's Ekklesia as a Civic Assembly: Understanding the People of God in their Politico-Social World*. WUNT 2/393. Tübingen: Mohr Siebeck, 2015.

Parott, R. L. "Paul's Political Thought: Rom 13:1–7 in the Light of Hellenistic Political Thought." PhD diss., The Claremont Graduate School, 1980.

Pearson, Birger. "1 Thessalonians 2:13–16: A Deutero-Pauline Interpolation." *HTR* 64 (1971): 79–94.

Poland, Franz. *Geschichte des grichischen Vereinswesens*. Leipzig: Teubner, 1909.

Porter, Stanley E. "Romans 13:1–7 as Pauline Political Rhetoric." *FNT* 3 (1990): 115–39.

―――. *The Apostle Paul: His Life, Thought, and Letters*. Grand Rapids: Eerdmans Publishing Company, 2016.

Price, S. R. F. *Rituals and Powers: The Roman Imperial Cult in Asia Minor*. Cambridge: Cambridge University Press, 1986.

Quaß, Friedemann. *Die Honoratiorenschicht in den Städten des griechischen Ostens: Untersuchungen zur politischen und sozialen Entwicklung in hellenistischer und römischer Zeit.* Stuttgart: Steiner, 1993, 355–65.

Rabens, Volker. *The Holy Spirit and Ethics in Paul: Transformation and Empowering for Religious-Ethical Life.* 2nd ed. Minneapolis: Fortress Press, 2013.

Ramage, Edwin S. *The Nature and Purpose of Augustus' "Res Gestae."* Stuttgart: Franz Steiner Verlag Wiesbaden GMBH, 1987.

Rich, J. W. *Declaring War in the Roman Republic in the Period of Transmarine Expansion.* Brussels: Latomus, 1976.

Rich, John. "Fear, Greed, and Glory: The Causes of Roman War-Making in the Middle Republic." Pages 38–69 in *War and Society in the Roman World.* Edited by John Rich and Graham Shipley. London: Routledge, 1993.

Richard, Earl J. *First and Second Thessalonians.* Edited by Daniel J. Harington. SP. Collegeville: The Liturgical Press, 1995.

Richardson, J. S. *Hispaniae: Spain and the Development of Roman Imperialism* (Cambridge: Cambridge University Press, 1986.

———. "Imperium Romanum: Empire and the Language of Power." *JRS* 81 (1990): 1–9.

Richardson, Peter. "Early Synagogues as Collegia in the Diaspora and Palestine." Pages 90–109 in *Voluntary Associations in the Graeco-Roman World.* Edited by John S. Kloppenborg and Stephen G. Wilson. London: Routledge, 1996.

Richter, Daniel S. "Plutarch on Isis and Osiris: Text, Cult, and Cultural Appropriation." *TAPS* 131 (2001): 191–216.

Riley, Ronald T. *The Emperor's Retrospect: Augustus' Res Gestae in Epigraphy, Historiography, and Commentary.* StHell 39. Leuven: Peeters, 2003.

Rives, James B. *Religion in the Roman Empire.* Oxford: Blackwell Publishing, 2007.

Rogers, Guy MacLean. *The Sacred Identity of Ephesos: Foundation Myths of a Roman City.* London: Routledge, 1991.

Rogers, Trent A. *God and the Idols: Representations of God in 1 Corinthians 8–10.* WUNT 2/427. Tübingen: Mohr Siebeck, 2016.

Russell, D. A. "Figured Speeches: 'Dionysius,' Art of Rhetoric VIII–IX." Pages 156–68 in *The Orator in Action and Theory in Greece and Rome: Essays in Honor of George A. Kennedy.* Edited by Cecil W. Wooten. Brill: Leiden, 2001.

Russell, D. S. *The Jews from Alexander to Herod.* London: Oxford University Press, 1947.

Rutgers, Leonard V. *The Jews in Late Ancient Rome.* Leiden: Brill, 1995.

———. *The Hidden Heritage of Diaspora Judaism: Essays on Jewish Cultural Identity in the Roman World.* CBET 20. Leiden: Brill, 1998.

Safrai, Shemuel and Malcom Stern, eds. *The Jewish People in the First Century: Historical Geography, Political History, Social, Cultural and Religious Life and Institutions.* 2 vols. CRINT 1/1–2. Philadelphia: Fortress, 1974–76.

Said, Edward W. *Culture and Imperialism.* New York: Vintage Books, 1993.

Sandmel, Samuel. "Parallelomania." *JBL* 81 (1962): 1–13.

Santangelo, Federico. "The Fetials and Their 'Ius.'" *BIHR* 51 (2008): 63–93.

Scheidel, Walter, ed. *The Cambridge Companion to the Roman Economy*. Cambridge: Cambridge University Press, 2012.

Schenck, Kenneth. *A Brief Guide to Philo*. Louisville: Westminster John Knox Press, 2005.

Schlier, Heinrich. *Der Römerbrief*, HThKNT 6. Freiburg: Herder, 1977.

Schmeller, Thomas. *Eine sozialgeschichtliche Untersuchung paulinischer Gemeinden und griechisch-römischer Vereine*. SBS 162. Stuttgart: Katholisches Bibelwork, 1995.

Schmidt, Daryl Dean. "1 Thess 2:13–16: Linguistic Evidence for an Interpolation." *JBL* 102 (1983): 269–79.

Schnabel, Eckhard J. "How Paul Developed His Ethics." Pages 167–297 in *Understanding Paul's Ethics: Twentieth-Century Approaches*. Edited by Brian S. Rosner. Exeter; Paternoster Press, 1995.

Schneider, Gerhard. "Die Idee der Neuschöpfung beim Apostel Paulus und ihr religionsgeschichtlicher Hintergrund." *TThZ* 68 (1959): 257–70.

Schreiner Thomas R., *Paul, Apostle of God's Glory in Christ: A Pauline Theology*. Downers Grove: InterVarsity Press, 2006.

Schumpter, Joseph. *The Economics and Sociology of Capitalism*. Princeton: Princeton University Press, 1991.

Schweizer, Eduard. *The Good News According to Mark*. Translated by Donald H. Madvig. Richmond: John Knox Press, 1970. Collins, Adela Yarbro. *Mark*. Edited by Harold W. Attridge. Minneapolis: Fortress Press, 2007.

Scott, James C. *Weapons of the Weak: Everyday Forms of Peasant Resistance*. New Haven: Yale University Press, 1986.

———. *Domination and the Arts of Resistance: Hidden Transcripts*. New Haven: Yale University Press, 1990.

Scott, James M. *Adoption as Sons of God: An Exegetical Investigation into the Background of ΥΙΟΘΕΣΙΑ in the Pauline Corpus*. WUNT 2/48. Tübingen: Mohr Siebeck, 1992.

Scroggs, Robin. *The Last Adam: A Study in Pauline Anthropology*. Philadelphia: Fortress, 1966.

Seaford, Richard. "Dionysiac Drama and the Dionysiac Mysteries." *ClQ* 31 (1981): 252–75.

Shatzman, Israel. "The Roman General's Authority Over Booty." *Hist* 21 (1972): 177–205.

Shogren, G. S. *1 & 2 Thessalonians*. Grand Rapids: Zondervan, 2012.

Sidebottom, Harry. "Imperialism: The Changed Outward Trajectory of the Roman Empire," *Historia* (2005): 315–30.

Simpson, J. W. "The Problems Posed by 1Thessalonians 2.15–16 and a Solution." *HBT* 12 (1990): 42–72.

Singgih, E. G. "Towards a Postcolonial Interpretation of Romans 13:1–7: Karl Barth, Robert Jewett and the Context of Reformation in Present-Day Indonesia." *AsJT* 23 (2009): 111–22.

Smallwood, E. Mary. *The Jews under Roman Rule: From Pompey to Diocletian*. SJLA 20. Leiden: Brill, 1976.

Stegemann, W. "Anlass und Hintergrun der Abfassung von 1 Th 2, 1–12." Pages 397–416 in *Theologische Brosamen für Lother Steiger*. DBAT 5. Edited by G. Freund and E. Stegemann. Heidelberg: Esprint, 1985.

Stegemann, Ekkehard and Wolfgang Stegemann. *The Jesus Movement: A Social History of its First Century*. Minneapolis: Fortress Press, 1999.

Stein, R. H. "The Argument of Romans 13:1–7." *NovT* 31 (1989): 325–43.

Steward, Charles. "Syncretism and its Synonyms: Reflections on Cultural Mixture." *Diacritics* 29 (1999): 40–62.

Stewart, Charles and Rosalind Shaw, eds. *Syncretism/Anti-syncretism: The Politics of Religious Synthesis*. London: Routledge, 1994.

Stuhlmacher, Peter. "Erwägungen zum ontologischen Charakter der ΚΑΙΝΗ ΚΤΙΣΙΣ bei Paulus." *EvTh* 27 (1967): 1–35.

———. *Paul's Letter to the Romans*. Translated by Scott J. Hafemann. Edinburgh: T&T Clark, 1994.

Svebakken, Hans. *Philo of Alexandria's Exposition on the Tenth Commandment*. Atlanta: Society of Biblical Literature Press, 2012.

Tatum, W. Jeffery. "Cicero's Opposition to the Lex Clodia de Collegiis." *CQ* 40 (1990): 187–94.

Taylor, Lily Ross. *The Divinity of the Roman Emperor*. Middletown: American Philological Association, 1931.

Taylor-Perry, Rosemarie. *The God Who Comes: Dionysian Mysteries Revisited*. New York: Algora Publishing, 2003).

Tcherikover, Victor. *Hellenistic Civilization and the Jews*. Grand Rapids: Baker Academic Press, 1999.

Tellbe, Mikael. *Paul between Synagogue and State: Christians, Jews, and Civic Authorities in 1 Thessalonians, Romans, and Philippians*. ConBNT 34. Stockholm: Almqvist &Wiksell International, 2001.

Theissen, Gerd. *Psychological Aspects of Pauline Theologie*. Edinburgh: T&T Clark, 1978.

———. *Sociology of Early Palestinian Christianity*. Translated by John Bowden. Philadelphia: Fortress Press, 1978.

———. *The Social Setting of Pauline Christianity: Essays on Corinth*. Translated by John H. Schütz. Philadelphia: Fortress Press, 1982.

Thiselton, Anthony C. *The First Epistle to the Corinthians: A Commentary on the Greek Text*. NIGTC. Grand Rapids: William B. Eerdmans Publishing Company, 2000.

Thomas, Richard F. "A Trope by Any Other Name: "Polysemy," Ambiguity, and Signification in Virgil." *HSCP* 100 (2000): 381–407.

Thurston, Bonnie B. and Judith M. Ryan. *Philippians and Philemon*. SP 10. Edited by Daniel J. Harrington. Collegeville: Liturgical Press, 2005.

Tobin, Thomas H. *Paul's Rhetoric in Its Contexts: The Argument of Romans*. Peabody: Hendrickson, 2004.

Turcan, Robert. *The Cults of the Roman Empire*. Translated by Antonia Nevill. Oxford: Blackwell, 1996.

———. *The Gods of Ancient Rome: Religion in Everyday Life from Archaic to Imperial Times*. Translated by Antonia Nevill. Edinburgh: Edinburgh University Press, 2000.

Usener, Hermann and Ludwig Radermacher, eds., *Dionysii Halicarnasei quae exstant opuscula,* vol. 6; Bibliotheca scriptorum graecorum et romanorum teubneriana. Stuttgart: B. G. Teubner, 1967–85.

Valadier, Paul. *Des versets encombrants.* «*Toute autorité vient di Dieu*» *(Epître aux Romains, 13,1) Théophilyon* 20 (2015): 99–113.

Van Nijf, Otto M. *The Civic World of Professional Associations in the Roman East.* Amsterdam: J. C. Gieben, 1997.

Venticinque, Philip F. "Family Affairs: Guild Regulations and Family Relationships in Roman Egypt." *GRBS* 50 (2010): 273–94.

Vogliano, Achille. "La grande iscrizione bacchica del Metropolitan Museum." *AJA* (1933): 215–31.

Walsh, P. G. "Making a Drama out of a Crisis: Livy on the Bacchanalia." *GR* 43 (1996): 188–203.

Walter, Nikolaus. "Gottes Zorn und das 'Harren der Kreatur,' Zur Korrespondenz zwischen Römer 1, 18–32 und 8, 19–22." Pages 219–28 in *Christus Bezeugen: Festschrift für Wolfgang Trilling zum 65 Geburstag.* Edited by T Holtz. Leipzig: St. Benno-Verlag, 1989.

Wanamaker, Charles A. *The Epistles to the Thessalonians: A Commentary on the Greek Text.* NIGTC. Grand Rapids: William B. Eerdmans, 1990.

Warren, Larissa Bonfante. "Roman Triumphs and Etruscan Kings: The Changing Face of the Triumph." *JRS* 60 (1970): 49–66.

Warrior, Valerie M., ed. *Roman Religion: A Sourcebook.* Newburyport: Focus Publishing, 2002.

———. *Roman Religion.* Cambridge: Cambridge University Press, 2006.

Weatherly, Jon Allen. "The Authenticity of 1 Thessalonians 2.13–16: Additional Evidence." *JSNT* 42 (1991): 79–98.

Wedderburn, A. J. M. *The Reason for Romans.* Minneapolis: Fortress Press, 1991.

Weima, Jefferey A. D. "An Apology for the Apologetic Function of 1 Thessalonians 2.1–12." *JSNT* 68 (1997): 73–99.

———. *1–2 Thessalonians.* BECNT. Grand Rapids: Baker Academic, 2014.

White, Joel R. "'Peace and Security' (1 Thessalonians 5.3): Is It Really a Roman Slogan?" *NTS* 59 (2013): 382–95.

———. "'Peace' and 'Security' (1 Thess 5.3): Roman Ideology and Greek Aspiration." *NTS* 60 (2014): 499–510.

Whitlark, Jason A. *Resisting Empire: Rethinking the Purpose of the Letter to "The Hebrews."* London: Bloomlsbury T&T Clark, 2014.

Wild, Robert. *Water in the Cultic Worship of Isis and Serapis.* Leiden: Brill, 1981.

Wilson, Stephen G. "Voluntary Associations: An Overview." Pages 1–15 in *Voluntary Associations in the Graeco-Roman World.* Edited by John S. Kloppenborg and Stephen G. Wilson. London: Routledge, 1996.

Winn, Adam, ed. *An Introduction to Empire in the New Testament.* Atlanta: SBL Press, 2016.

Witherington, Ben. *1 and 2 Thessalonians: A Socio-Rhetorical Commentary.* Grand Rapids: William B. Eerdmans, 2006.

Witt, R. E. *Isis in the Graeco-Roman World.* Ithaca: Cornell University Press, 1971.

Wright, N. T. "Adam in Paul Chronology." Pages 359–89 in *SBL Seminar Papers*. Vol. 22. Chico: Scholars Press, 1983.

———. "Paul's Gospel and Caesar's Empire," Pages 160–83 in *Paul and Politics: Ekklesia, Israel, Imperium, Interpretations: Essays in Honor of Krister Stendahl*. Edited by Richard A. Horsley. Harrisburg: Trinity Press International, 2000.

———. *The Resurrection of the Son of God*. Vol. 3 of *Christian Origins and the Question of God*. London: SPCK, 2003.

———. *Paul in Fresh Perspective*. Minneapolis: Fortress Press, 2005.

Yavets, Zvi. *Julius Caesar and His Public Image*. London: Thames & Hudson, 1983.

Index

About the Author

Najeeb T. Haddad is chair and assistant professor of the Department of Religious Studies at Notre Dame of Maryland University. Najeeb was born in Chicago to Jordanian immigrants. He received his BA in religious studies and philosophy from Saint Xavier University in Chicago. He also received an MA in theology in biblical languages and literature, and a PhD in New Testament and Early Christianity from Loyola University Chicago. He is an active member of the Catholic Biblical Association, Chicago Society of Biblical Research, and the Society of Biblical Literature. His current interests include the Pauline letters, empire criticism, and Hellenistic Judaism.

CPSIA information can be obtained
at www.ICGtesting.com
Printed in the USA
BVHW040054180423
662500BV00001B/4